AUTUMN OF THE MATRIARCH

DIEGO MAIORANO

Autumn of the Matriarch

Indira Gandhi's Final Term in Office

HURST & COMPANY, LONDON

First published in the United Kingdom in 2015 by
C. Hurst & Co. (Publishers) Ltd.,
41 Great Russell Street, London, WC1B 3PL

Printed in India

A Cataloguing-in-Publication data record for this book is available from the British Library.

ISBN: 978-184904-430-1

www.hurstpublishers.com

CONTENTS

ACKNOWLEDGEMENTS

The list of people that contributed in one way or the other to shaping this book is much longer than what I can recall. Numberless casual conversations shaped my views, gave me new ideas, made me reconsider some of the arguments, or opened new paths. The first word of thanks must go to all the people that talked with me about Indira Gandhi or about India's politics over a coffee, on a train or a plane, in a restaurant or at a tea stall. Your contribution is much more significant than what I can possibly acknowledge.

The research on which this book is based was possible thanks to a Ph.D. scholarship granted by the Italian Ministry of Education, University and Research through the Department of Political Studies at the University of Torino (Italy).

I would like to thank Michael Dwyer from Hurst and Co. for guiding me through the revision of the manuscript and for all the support he provided.

A lot of people found some time in their busy schedule to talk with me about Indira Gandhi. Some of them asked to remain anonymous. Others who made decisive contributions to my understanding of the complexities of Indian politics are Subash Agrawal, Naresh Chandra, Salman Haider, Sanjoy Hazarika, Jagmohan, Inder Malhotra, S. K. Mishra, Ajit Mozoomdar, Ashish Nandy, Prem Shankar Jha, Mark Tully, the late Vasant Sathe, N. C. Saxena, Bishma Narayan Singh, Natwal Singh, E. Sridharan, Uma Vasudev, George Verghese, and Yogendra Yadav. I also would like to thank numberless Congress party workers to share with me their views on Mrs Gandhi.

I benefited from many casual conversations with a number of academics in Italy, the UK and India. In particular, I would like to express my gratitude to Rochana Bajpai and Amrita Shodhan. You both were critical in putting me on the right path during my time at SOAS. Germano was a great source of inspiration during numerous difficult moments.

The staff of the Asian and African Studies Reading Room at the British Library were an example of what public service should be. I really would like to thank them for their kindness, expertise and advice during the long months spent scrutinizing endless microfilms. Another word of thanks must go to the staff of the Nehru Memorial Museum and Library in Delhi. My deepest gratitude goes to Chloe Mackin, who made an invaluable work of proofreading. Her generosity significantly helped making this book more readable.

Two persons shaped my views on India's politics and history more than anyone else. These are my two doctoral supervisors, Michelguglielmo Torri and James Manor. I do not think that I will ever be able to express my gratitude in fullness to Michelguglielmo. He introduced me to the study of India, for which I will never thank him enough. He also shaped my view of the world to a great extent. He encouraged me in any possible way, going much beyond his role as a scientific advisor. He also offered me a model for what the relation between students and teachers should be.

One afternoon back in 2009 I wrote an email to Jim Manor saying what my doctoral research was about. To my great surprise, he answered that email, and invited me to his office for a chat. He has been a major source of inspiration ever since. My understanding of India's politics owes much to the passion with which he guided me through my research. Again, I owe him much more than I could possibly acknowledge. I could have never hoped for two better gurus.

Special thanks to my family, who supported me despite the fact that I chose to undertake an academic career in the midst of the worst economic crisis since the 1930s. From a rational point of view it made little sense; but they never stop saying that I should pursue whatever career I felt as mine.

Finally, there is one person that contributed to this book at least as much as I did. This is my partner Alice. I still do not quite understand where she found the strength to support me through the ups and downs of academic research. I thank her for making me feel it was easy spending long periods away from home and for encouraging me not to give up, even when my prospects of finding a job in academia looked gloomy. I thank her for never stopping believing in me and for making me appreciate the romantic side of India even when I could not tolerate reading about yet another bad story from Indira Gandhi's times. I thank her because she familiarised herself with Indian politics and because she surprises me when she comments—very competently—on India's political life. To her this book is dedicated.

Torino, 28 May 2014

INTRODUCTION

In January 1980 India went to polls. Indira Gandhi and her Congress (I) party secured a two-thirds majority in the Lok Sabha.[1] Just a couple of months later, the party obtained another impressive victory in a series of state-level elections. Judging by the numbers, the Congress (I) seemed to have restored its dominance over India's political system, and Indira Gandhi was apparently re-crowned as its Empress.[2]

However, the Congress (I)'s dominance was fragile. This book narrates the story of the fragility of Indira Gandhi's dominance over the political system, the implications that such fragility had, and the process of deep political and economic change that characterised Mrs Gandhi's final term in office, from January 1980 to her assassination on 31 October 1984.

The Indian National Congress[3] dominated India's politics for a long time. The party led the struggle for independence against British domination. When India broke free from colonialism in August 1947, the Congress turned from an anti-colonial movement into a governing party. Jawaharlal Nehru, one of the leaders of the freedom struggle, became the first prime minister of the country. A combination of genuine popularity with the party's remarkable ability to extract votes in exchange for patronage distribution ensured the Congress's dominance over India's political system for the first two decades after independence.

Things started crumbling in the late 1960s. Nehru, who had been the prime minister uninterruptedly from 1947 till his death in 1964, left a void that the Congress found difficult to fill. Nehru's successor as Prime Minister, Lal Bahadur Shastri, unexpectedly died in Tashkent in 1966. Therefore, for the second time in less than two years, the Congress party had to choose its leader, a process that, inevitably, tests the party cohesiveness and, usually, leaves many disgruntled leaders behind.

In 1966 the party's leadership chose Indira Gandhi as the next prime minister. She had several advantages. First, she was the daughter of Jawaharlal Nehru. Second, the marriage with a long-time friend, Feroze, had given her the surname "Gandhi", which could not but remind the people of the Mahatma, India's only undisputed father of the nation. Third, being a woman, the Congress leadership thought that she would be easily controllable and thus would not pose a threat to the structure of power within the party (Malhotra 1989). As it will become very clear in the course of this book, nothing could be further from the truth.

The dominance of the Congress party was seriously challenged for the first time during the 1967 general elections. As we will see in greater detail in chapter 1, this election marked a watershed in Indian politics. The Congress managed to secure a wafer-thin majority in the Lok Sabha, but lost the control of a number of state governments. The "Congress system" (Kothari 1964) was shaken to its foundation.

The years that followed were marked by intense change within the Congress party. Indira Gandhi, rather than being the "dumb doll" that many senior politicians had believed, turned out to be a cynical and skilful politician. She first orchestrated a split in her own party (in 1969), which brought her to assume control of the organisation. She then conducted the Congress to a massive electoral victory in 1971 and the country to a major success in the war against Pakistan. In the early 1970s Indira Gandhi did look like the Empress of India.

However, the honeymoon with India's society did not last long. A combination of bad economic conditions, unwise policy decisions and profound changes in society contributed to make India less and less governable. Indira Gandhi's response consisted of a marked shift towards authoritarianism, which eventually led her to suspend democracy in July 1975 and to declare a state of emergency. However, India had enough antibodies to restore democracy. In 1977 the electorate rejected Indira Gandhi and, for the first time since 1947, elected a non-Congress government.

The election of the Janata Party (an alliance of all major non-Congress parties, barring the communists) led many to think that the one-party-dominant party system had come to an end and that Indira Gandhi had been "consigned to the dustbin of history", as Atul Vajpayee, Foreign Minister of the Janata Party, said (BBC News, 28 October 2004).

However, the government lasted for just a little more than two years before disintegrating under the weight of its own internal contradictions. Indira Gandhi made a spectacular comeback at the 1980 general elections. It is with the apparent restoration of the party's dominance over India's political system that our story begins.

A Strange Decade

The 1980s was a "strange decade".[4] The strangeness of the period stemmed from two sets of reasons. First, as I will try to show in this book, the 1980s was a period of intense political and economic change. A brief comparison with some recent events will clarify the point.

In early December 2011, the Congress-led United Progressive Alliance (UPA) government decided to permit foreign direct investment (FDI) in the multi-brand retail sector. The decision sparked off vehement protests not only among the opposition ranks, but also within the UPA itself. The opposition managed to paralyse Parliament for several days. Mayawati, leader of the Uttar Pradesh-based Bahujan Samaj Party (BSP), accused Rahul Gandhi, Congress's General Secretary and great-grandson of Jawaharlal Nehru, of pushing for allowing FDI in the retail sector to favour his "foreign friends" (*The Hindu* 26 November 2011). Within the UPA, Mamata Banerjee, the leader of the Trinamool Congress—a regional party from West Bengal—managed to put enough pressure on the Prime Minister, Manmohan Singh, and his Finance Minister, Pranab Mukherjee, to make them "suspend" the decision until all stakeholders—political parties and chief ministers—reached an agreement (*The Hindu* 07 December 2011).

Long-time observers of Indian politics will not fail to see how the way in which events unfolded in the just mentioned episode would have been inconceivable in 1980. First, opening the ownership of the retail sector to foreign investors was just not imaginable in the early 1980s, especially for a Congress government, whose leader did not miss a chance to see a "foreign hand" in whatever problem arose in India. Second, that a regional party had the strength to block a central government policy was out of the question, given the absolute majorities enjoyed by the ruling parties at the centre from 1952 to 1989. Indeed, the very attempt by a regional party to block a national policy was not imaginable in the political scenario of the 1980s. Such a party would have been dubbed as secessionist or anti-national. Third, the government would have not risked its stability for a policy that could easily be seen as one favouring exclusively the urban middle class and the big industrialists. Fourth, although few doubted that Mrs Gandhi planned to pass the prime ministership to her younger son, Sanjay Gandhi, dynastic politics was by no means rooted yet.

If all this was not conceivable in 1980, just five years later, the seeds of political change had been sown, as we will see in the course of this book. Steps had been taken to liberalise India's economy; regional parties had acquired national relevance; the middle class and the big industrialists had been chosen as the government's major allies in the process of growth; the extremely smooth succession of Rajiv Gandhi to his mother as prime minister had "institutionalised" dynastic rule. The 1980s was a "strange" decade because it was an age of transition between an "old" and a "new" political scenario.

The second set of reasons why the 1980s was a "strange decade" refers to the nature of the dominance of the Congress (I) that was restored with the 1980 general elections and to the configuration of the party system. A fundamental theoretical assumption of this study is that "the way in which parliamentary democracy works depends, more than we may like to admit, on the balance of powers between political parties" (Morris-Jones 1957, 113).

During the first two decades after independence, the configuration of India's party system as a "Congress system" (Kothari 1964) allowed the party to function as a consociational mechanism (Lipjhart 1996). In short, the Congress party, through an extensive and complex patronage system, ensured the inclusion of most groups of India's society within its fold (Brass 1984a; Brass 1984b; Weiner 1967). This was one of the key reasons why democracy consolidated in a highly fragmented and extremely poor society. In fact, in the 1950s, few were ready to bet on the sustainability of democratic rule in India. However, the dominance of the Congress party and its vibrant internal democracy helped in democratising the whole political system. The Congress organization became an impressive machine for patronage distribution and the extraction of votes, contributing to the permanence of the party in a dominant position and to the governability of the political system.

However, a fundamental reason why the "Congress system" had been working was that a sizable part of Indian society was politically asleep. Powerful actors at the local level were able to control sizable "vote banks". The lower sections of India's society, by and large, did not dare question the social order. However, starting from the late 1960s, a demand for political representation arose among large strata of the electorate, as we will see in greater detail in chapter 1. The Congress party could not manage such an awakening of India's society on its own. On the one hand, rising expectations and the growing sophistication of India's electorate made it increasingly difficult to be "something to everyone" (Kohli 1990b, 379) and to rely exclusively on clientelism to win popular support, especially since the memories of the anti-colonial struggle were fading rapidly. On the other hand, Mrs Gandhi deliberately pursued a policy of destabilisation and de-institutionalisation of her own party, which she saw more as a threat to her project of personal domination than as an instrument through which to govern.

Mrs Gandhi tried to respond to this challenge by transforming the Congress from the party that had conducted the struggle for independence into the party of the poor. The slogan for the 1971 general elections *"garibi hatao!"* (abolish poverty!) skilfully exploited a growing sense of frustration with India's developmental path arising from the lower sections of India's socio-economic system. Before 1971, poverty had never been a major issue around which electoral campaigns had been fought nationally. Mrs Gandhi's direct appeal to the poor showed them that politics was responding—at least at the rhetorical level—to their concerns. Moreover, the launch of the green revolution redirected substantial resources from the industrial to the rural sector, providing in the process enormous patronage resources to distribute at the local level.

However, this strategy was not long-lived. Growing authoritarianism within the party and in governance—ultimately leading to the imposition of the emergency regime in July 1975—further decreased the Congress's (and the state's) ability to respond to the growing demand for political representation. Non-Congress parties began representing a threat to Indira Gandhi's power position and to the Congress's dominance over the party system. Eventually, the Janata Party managed to win a parliamentary majority in the 1977 general elections.

The brief Janata interlude (the party imploded in 1979) severely altered the political equilibrium in north India, leading to a virtual collapse of the structure of dominance upon which the Congress party had rested in the previous decades. As a consequence, the Congress (I) that won the national and most state elections in the first months of 1980 was a giant with feet of clay. Its electoral strength did not match its ability to represent different interests and groups in India's society, leave alone mediate between them. In a context where, as Ashis Nandy puts it, the state had come to hold a threefold role "as a protector, as a moderniser and as the arena where social relationships could be renegotiated" (*Seminar* No. 269, January 1982), the inability of the Congress party to function as a power-sharing mechanism had severe consequences on the governability of the system and on the quality of democracy.

This rather long digression puts into a broader context the second reason why the 1980s was a "strange" decade. In short, the party system and the broader political system did not match. The former was still dominated by the Congress (I); however, other political forces—expression of the growing demand for political representation coming from below—began to play a crucial role within the broader political system. As we shall see in the course of this study, the political and the party systems tended to re-align in the course of the early 1980s. New forms of political mobilisation, that would constitute the most important ways of winning electoral support for the following thirty years, emerged. However, Mrs Gandhi did not hesitate to use the institutions of the state to force the maintenance of an "artificial" one-party-dominant party system controlled by the Congress (I). Or, to put it in slightly different terms, Mrs Gandhi used all the power stemming from her dominance over the state apparatus to prevent the emergence of a multi-party system.

To sum up, the 1980s was a "strange" decade because these were years of profound change. In January 1980 the political and economic systems were similar to the ones born at independence. When Indira Gandhi was assassinated five years later, the country was more similar to today's India. Leading this process of change—sometimes intentionally, sometimes not—there was an apparently strong leader who used her power position at the top of the system not to drive the country through the process of change, but to prevent a new party system from emerging—a system that was much less congenial to her project of personal domination of India's polity, but much more in line with the changes occurring within India's society.

Institutions and Political Agency

During Indira Gandhi's years as prime minister, India's institutions were under severe stress. The interaction between Mrs Gandhi's actions and

India's institutions is the leitmotif of this book. As I will try to show, Mrs Gandhi's dominance over India's politics in the early 1980s allowed her to shape the way institutions worked to a significant extent. On the other hand, this study will also show how institutions, although severely weakened or functioning in a distorted way, never stopped being a counterforce to Mrs Gandhi's project of personal domination.

Mrs Gandhi's attempts to subjugate India's institutions are a recurring theme throughout the book. We will see in chapter 1 how the most important institution of the country, the Indian National Congress, was transformed from a formidable political organisation into a personal property of the Gandhi family during the 1970s. The "I" (for "Indira") that was attached to the party's name in 1978 best represents this state of affairs. In chapter 2 we will see, on the one hand, how the deinstitutionalisation of the Congress (I) continued throughout the early 1980s; but, on the other hand, I will also show how the party did not cease to be a constraining force on Mrs Gandhi's projects. On the surface, she was able to impose her will; however, especially at the state level, legislators had their own agenda that was often in contrast with Mrs Gandhi's. The political machinations of Congress (I) politicians often forced her to change her plans, or to take a different course of action. In some cases, political dynamics within the Congress (I) at the state level had a direct impact on the central government's policies. Also, although she had managed to nullify internal opposition to her leadership, factionalism at the state level and between the centre and the states became a major problem. This not only consumed much of Mrs Gandhi's time, leaving less space for governing; but rampant factionalism also caused major governance problems at the state as well as at the central level and contributed to make the whole political system less responsive.

The formal institutions of the state were under similar stress throughout the early 1980s. Mrs Gandhi was able to severely weaken the Parliament, the presidency, the Constitution, the Bureaucracy, the Supreme Court and the federal setting. I will analyse these processes in chapter 4. I will show how some institutions (in particular the presidency and the Parliament) simply stopped being a counterweight to the executive's power and became docile instruments at Mrs Gandhi's disposal.

Other institutions, although significantly subjugated, remained a constraining force for Mrs Gandhi. The bureaucracy, for instance, was politicised to a significant extent. According to the prime minister, a "committed" bureaucratic apparatus was necessary for the project of social and economic transformation that she claimed to be pursuing. However, the distorted way in which the bureaucratic apparatus was working severely impacted on the state's (and Mrs Gandhi's) ability to implement policies. In particular, two things are worth noting. First, in the very confused political situation of the early 1980s, bureaucrats often did not know which orders to implement and which to disregard. This caused a severe limitation in the government's governing capacity and in Mrs Gandhi's ability to impose her will. Second, it became very clear among the ranks of the bureaucracy that their career prospects were dependent on political dynamics. This meant that bureaucrats started fearing to communicate information that the Gandhi family was not happy to hear. Therefore, the prime minister found herself in a situation where it was extremely difficult for her to evaluate what information was reliable and what was not. This further isolated Mrs Gandhi at the top of the system and further decreased her ability to govern, especially because her own party had stopped functioning as an effective information-gathering machine.

The Supreme Court was systematically attacked too. Mrs Gandhi was aware that the court was a major source of limitation to her project of personal domination. In fact, a prolonged conflict between the court and the prime minister characterised Mrs Gandhi's entire political career. During the 1980s, she tried, partially successfully, to limit the Supreme Court's independence, especially through the appointment of friendly judges. However, the Supreme Court managed to remain the main safeguard of the democratic order and, paradoxically, it emerged out of the conflict with Mrs Gandhi stronger than before, as its interventionist role since the 1990s demonstrates (Rudolph and Rudolph 2001).

Perhaps the institution that was put under the toughest pressure was federalism. Since the late 1960s the main political challenge to the Congress party had come from the Indian states. A number of regional parties began to win state elections, thus undermining the one-party-dominant party system. However, it was in the early 1980s that state-level parties started playing a prominent role in national politics too. Mrs Gandhi's strategy was twofold. On the one hand, she centralised power significantly and refused to manage centre-state relations within an institutional framework. On the other hand, Mrs Gandhi used the state apparatus—including the military—to prevent regional parties from becoming a national force. The severe crises that erupted in Assam,

Andhra Pradesh, Jammu and Kashmir and Punjab had one thing in common: a political solution was not pursued because this would have strengthened regional parties and therefore accelerated the emergence of a multi-party system. This was something that Mrs Gandhi was not ready to concede. However, despite the massive abuse of power that characterised Mrs Gandhi's policy toward the states, regional parties remained a major political challenge for the Congress (I) that, eventually, cost Mrs Gandhi not only the popularity of the party, but also her own life. Paradoxically, Mrs Gandhi's attempts to prevent regional parties from playing a larger role in national politics accelerated the coming into being of a multi-party system and the transition from a Delhi-centred polity to a state-centred one.

To sum up, this study shows that institutions do matter, but political agency matters too. Mrs Gandhi's actions had a profound impact on the working of the country's democratic institutions. Some of them just succumbed. Some others resisted the attacks and safeguarded the democratic order. Still others, although severely weakened, constrained Mrs Gandhi's project of personal domination and shaped her political strategies. It is from the interplay between Mrs Gandhi's actions and the country's institutions on the one hand, and the pressures coming from a rapidly changing society on the other hand, that the processes of political and economic change that characterised the early 1980s come from. Or, to put it in different terms, it is from this complex dynamic that some of the key features of today's India stem.

I

INDIAN POLITICS AND SOCIETY IN THE 1970S

Introduction

Rajni Kothari (1970a), writing in the aftermath of the Congress's poor electoral performance three years earlier, defined the 1967 elections as "a watershed in Indian Politics" (940). The party led by Mrs Gandhi could barely secure an absolute majority in the fourth Lok Sabha[1] and lost six of the largest states to the opposition.[2] In Rajasthan, the Congress was able to form a government only after having "persuaded" several independents to join the party. In the following weeks, the coming into being of what Morris-Jones called "a defectors market"[3] (1978a, 155) caused the fall of the Congress governments in three other states—Haryana, Madhya Pradesh, and Uttar Pradesh.

The outcome of the 1967 elections was a sign that something had been changing in Indian politics and society in the previous twenty years. First, for millions of voters the Congress was now just a political party, rather than the soul of the nationalist movement. As such, they were less inclined to forgive the party's shortcomings in the name of the role it had played in bringing the colonial regime to an end.[4]

Second, the politics of patronage, which had sustained the "Congress system" (Kothari 1964) during the first twenty years of independence, began to show its limits. This was made clear by the electoral fiasco of a large part of the so-called "syndicate".[5] Apparently their politics of accommodation towards "existing and potential clients in exchange for their political support" (Manor 1997, 101) was no longer a necessary and sufficient condition to win a seat in the Lok Sabha (Kothari 1970a, 937–8).

Third, the Congress party started "losing its capacity to function as an umbrella organisation" (Frankel 2005, 343) well before the Congress split in 1969 and the suspension of internal party elections in 1972. Therefore, the "parties of pressure", as Kothari (1964) calls them, gradually stopped trying to influence "like-minded...groups in the dominant party" (Morris-Jones 1978b, 218) in order to pursue their political goals, and started acting outside the Congress party. At the national level, the challenge faced by the Congress came from both the right—the Swatantra Party and the Jana Sangh became the second and third force in the fourth Lok Sabha—and the left—the communist and the socialist parties conquered a total of 78 seats. At the state level, on the one hand, splinter groups from the Congress mushroomed;[6] on the other hand, opposition forces started realising that the only way they could pose a threat to the ruling party was by avoiding a division in the anti-Congress vote. Indeed, in most states Mrs Gandhi's party faced a united opposition. In West Bengal and Kerala the Congress was defeated by united fronts led by the parties of the left; in Bihar, Orissa and Punjab, victory went to united fronts comprising all opposition parties barring the communists; in Rajasthan the challenge to the Congress came from the right, in the form of an alliance between the Jana Sangh and the Swatantra Party. The only state where the Congress was defeated by a single party was Tamil Nadu, where the Dravida Munnetra Kazhagam (DMK) swept the polls.

All these changes were symptoms of a deeper transformation of Indian society and politics. What became apparent at the end of the 1960s was that a growing demand for political representation was shaking the foundations of Indian democracy.

The Socio-economic Context

The demand for political representation was precipitated by the difficult economic situation of the mid-1960s. It is in this period that some of the limits to the strategy of rapid industrialisation pursued by the government since independence began to emerge. In the first place, slow economic growth—at a "Hindu rate" (Rodrik and Subramanian 2004)—especially in the primary sector, led to a serious food crisis in 1965–66.

Second, the war with Pakistan in 1965, while draining significant financial resources, did not bring any significant military or political results. Third, the devaluation of the rupee in 1966 did not result in notable economic benefits, whilst seriously affecting the government's popularity. Fourth, from the mid-1960s onwards the Indian government lost control of the price situation and two-digit inflation critically eroded the purchasing power of most of the population. All these factors, on the one hand, contributed to the poor electoral performance of the ruling party in 1967 and, on the other, exacerbated socio-economic tensions throughout the country (see Raj Narain 1975).

There was another factor that greatly contributed to the process of generating political demands. The Indian historian Ramachandra Guha (2007, 417–8) maintains that by the end of the 1960s "elections were no longer a top-dressing on inhospitable soil; they had been fully indigenized, made part of Indian life, a festival with its own unique set of rituals, enacted every five years". In other words, in the first twenty years of independence, democratic values had been penetrating down the social body, reaching every layer of the socio-economic order. Both factors—difficult economic conditions and the democratisation of Indian society—persisted throughout the following decade. The third Indo-Pakistan war, the first oil shock and bad weather conditions leading to the food shortages of the first half of the 1970s seriously compromised the economic situation; at the same time, the rise of plebiscitary politics promoted by Indira Gandhi contributed to the further political emancipation of subaltern groups.

By all accounts, the Congress party could not respond to this fast-growing demand for political representation, at least in the way it had done since independence. Pranab Bardhan (1998) argues that in 1947 Indian democracy was captured by a coalition of "dominant proprietary classes", namely industrial capitalists, rich farmers and the middle class. These groups—or, better, important sections within these groups—had been able to set up a peaceful coexistence under the umbrella of the Congress party through which they were able to influence—if not to determine—the functioning of the state apparatuses. However, from the 1960s, the reciprocal relations among the groups and of those with the ruling party underwent some changes. To begin with, a sizeable section of the industrialists were not happy with the adoption in 1954 of "a socialistic pattern of society" as one of Congress's goals (Jha 1993, 28).

Second, a significant part of the rural elite, which had huge electoral influence, had been alienated following the choice in favour of the rapid industrialisation strategy that marked the Second Five-year Plan (Kaviraj 1988). Third, part of the middle class began to feel that the promises made by the Congress government concerning a rapid modernisation of the country were not going to be fulfilled in the foreseeable future. In addition, a fourth actor started claiming its place at the centre of Indian politics: the Indian masses (Manor 1983a and 1983b; Vanaik 1990, 82; Khilnani 1997, 48). If the industrialists possessed the capital, the rich farmers possessed the land, and the middle class the knowledge, then the Indian masses could count on their numerical strength to make their voice heard. In this sense, the subaltern strata can be seen as a fourth "proprietary class" which aspired to become "dominant" or, at least, more and more determined not to allow the three other groups to systematically exclude them from the distribution of state resources.[7] Starting from the late 1960s and, even more so, the early 1970s, the Indian masses became a central protagonist in Indian politics, not only as subjects prone to the will of their semi-feudal lords, but also as agents of a political will of their own.[8]

The overall effect of these changes was that these groups had to renegotiate their relations with the ruling party, which, in turn, was then in a process of deep transformation in the aftermath of Nehru's death and the rise to power of his daughter. As we shall see in the next section, the demand for political representation pervaded the whole spectrum of Indian society and took various forms. Even though, for analytical reasons, different kinds of demands will be treated separately, in fact in most cases the boundaries between these demands and between the social groups that advanced them were blurred and overlapping.

Demands for Political Representation

Perhaps the best example of demand for political representation emerging in the mid-1960s was that of parts of the peasant proprietors[9] of the Hindi belt. This social group had constituted the backbone of the Indian National Congress in the countryside during the freedom struggle. Not surprisingly, the middle and upper peasantry had also been the main beneficiary of the Congress's agrarian policies in the 1950s and of the land reform.[10] However, this social group was far from being a homogenous one. Caste differences were crucial in determining the power relations within this stratum. As Christophe Jaffrelot (2003, chs 2 and 4) shows, the caste composition of the Legislative Assemblies throughout the Hindi belt was overwhelmingly in favour of the upper-caste groups.[11] This was true also for the lower tiers of the administration, at the district, block and *gram panchayat*[12] levels (Brass 1985). Therefore upper-caste dominance coincided with Congress dominance of these institutions. Such a coincidence, on the one hand, was the main reason why the party was so "popular" in the countryside; on the other, it left out important caste groups which were either excluded or limited in their access to state resources, because they were kept out from the control of the key posts in the Congress party. In many cases such groups belonged to intermediate or lower peasant castes.

With the Second (1956–61) and Third (1961–66) Five-year Plans, the Indian government adopted a strategy of rapid industrialisation through massive public investments in the secondary sector. As a consequence, public investments in agriculture severely diminished. In this context, the conflict over the allocation of agricultural inputs (like fertilisers, seeds, etc.) became even more bitter. It is plausible that upper castes were able to intercept the greatest share of (shrinking) developmental resources, thus further alienating intermediate- and lower-caste peasants. Furthermore, Nehru's Government pushed for the establishment of a cooperative system in the countryside and this was strongly opposed by the whole spectrum of rich farmers.

In short, the first "dominant class" of the "ruling coalition" was united only as far as its main economic interests were concerned—boycotting the implementation of the land reform and intercepting the greatest possible share of developmental resources. However, the ability to intercept such resources depended on the political control of local institutions, which were dominated by Congressmen usually belonging to upper-caste groups. The adoption of the Second Five-year Plan and the attempts to impose a cooperative system resulted in widespread resentment in the countryside, not only among groups traditionally hostile to the Congress party, but also among its core supporters (Kaviraj 1988).

Resentment among rich farmers towards the central government economic policies found expression in the emergence of the Samyukta Vidhayak Dal (United Legislature Party) coalition that formed the government in many states after the 1967 elections (Guha 2007, 427). In some states of the Hindi belt, middle- and lower-caste peasants organised themselves in more structured ways. Charan Singh's various political formations and Rammanohar Lohia's socialist parties constitute the best examples of answers to the grievances coming from economically powerful (but politically weak) social groups in the countryside.

Mrs Gandhi's party reacted to such a loss of support in the countryside. Indeed, the implementation of the Green Revolution, which redirected enormous resources towards the rural sector (2FYP (1956–61), ch 3; 3FYP (1961–66), ch 5; 4FYP (1969–74), ch 3), can be seen as the core of a political strategy aimed at winning back the support of the rural elites (Kaviraj 1988, 77). In addition, it has been argued (Torri 1975) that the nationalisation of the banking sector in 1969, apart from generating waves of enthusiasm among a whole section of the population who had never entered a bank, redirected a substantial amount of credit towards the rural world.

In short, after the adoption by the Union government of an economic strategy based on massive investments in the industrial sector and the subsequent alienation of important sections of the rural elites, a demand for political representation arose among rich farmers. Mrs Gandhi's party was able to respond to such a demand by adopting a set of economic policies that shifted the emphasis of the planning process onto the agricultural sector.

However, caste groups who were economically powerful but politically weak—and were therefore excluded from the control over the distribution of state resources—could not, in many cases, be accommodated within the ruling party, mainly because those in power at local and state level were strong enough to resist the challenge. These groups found other ways to express their grievances, especially in the highly populated Hindi belt. In particular, in the two key states of Uttar Pradesh and Bihar, peasant parties (the Bharatiya Kranti Dal, the Socialist Party and, after the merger of these and other parties in 1974, the Bharatiya Lok Dal) which defended the interests of intermediate and lower castes (Byres 1988) have "from 1969 to 1984 constituted a persistent, stable source of opposition to the Congress" (Brass 1985, 26) through the political message conveyed by two former Congressmen, Charan Singh and Rammanohar Lohia. In other cases, for example in Rajasthan, middle-caste peasants (mainly Jats) were accommodated within the Congress party and no peasant alternative arose. In the south, the situation was quite different. Here, the hold of upper-caste groups on land and political institutions had been less pervasive. Moreover, the proportion of the upper castes in the total population was negligible. Therefore, political accommodation of middle- and lower-caste groups controlling a significant amount of land had been easier. In Maharashtra, the Marathas were able to dislodge Brahmins from the control of the Congress party at least from the 1950s (Lele 1990). In Karnataka, the process of integration of non-Brahmin groups in the party started even earlier, with the inclusion of the dominant cultivating castes of the Vokkaligas and the Lingayats (Manor 1989). In Andhra Pradesh, the inclusion of the Kapus and the Kammas had shaped the local Congress party since the late colonial period (Reddy 1989).[13]

Another important social group that started looking for an alternative political representative starting from the late 1950s was the business community. Although part of the business elite (in particular the Calcutta-based Marwari business houses led by G. D. Birla) remained "loyal" to the Congress because it was seen as the best insurance against the peril of a communist revolution, important sections of the business community (a series of Parsi and Gujarati businessmen among whom the most prominent were the Tatas) chose to challenge the Congress from the outside. The foundation and the financial support of the Swatantra Party[14] (and, in part, of the Jana Sangh) represented the attempt by a series of socially conservative and economically liberal groups to oppose the "socialistic" pattern undertaken by the Congress since the mid-1950s.

Indeed, Mrs Gandhi's party chose a confrontational approach toward big business. Two developments are worth noting in this respect. First, private companies had been the principal sources of funding for all political parties. A government study (cited in Kochanek 1987, 1286) showed that between 1962 and 1968 private companies officially donated to political parties more than Rs 2.5 crore.[15] Out of this sum, Rs 2 crore went to the Congress party, Rs 4.6 lakhs to the Swatantra party, while the remaining 45 parties received slightly more than Rs 8 lakhs in total. Another study (cited in the same work) showed that the 126 largest companies contributed more than Rs 1 crore to political parties in 1967, of which Rs 73.7 lakh went to the Congress and Rs 2.5 lakh to the Swatantra. All this changed in 1969, when Mrs Gandhi chose to starve the opposition of funds by banning corporate donations to political parties.[16] This, together with the abolition of the privy purses of the former princes in the same year, severely reduced the flow of funds towards the opposition. The death blow, which reduced the possibilities of most opposition parties competing with the Congress to nil, came from the sudden doubling of electoral expenses, following the de-linking of state and national elections in 1971. The first "casualty" of such a strategy was the Swatantra Party (Jha 1993, 40) whose cadres later merged with the Jana Sangh and the Lok Dal.

Second, in the context of the struggle for supremacy within the Congress party against the so-called syndicate, Mrs Gandhi chose to undertake a marked move towards the left. Here, the prime minister found a valuable ally in leftist party workers—gathered in the Congress Forum for Socialist Action (CFSA)—who resented the mutually dependent relationship between the Congress party and the big business houses and, perhaps more importantly, begrudged the control that the members of the syndicate had over the flow of funds. Mrs Gandhi's decision to align with the leftists inside her party (and, for that matter, outside of it, as after the split of the Congress party in 1969 her government was supported by the Communist Party of India (CPI)) was followed by the adoption of a radical and populist rhetoric, of which "*garibi hatao*" was perhaps the best example.

Indeed, concrete policy measures substantiated the prime minister's anti-capitalist approach. The enactment of the Monopolies and Restricted Trade Practices Act (MRTP) and the nationalisation of banks in 1969, the nationalisation of coal and oil products in 1973, and a set of other measurers which further tightened the grip of the state over the economy, contributed to the creation of "one of the most comprehensive systems of control and regulation of the private sector of the non-communist world" (Kochanek 1987, 1283). In other words, the central government had a firmer control than ever on the "commanding heights" of the economy. Moreover, the business community did not appreciate the signing of the Indo-Soviet Treaty of Peace, Friendship and Cooperation in 1971, and Mrs Gandhi's further advancement towards the Soviet Union.

As a consequence, the business community was forced to go on the defensive. If the business houses were dependent on the government even before Mrs Gandhi's left turn, such a dependency became a sort of domination by the state in the early 1970s. With the appointment of L. N. Mishra as foreign trade minister in 1970, (illegal) "donations" to the Congress party (which started resembling extortion more and more) became a prerequisite for all contact with the public administration.[17] This, on the one hand, resolved the Congress party's problem of fund-raising; on the other, it generated a massive amount of black money that, in turn, decisively contributed to the emergence of a system of corruption that still pervades the Indian polity.

Most of the industrialists could not but adapt to the new system. In fact, they simply had to consider the cost of the "donations" to the Congress party as any other cost involved in any given investment. On the other side, the protected industrial environment guaranteed by the government assured private industrialists high profit margins and virtually non-existent competition from abroad. However, a part of the business community did not stop looking for an alternative representative. The agitation of the mid-1970s that developed in the JP movement had the support of a section of the business community. Perhaps it is not a coincidence that the agitations began in Gujarat, a state where business was strong and where the Swatantra party had polled 39.92 per cent of the votes in the 1967 elections.

The third component of the ruling coalition—the middle class—was also in the process of renegotiating its relationship with the Congress party. In the first decades of independence, the middle class developed a relationship with the state that eventually resulted in a reciprocal dependence. Indeed, "the middle class both benefited from specific forms of support from state-led development and simultaneously were incorporated into the institutional and economic apparatus of a rapidly expanding set of state structures at both local and national levels" (Fernandes 2006, 22).

One very important factor in the structuring of such a relation was the educational policy adopted by the central government. Higher educational institutions received a disproportionate amount of resources (Rudolph and Rudolph 1987, 297) when compared to primary and secondary education, which was highly underfunded (Kohli 2004, pt. III). Responding to the demands articulated by the urban and rural middle classes, the political elite had created an extensive network of university-level institutions, which contributed to a skyrocketing increase in the enrolment rates. One only has to think that in 1951 there were 816 colleges and 27 universities throughout India; by 1975 the former had increased to 8,395 while the latter to 119. In the same period, students enrolling in higher educational institutions rose from 423,326 to 4,615,992 (Rudolph and Rudolph, Tabs. 31 and 32). However, the high rate of enrolment did not only appease the hunger for education in the middle classes. It also led, on the one hand, to a deterioration of the living conditions in the campuses and, on the other, and more importantly, to a widening of the gap between the number of educated people and the number of available white-collar jobs. This seems to be the root of the students' "unrest" (as it is usually euphemistically called) that characterised the second half of the 1960s and the 1970s. The number of reported incidents involving students increased from 109 in 1963, to 607 in 1966, to 4,380 in 1971 and to 11,540 in 1974 (Rudolph and Rudolph 1987, tab. 33 and Ch. 11) when the JP movement reached its height.

Another manifestation of the growing alienation of the middle class youth and the inability of Mrs Gandhi's party to respond to its demands in the short term was the growing importance of the "sons-of-the-soil" movements in various parts of the country (most notably in Maharashtra, Assam and Karnataka). The most visible example was the Shiv Sena in Maharashtra which, before concentrating its efforts on anti-Muslim propaganda, had played an important role in responding to the demand for political representation of a middle class, Bombay-based, young constituency, which was (or was felt to be) excluded or kept at the margin of the labour market. A similar, chauvinistic expression of the middle class's grievances was the relative improvement of the Jana Sangh electoral force in the 1960s and 1970s (Jaffrelot 1996, pt. 2).

Other sections of the middle class started expressing other types of political demands which were not included in any party agenda and found expression in a set of "new social movements" (Guha 2007, 542). These included women's movements (Calman 1989), and a series of "civil rights movements" (Guha, 543). Some of these converged into the all-embracing and predominantly urban JP movement which involved "students, youth, university and other teachers, journalists, lawyers, doctors, housewives and ordinary citizens" (Wood 1975, 318) and which threatened to undermine the political and social stability of the country.

There were important sectors of the middle class that did not look for a political alternative to the Congress. In particular, Mrs Gandhi's centralising policies had the effect of giving more power to the higher echelons of the bureaucracy. Even at the lower levels of the administration, the progressive destruction of the Congress party organisation[18] had augmented the discretionary powers of most government employees and hence their opportunities to supplement their income with bribes (Kaviraj 1988, 72–5). Finally, Mrs Gandhi's appeal to the youth, intellectuals and minorities resulted in genuine support among middle class leftists.[19]

From the 1960s, a fourth group was about to become a protagonist in Indian politics, namely the Indian masses. Although universal franchise had been established in 1947, by all accounts, the first general elections had been more democratic in words than deeds. In fact, vertical "faction chains" (Kothari 1964, 1163) and vote-banks were a structural feature of the "Congress system". Support for the party was acquired not only through a political message based on the nationalist struggle and on the politics of patronage to which we referred above. Many other (often illegitimate) means were used to win the support of the Indian masses, including coercion. In many cases, however, the oppressive social structures in the Indian countryside made subaltern strata inclined to follow the political advice of the village headmen on a completely voluntary basis. James Manor (1981) reports an anecdote that occurred in a village in the south of India in late 1979 where poor villagers felt somewhat obliged to go to the village headman to "humbly ask for his guidance on how they should vote since he alone possessed the wisdom to enlighten them" (29). However, by the late 1970s, such a request was a mere formality. The headman himself knew that "the old times and old ways had gone for good" (29) and that villagers would have voted the way they liked.

Scholars are quite unanimous in locating the first signs of the emancipation process of the Indian masses from their semi-feudal lords in the late 1960s and early 1970s (Frankel 2005; Corbridge and Harris 2000; Manor 1981). This process was reflected not only in growing participation in the electoral process itself—voter turnout increased from 44.87 per cent in 1952 to 60.49 per cent in 1977—but also in the declining importance of factional networks in determining voters' behaviour.[20] In many senses, what Indian society was experiencing was an "awakening" (Manor 1983a) of its till then silent majority. In the framework of Bardhan's "ruling coalition" it can be said that the Indian poor were in the process of becoming the fourth "proprietary class". The "capital" that they owned was the realisation that the democratic framework could be worked—at least in theory—in their favour.

Mrs Gandhi played a major role in this process. Indeed, she was the first to read the signs of this change in Indian society and consequently respond to the masses' demand for political representation. It is true that the politics of "*garibi hatao*" transformed Indian elections into populist referenda; but, on the other hand, it contributed to the political awakening of many till then subordinated voters. In 1971, "in a significant sense, it can be said that large numbers of the peasantry directly participated in the national political process for the first time" (Frankel 2005, 458). Mrs Gandhi "virtually said that the Indian institutional model of reconciling interests and being all things to all people was responsible for growing disparities and the need was to mobilise the poorer and underprivileged and discriminated strata into a new coalition of interests that would provide the basis of the Congress Party's new appeal" (Kothari 1988, 2226). Further, Indira Gandhi's truly national appeal contributed to the realisation by the Indian poor that a collective "we" not only existed, but that in electoral terms it was far more important than any other "we" in the country. It is likely that Mrs Gandhi's massive victory in 1971 was the result of a mix of such a "new" form of political mobilisation of the masses and of the building up of a broad coalition of rich farmers in the wake of the nationalisation of the banks and the implementation of the green revolution. The relative weight of each component is rather difficult to assess.

Needless to say, the Indian poor did not act in a coordinated manner. Many of them remained embedded in a network of semi-feudal relations, while others supported opposition parties, while still others actively participated in the JP movement. One of the expressions taken by the poor's assertiveness that is worth mentioning was the movement born in Naxalbari, in northern West Bengal. By March 1967 "direct actions" against landlords started being set up by bands of landless tribe members, organised under various labels of maoist inspiration. Later, in the same year, the so-called Naxalite movement took the form of an armed struggle and, since then, spread significantly throughout East and Central India. The insurrection was brutally repressed several times, but it has resurfaced regularly, including in very recent years. Today, Naxalite groups are present in about one third of the districts of the country.

The last development that is worth mentioning here is the growing importance that regionalism assumed from the late 1960s. It is important not only because regional issues have been shaping Indian politics ever since, but also because centre-state relations would become one of the major lines of conflict in the 1980s. Furthermore, after the definitive collapse of Congress dominance in 1989, local parties expressing regional concerns and issues would become a fundamental element of the national party system.

In the 1950s the Congress party had been able to manage regional issues within its fold. Although reluctantly, the demand for the reorganisation of the states along linguistic lines had been accommodated in the 1950s and early 1960s. Such a demand had been managed within the party and, most importantly, it was the Congress that collected the political dividends of the entire operation.

However, language and regional politics did not end there. As envisaged by the Constitution, in 1965 Hindi should have become the only official language of the Union. This sparked violent protests in Tamil Nadu, where the DMK was able to organise a students' movement against the central government and subsequently to win the state election on the basis of an electoral appeal to Tamil nationalism. In Punjab, the Akali Dal—the political party of the Sikhs, in particular belonging to the rurally dominant Jat caste cluster—kept demanding a state for Punjabi speakers that was ultimately granted in 1966. That very year, another ethnic-based party, the Shiv Sena in Maharashtra, was formed. In the northeast of the country events took a similar course. Tribal groups in the hills of Assam resorted to violent struggles protesting against exploitation by the people of the valley. Within a few years, two states were carved out of Assam, namely Nagaland (in 1963) and Meghalaya (in 1967). In 1966, the Mizo National Front successfully established itself in the countryside, in the wake of a major armed uprising that was based on ethnic nationalism. Indeed, the Congress party itself was deeply affected by the growing importance of regional and local issues in politics, to the point that it can be argued that rather than a truly national party, the Congress had become a constellation of regional parties (see Chhibber and Petrocik 1990). The de-linking of national and state elections in 1971, moreover, "added a structural determinant to longer-term processes differentiating national and regional politics" (Rudolph and Rudolph 1997, 204), thus further facilitating the emergence of regional arenas of competitive politics.

All these examples also show how the demands for political representation overlapped the boundaries of the social groups mentioned above. The DMK was not just an expression of regionalism. It responded also to the demands of students who feared that the usage of Hindi in the selection procedures for public jobs would have kept them on the edge of the labour market; and it responded to the demand for a share of the power at the state level by the backward castes. Similarly, the agitation for a Punjabi suba was also the expression of demand by rich Jat farmers for a state in which they could be in a dominant position.

To sum up, during the 1960s and the 1970s there was a reshaping of the relations between the most powerful social groups in the country—Bardhan's "dominant proprietary classes"—and the ruling party. Such a reshaping stemmed from the rise of a demand for political representation that characterised virtually the whole spectrum of Indian society. Furthermore, a fourth actor started knocking at the ruling coalition's doors, namely the Indian masses. As a consequence, a reshaping of the ruling coalition itself occurred, as Indian masses could not be excluded any longer. Mrs Gandhi, in the context of the struggle for power within the Congress party and in order to ensure her political future, well interpreted these demands and chose to open the doors to the Indian poor while, at the same time, appeasing the rich farmers with the redirection of public credit and funds towards the rural sector. This does not mean that the other two dominant proprietary classes were completely excluded from the social coalition that supported Mrs Gandhi's party. But the emphasis was definitely on "Bharat" rather than on "India". As we shall see in chapter 3, a similar change of emphasis would take place in the first half of the 1980s, when the Congress (I) would move towards the urban world.

In the next section we will briefly see how the Congress party was, to use a euphemism, "transformed" during such a reshaping of its relations with Indian society.

The Deinstitutionalisation of the Congress Party

The deinstitutionalisation of the main political institution in India—the Indian National Congress—has been the subject of endless research.[21] For this reason, what follows is just a brief overview of the principal developments which transformed Mrs Gandhi's party from "the largest and most formidable agency for the distribution of patronage and extraction of loyalty that the world has ever seen or is ever likely to see" (Manor 1983b, 727) into "a loosely-knit cabal of warlords[22] who commanded what were virtually private armies of supporters" (Jha 1993, 46).

The origin of the destruction of the Congress party by its own leader was the struggle for the control of the party which took place between 1966 and the proclamation of the emergency in 1975. Since the Sino-Indian war in 1962, conflicts emerged among the party bosses. The situation was worsened by the power struggle that followed Bahadur Shastri's death which, on the one hand, resulted in the election of Indira Gandhi to the prime ministership, but on the other, deepened the fracture between her supporters and Morarji Desai's. After the 1967 general elections, the dualism at the top of the party was manifested by the appointment of Desai as Deputy Prime Minister and Finance Minister.

In 1969, the Congress Party ceased to be a unitary formation: the first branch (Congress (R)), comprising about two thirds of the Parliamentary Party, decided to follow Mrs Gandhi. The second branch (Congress-(O)) chose Morarji Desai, who was backed by the syndicate, which, in turn, controlled most of the factional network.[23]

Mrs Gandhi's strategy was made up of two elements. In the first place, the prime minister was able to portray the struggle for the control of the party that eventually led to the split in 1969, as a "bitter struggle between the common people and the vested interests in the country" (Indira Gandhi quoted in Hardgrave and Kochanek 2008, 279). Indeed, the first measures taken by Mrs Gandhi in the course of such "struggle" won her a huge amount of popular support. In particular, the nationalisation of the banking sector, the abolition of the princes' privy pursues and the promise of effective implementation of the land reform put the syndicate on the defensive. Second, following the split, Mrs Gandhi skilfully managed to gain control not only of the so-called party high command—the Congress Working Committee, the President of the party, the Congress Parliamentary Board, and the Congress Election Committee—but also of the most important institutions of the state apparatus, in particular the Cabinet and the presidency.[24]

The split of the party did not put an end to the conflicts within the ruling party. Indeed, Mrs Gandhi's massive—and, to a significant extent, personal—victory in 1971 paradoxically made things more complicated. In the first place, following the restoration of the party to a dominant position, most of the notables and local party bosses who had chosen to support the Congress (O) in 1969 decided to join Mrs Gandhi's bandwagon, in order not to be excluded from the administration of patronage. Second, given the fact that Mrs Gandhi's idea of the party did not include any form of internal opposition or challenge to her rule, she started destroying those powerful party leaders who could eventually turn into enemies. The first casualties were those very state leaders who had made her victory against the syndicate possible—Mohanlal Sukhadia from Rajasthan, K. Brahmananda Reddy from Andhra Pradesh, Mohinder Mohan Chandhury from Assam, S. C. Shukla from Madhya Pradesh and V. P. Naik from Maharashtra (see Kochanek 2002, 96). Shortly after, the CFSA was to be sidelined. Third, Mrs Gandhi began to impose chief ministers from above. The new ideal-type chief minister was a powerless party worker who could not but assent to any wish of the central leadership (i.e. Mrs Gandhi), which was his/her sole source of legitimation. Moreover, following the suspension of internal elections in 1972, Mrs Gandhi started placing her men—loyal but not necessarily competent—in key positions in the party's apparatus.

The overall result of these developments was that factionalism exploded. However, it was of a different kind compared to what classic works on the Congress party had described (e.g. Brass 1984b; Weiner 1967). In the Nehru years, factional leaders were those who mediated between politicians and voters through the dominance over a set of local social institutions that let them exercise authority over local rural realities (see Frankel and Rao 1989, Introduction, for an elaboration of the concept of "social dominance"). Their close links with the ruling party allowed them to combine socio-economic with political power. In the early 1970s the situation had changed. Those who once exercised dominance in the countryside were challenged not only by the growing assertiveness of rising social groups and castes, but also by a series of "newcomers" who had supported Mrs Gandhi in the struggle for control of the Congress party and who therefore broke the old guard's monopoly over the control of the Congress organisation. In addition, following the ban on corporate donations to political parties and the subsequent criminalisation of politics described above, a new class of political "entrepreneurs" asserted itself. In fact, those who were able to bring money to the party's coffers could not be excluded from a share of power. Finally, Mrs Gandhi's style of government and the centralisation of powers in her hands, established loyalty to the Gandhi family as an essential prerequisite to holding a position of power both in the Congress and in the state apparatus. As a consequence, not only did the list of disgruntled people within the party lengthen, but the sources of "legitimation" of power multiplied—social dominance, "fundraising", loyalty to Mrs Gandhi—while the means till then used to test each faction's strength—internal elections—were suspended. A state of war of all against all broke out. The prime minister—that assumed the role of supreme arbiter—found her position strengthened as that of her party was weakened. The whole process took place at a time when the myth of the nationalist struggle—the only real ideological foundation the Congress party ever had—was waning, and the bitter struggle for the control of the party impeded its replacement with an alternative, credible ideological commitment for the party's cadres.

Needless to say, state governments became more and more ineffective, as chief ministers had to spend most of their time trying to remain in power. The remaining time was usually spent trying to accommodate as many followers and relatives as possible in the shortest time possible, since nominated chief ministers and state cabinet members knew that their destiny could change at any moment. In three cases (Andhra Pradesh, Uttar Pradesh and Orissa in 1973) President's Rule had to be declared. This, on the one hand, further strengthened Mrs Gandhi's position as the final arbiter of every dispute and as the principal source of legitimation; on the other, it severely reduced Congress governments' performances in the states, which resulted in the mismanagement of the difficult economic situation of the first half of the 1970s.

In the process, the Congress organisation decayed severely. It did not take the form of a pyramid (Kochanek 2002), nor did a duality between the parliamentary and the (nominated) organisational wings develop (Rudolph and Rudolph 1987). In fact, below Mrs Gandhi's narrow circle, anarchism prevailed, while power shifted rapidly. Indeed, not even those upon whom such a "system" relied, the closest advisers to Mrs Gandhi, could think that their positions in the power structure were assured. The Congress party started to be seen, not as a resource, but as a prerequisite to contest elections under Mrs Gandhi's name—by far considered the best political asset. The party organisation was deliberately permitted to degenerate. If in the political situation of the 1970s, an efficient party machine was not an essential asset to win an election, it was still a fundamental tool for channelling the flow of information from the localities to New Delhi. Mrs Gandhi's populist appeal might have replaced the Congress machine in mobilising electoral support. But neither her advisers, nor the intelligence agencies, which have repeatedly been shown to be unreliable sources of political information could substitute for that immensely formidable machine of gathering information that the Congress party had been.

The Emergency 1975–77

By the mid-1970s, the Congress party had ceased to be an instrument for effective governance, let alone for bringing about a degree of social change. As far as electoral mobilisation was concerned, the party had not only stopped being an asset, but the continuous infighting and the subsequent poor performance of the state governments negatively affected its electoral prospects. Growing allegations of corruption supported by dissident party workers in Gujarat set the stage for the massive upheaval that would lead to the dismissal of the state government in 1974. Similarly, in Uttar Pradesh it was only thanks to Mrs Gandhi's enduring personal popularity that the Congress could retain a majority in the elections in 1974. Francine Frankel (2005, 522), on the basis of her own fieldwork in Uttar Pradesh in the summer of 1973, argues that landless workers and poor peasants were distinguishing between "Indiraji" and the rest of the state administration. While attributing positive developments to the prime minister, they tended not to blame her for other government failures, on the basis of the rather reasonable belief that she could not do everything herself. Indeed, it is likely that Mrs Gandhi's personal popularity had not eroded much throughout her prime ministership.[25]

Nevertheless, it is undeniable that 1974–75 were years characterised by growing social unrest. However, it was mainly an urban phenomenon. The major cause of grievances among the urban middle classes was the bad economic situation that the country was facing, especially after the first oil shock in 1973. In particular, the wholesale price index rose by 19.2 per cent in 1973 and 27.3 per cent in 1974 (Ministry of Finance: Economic Survey, 1974–75). Salaried employees were further affected by the series of anti-inflation ordinances enacted in 1974. Compulsory deposit schemes were implemented, while a tough credit policy reduced the amount of capital available to the business community (Frankel 2005, 516). In short, although the social unrest that produced the JP movement certainly had a mass character, it was nevertheless limited to the urban world in a small number of states.

The proclamation of the emergency in June 1975, more than being the outcome of "the radical erosion of Mrs Gandhi's plebiscitary support"

(Rudolph and Rudolph 1987, 137) was the last in a series of authoritarian measures taken after 1971, when the adoption of the Maintenance of Internal Security Act (MISA) inaugurated the process of erosion of the democratic framework.

To make a long story short, Mrs Gandhi could just not tolerate any kind of limitation to her range of action. This is not to say that her "nature" was dictatorial (as her cousin maintains (Sahgal 1978)), but that if there is one thing she showed during her entire political career, it was that she wanted the chance to do whatever she thought necessary in any type of situation. In this respect, the Constitution, the rule of law, the judiciary, the Parliament, the Cabinet, the chief ministers, the party colleagues, the opposition, the bureaucracy, the press et cetera were all potential sources of limitations. Mrs Gandhi's main political objective[26] from her election as prime minister in 1966 till the enactment of the notorious Forty-second Amendment of the Constitution ten years later (see Austin 1999, ch. 17) was to subject every single institution in the country to her will, not necessarily because she wanted to exercise absolute power, but because she wanted the option of doing so, if need be.

We have already seen how Mrs Gandhi was able to take the control of the party—at the cost of splitting it—and to disempower the opposition—at the cost of generating a huge parallel economy. In the years between 1971 and 1977 she was able to take control of the other state institutions.[27] The most resilient were the judiciary and the press. Both could be subjected only with the imposition of the emergency. While no serious attempt had been made to curb the freedom of the press before 1975, the war on the judiciary had begun much earlier (Austin 1999, pt. II). Judges had been transferred or superseded according to their attitude towards the government. A "committed" judiciary—beside a "committed" bureaucracy—was reputed to be necessary in order to pursue the "social revolution" that the government had promised to its electorate. However, even when the Supreme Court upheld the Twenty-fourth and Twenty-fifth amendments, which gave the Parliament enough power to enact any kind of progressive legislation, Mrs Gandhi's war on the judiciary did not stop. The problem here was that the Court, while upholding the two amendments, had affirmed that the Parliament could not alter the "basic structure of the Constitution",[28] thus posing a limit to the legislative power of the Lok Sabha. This was a clear sign that more than the specific amendment or any piece of legislation, what the Prime

Minister was interested in was to confer on Parliament the right to "preserve or destroy the Constitution" (Austin 1999, 374), which was ultimately done with the Forty-second Amendment in 1976.

The erosion of the democratic institutions was accompanied by a complementary centralisation of power in the hands of the prime minister. During Mrs Gandhi's prime ministership power shifted from the Parliament to the Cabinet, from there to the prime minister's Secretariat and, on the eve of the emergency, to the prime minister's house, from where a small coterie of individuals pretended to run the country. Moreover, the prime minister brought under her control the police and the intelligence services, which were strengthened by the creation of the Research and Analysis Wing (RAW). The multiplication of the paramilitary forces was another sign of growing authoritarianism, as was the enactment of preventive detention laws like the MISA (whose scope was broadened in 1974) and the Conservation of Foreign Exchange and Preventing of Smuggling Activities Act (COFEPOSA) the same year. Parallel to these developments, there was a gradual analogous centralisation of power from the states—the power base of the syndicate—to the centre, which weakened India's federal structure.

The declaration of the emergency, however, had one single immediate cause: the decision by Justice Jagmohan Lal Sinha of the Allahabad High Court that the prime minister had violated the electoral law during the election campaign in 1971.[29] Even though we now know that Mrs Gandhi's closest advisors—Siddharta Shankar Ray, Rajni Patel, D. K. Barooah and, of course, Sanjay Gandhi—had been actively working on a resolution for the imposition of an internal emergency at least since the beginning of January 1975 [*Outlook*, 2 November 2009], this was not actually imposed until there were no other options left. Apparently Mrs Gandhi thought she could manage the situation brought about by the JP movement with the existing legislation and the coercive means at her disposal, especially because an externally based emergency had already been in place since the Indo-Pakistan war in 1971. Moreover, as shown by the sudden disappearance of the JP movement after the proclamation of the emergency, it is quite clear that the unrest was not the "major threat" the government had tried to portray.

The declaration of the emergency was the only way for Mrs Gandhi to avoid stepping down. This could have resulted in a permanent exclusion from power. Indeed, despite Mrs Gandhi's apparent control over the

Congress organisation at the centre, her power was far from unchallenged. James Manor (1997, 102) even asserts that this was "the main threat" to Mrs Gandhi's power position. The prime minister was primarily challenged by the so-called "Young Turks"—who had been so instrumental in Mrs Gandhi's ascent to power—led by Chandra Shekhar, Ram Dhan and Mohan Dharia. The latter was even sacked from the Cabinet after he publicly expressed the group's view that the accommodation of Jayaprakash Narayan should have been pursued. Moreover, it is likely that Jagjivan Ram—one of the few leaders with a relatively wide independent power base (among the Dalits)—would have attempted to replace Mrs Gandhi, once she had stepped down.[30]

In short, the emergency came as the final step in the deterioration of the quality of Indian democracy that started with the coming to power of Mrs Gandhi. Such deterioration was, in a sense, caused by the very way in which Mrs Gandhi managed to secure her power. The destruction of the Congress party as an instrument for information gathering made the leadership more and more insecure and therefore more inclined to make the power of the state more and more authoritarian in order to maintain law and order—and, perhaps more importantly, to preserve its hold on power.

The emergency regime had two consequences for this discussion, regarding various groups' support for Mrs Gandhi and the condition of India's state institutions. First, it alienated two important social groups who had supported Mrs Gandhi throughout the 1970s. On the one hand, the poor of the Hindi belt clearly understood that they would have been the first victims of an authoritarian regime. The family planning programme—"a terrifying campaign of forced sterilization" (Frankel 2005, 563)—and the "beautification" of cities[31] made clear that the only institutional framework that could protect the poor was democracy. On the other hand, rural elites, again most notably in the Hindi belt, probably resented the acceleration in the implementation of the land reform. According to Francine Frankel (2005, 550) who cites official reports, during the emergency 1.7 million acres were appropriated by the state and 1.1 million acres were actually redistributed. This was a remarkable result, if compared to the 62,000 acres redistributed between 1972 and 1975.[32] Nevertheless, even such a sharp acceleration in the pace of redistribution of agricultural could hardly result in any noticeable decline in the number of poor. It was, more simply, an attempt to give some concreteness to the politics of "*garibi hatao*"; populism can only be pushed to a certain point. However, it is plausible that many within the rural elites began to fear that proper land reform was about to be implemented. It is probably not a coincidence that Mrs Gandhi abandoned any reference to the land reform after her electoral defeat in 1977.

The middle class was divided on the emergency. On the one hand, the intelligentsia resented the suppression of democracy; on the other, part of the middle class appreciated the end of lawlessness and disorder (Malhotra 1989, ch. 10) that had characterised the years immediately preceding the regime. In addition, Sanjay Gandhi's reputation as a "doer" did conquer many hearts among much of the urban youth.

Much of the business community was pleased by the imposition of the emergency regime. Strikes and bandhs stopped immediately and some concessions were made to promote economic growth. Moreover, big business must have appreciated the brutal suppression of the railway strike in 1974 and, in general, of the weakening of the trade unions.

Second, institutions were severely damaged. The emergency had been imposed in accordance with the constitutional provisions; it had been authorised by the President of the Republic; the Cabinet had approved it; the Parliament had ratified it; most of the press had accepted to submit to the censorship; the bureaucracy abjectly implemented the most extreme decisions of the authorities. In short, the emergency, although imposed by a single person for what were ultimately personal reasons, showed the weakness of the entire institutional structure of the country.

However, Indian democracy was strong enough to abandon the authoritarian experiment and not to follow the path undertaken by most of its neighbours. In the next chapter we will see how the two processes described above—the articulation of a demand for political representation among important sectors of Indian society and the deinstitutionalisation of the Congress party—resulted, on the one hand, in a bad and deteriorating law and order situation, and, on the other, in the further erosion of the Congress party.

2

THE PARTY THAT DIDN'T WORK

THE CONGRESS (I) IN THE EARLY 1980s

Introduction

James Manor argues that, by the end of the 1970s, India had become "increasingly democratic and increasingly difficult to govern" (1997, 104). This was due, the argument continues, to both the "awakening" of large strata of Indian society and to the parallel incapability of the institutions to respond "rationally, creatively, or even adequately to pressures from society". This was true especially for the principal political institution of the country, namely the Indian National Congress that, as we have seen, entered a phase of serious decay during the 1970s.

In the first chapter we argued that the "awakening" of Indian society was translated into a demand for political representation to which the Congress partially responded. In particular, Mrs Gandhi, in the process of making her party a personal tool for the collection of money for financing her electoral campaigns, responded to the demand for political representation coming from the rural world. The politics of "*garibi hatao*" made her incredibly popular among the Indian poor, while the implementation of the new agricultural strategy won her a solid base of support among the rural elite.

It is likely that in 1977, when Mrs Gandhi called for fresh elections, both groups rejected the Congress party. Subaltern strata—Scheduled

Castes and Tribes, Muslims, landless labourers, urban slum-dwellers—had been the first victims of the emergency regime, at least in the Hindi belt. Moreover, the defection of Jagjivan Ram, who was quite popular among the Dalits, "dealt a devastating blow to the Prime Minister" (Frankel 2005, 569). The rich peasantry, on the other hand, was probably alarmed by the steep acceleration in the implementation of the land reform during the emergency, again most notably in north India. The result of the elections surprised most observers, including Mrs Gandhi who, having destroyed her own party as an instrument for information gathering at the local level, was not aware of the resentment pervading the Indian countryside.[1]

The Janata Party—a coalition of all major non-communist parties[2]—swept the poll. Morarji Desai finally realised his life-long dream of becoming the Prime Minister of India. However, more than a positive vote, that of 1977 was an "anti-emergency wave",[3] as the rapid decline in the party's popularity showed. Moreover, although the Janata Party's performance was remarkable throughout the country, it owed its victory to the highly populated regions of north India. In the south, Mrs Gandhi's party remained dominant in Andhra Pradesh and Karnataka and improved its performance (compared to that in 1971) in Kerala and Tamil Nadu. In west India, the Congress survived the anti-emergency wave.[4] In any case, the Janata Party's result was remarkable, especially if one takes into account the good economic conditions and the good monsoons of the previous two years.

The Janata interregnum,[5] brief as it was, changed Indian politics in at least four ways. First, as "no Indian alive in 1977 knew what it was like not to have the Congress as the country's dominant and ruling party [and] few knew what it was like not to have Nehru or Indira Gandhi as its dominant and ruling political figure" (Guha 2007, 525), the very fact that the opposition won the elections brought about a deep change in the political culture of the country. Life without the Congress turned from being a remote, theoretical possibility, to a reality.

Second, the central government restored the democratic character of the constitutional set up of the country. The Forty-third and Forty-fourth amendments eliminated all those undemocratic provisions enacted during the emergency and made it more difficult for the executive to abuse its powers, especially in relation to the emergency provisions and the declaration of President's Rule; the external emergency, which was still in force since the Bangladesh crisis in 1970–71, was revoked; the MISA was repealed;[6] measures were taken to protect the independence of the judiciary; and censorship was immediately lifted.

Third, in the Hindi belt, the precarious equilibrium among dominant or aspiring dominant groups in the countryside reached a critical point. The electoral dominance of the Congress party at state and national level had assured the dominance in the localities of those landowning groups—overwhelmingly upper-caste—which formed the core of its support base. Indeed, it was a two-way process—the dominance of the latter assuring the dominance of the party. As Blair (1980, 70) rather cynically puts it, "with the main power groups at the state level and in the countryside both wanting above all to maintain their control, and both being composed primarily of the same caste groups, it is not surprising that a tacit agreement developed between them, whereby each assisted the other".

In 1977, following the defeat of the Congress at the centre and in ten states,[7] the thread linking the localities to the upper levels of the polity was cut. In other words, dominant social groups at the local level were not "protected" from above any longer. On the other hand, economically powerful groups who had had limited access to political power in the previous decades—namely the middle and upper peasantry belonging to middle- or lower-caste groups—could assert themselves with the awareness that the weight of the state was now behind them (*Economic and Political Weekly*, 8 April 1978). This was evident from the caste composition of the MPs coming from the Hindi belt, who, in all but three cases, belonged to the Janata Party. For the first time, MPs belonging to upper-caste groups made up less than 50 per cent of the total, while intermediate and lower-caste members increased to one fifth (Jaffrelot 2003, 311).

At the state level, the new political equilibria reflected the process of bargaining that took place in Delhi. Whereas in Rajasthan, Himachal Pradesh and Madhya Pradesh former members of the Jana Sangh were chosen as chief ministers, in Haryana, Bihar and Uttar Pradesh it was Charan Singh who had the last word on the appointment of the heads of the governments. In the former case, upper-caste dominance remained unchallenged, given the fact that both the Congress (O) and the Jana Sangh (the two strongest components of the Janata Party in these states) were both dominated by upper-caste groups. However, a certain degree of realignment within the dominant upper-caste groups occurred. In the heart of the Hindi belt, the situation was completely different. In Uttar

Pradesh, even though the proportion of the members of Cabinet belonging to upper-caste groups was still overwhelmingly in their favour, the share of members belonging to the Other Backward Classes (OBC) increased to 17.4 per cent (Jaffrelot 2003, tab. 9.4). More importantly, the chief minister himself (Ram Naresh Yadav) was an Ahir (Yadav). In Bihar, the percentage of OBCs in the Cabinet was 42 per cent, 13 points higher than the upper-caste figure (Blair 1980, 69).

It was in these two states that the most serious conflicts arose. In Bihar, the chief minister Karpoori Thakur (an OBC himself) tried to implement a policy of reservation for the lower castes, which "called the social order into question" (Jaffrelot 2003, 316) and which was vigorously resisted by upper-caste groups. Students resorted to violent actions, while upper-caste politicians, including those belonging to the Janata Party, not only supported the agitations, but started conspiring against their own government. Eventually, in April 1979, Thakur was toppled. His successor, Ram Sunder Das, restored the "traditional" proportion of upper-caste members in the Cabinet (50 per cent), severely reduced that of the OBCs (to 20 per cent), and amended Thakur's reservation policy so that its impact would be less acute (Blair 1980). A similar course of events occurred in UP, where the chief minister Ram Naresh Yadav, one of Charan Singh's men, was toppled following the wave of protests that his reservation policy had aroused.[8]

A longer-term consequence of the "quota politics" was that a distinct OBC identity began to take shape. This was true not only at state level, but, with the appointment of the Mandal Commission in 1978, the seeds for the mobilisation of the OBCs at national level were sown, even though it would take more than ten years for the central government to implement the recommendations of the Commission.

The struggle for the control of cabinets and legislative assemblies was just the tip of the iceberg. Another very sought-after prize was the control of the local institutions which gave access to developmental resources, namely cooperatives, rural banks, panchayats and the like. Indeed, Thakur's government conducted panchayat elections and it is likely that many of his supporters were accommodated, thus seriously threatening the control exercised by hitherto dominant groups.

These developments contributed in many cases to the rupture of the structure of dominance, which was a fundamental instrument of social control in the countryside. The police, for instance, found themselves caught between formal (i.e. the state government) and informal authorities (i.e. local notables), which in many cases acted against each other's interests. The same situation applied to many other actors. The overall effect of the breakdown of the structure of dominance in the countryside was that the law and order situation severely deteriorated as no one was able to control a great number of actors—Dacoits, police, violent mobs of various natures, et cetera—which started to act either independently or on behalf of conflicting interests. As we shall see in the last part of this chapter, lawlessness and disorder was to last for the entire length of Mrs Gandhi's final term.

Fourth, the Congress party lost power and, consequently, depleted the fuel which had supplied the party's engine since independence, namely the possibility to distribute patronage. Given the fact that the Congress was an ideology-less party with a completely discredited leader at the top, it is not surprising that it started breaking apart. During the emergency, the tendencies towards disintegration within the Congress intensified, as we will see in the next section. The further deinstitutionalisation of the party contributed to the rise of a parallel organisation—Sanjay Gandhi's Youth Congress—which threatened, in the short term, to become the party's largest faction and, in a longer perspective, to substitute what remained of the Congress itself.

The Rise of the Youth Congress

The emergency was the ideal political humus for an extra-constitutional authority to flourish. It is in this period that Mrs Gandhi's dynastic ambitions started taking a more concrete shape. Not only was Sanjay Gandhi left free to empower selected members of the Congress party and the bureaucracy—Bansi Lal, Om Mehta, Jagmohan to name just a few—with virtually limitless authority in implementing his 5-point Programme,[9] but his mother gave him a free hand to build up his own base of supporters, through the enlargement and the strengthening of the Youth Congress, hitherto "a paper-organisation outside West Bengal" (Masani 1975, 310–7). The rise to prominence of what would come to be known as Sanjay's brigade intimidated many Congressmen, but, given the suspension of democratic rights, most of them did not explicitly oppose the prime minister's son.

However, resentment within the ranks of Congress mounted. Indeed, shortly after the relaxation of the emergency provisions in January 1977, a first defection occurred. Jagjivan Ram, one of the few Congress leaders with an independent power base (among the Dalits), denounced the emergency and the lack of democracy in Mrs Gandhi's party and announced the formation of the Congress for Democracy (CFD). Following Ram's defection, two other important leaders decided to join the newly born party. These were Hemvati Namdan Bahuguna (a Brahmin with a strong support base among Muslims in Uttar Pradesh) and Nandini Satpathy (a social worker and political activist from Orissa). The haemorrhage of party men could only be stopped after Mrs Gandhi agreed to reduce the number of party tickets allocated to Sanjay's followers to about twenty (Weiner 1978a, 15).

The electoral defeat, needless to say, made Mrs Gandhi's control over her own party even more tenuous.[10] Having been thrown out of power—she was not even an MP—Mrs Gandhi lost the authority to sack powerful and potentially dissident party leaders like Y. B. Chavan and Brahmananda Reddy, and, perhaps more importantly, lost the control over the political economy of corruption, which had been a fundamental element in the functioning of the party. Moreover, former ministers C. Subramanian and T. A. Pai explicitly accused Mrs Gandhi of being chiefly responsible for the emergency excesses. Indeed, many congressmen reputed Mrs Gandhi—even more so, her son and his coterie—for being responsible for the miserable state of the party.

A few days after the elections, at the end of March 1977, 125 Congress leaders met at Chandrajit Yadav's house to ask for a change at the top of the party organisation. In particular, they wanted Dev Kant Barooah—the inventor of the slogan "Indira is India. India is Indira"—to be removed from the party presidency and people like Bansi Lal and Om Mehta to be sidelined or expelled. In the following months, after the resignation of Barooah and the expulsion of Bansi Lal, accusations against the coterie continued and even some timid critiques of Mrs Gandhi herself were expressed.

The situation deteriorated till the point that, during the first days of 1978, the party split. Among those who chose not to follow Mrs Gandhi were Y. B. Chavan, Brahmananda Reddy, and Swaran Singh. In general terms, all those who could—or thought they could—win an election irrespective of their association with Mrs Gandhi's name, left the party. A notable exception was Devraj Urs in Karnataka who, for the time being, remained loyal to her. Although only a minority of the members of the AICC followed Mrs Gandhi in the Congress (I), it soon became clear that a sizeable part of the electorate recognised her party as the "legitimate" Congress. In February 1978, five states[11] went to the polls. Mrs Gandhi managed to secure an absolute majority in Andhra Pradesh and Karnataka and obtained a good result in Maharashtra. In April 1978, the Congress (I) was recognised as the main opposition party in the Lok Sabha.

After having demonstrated that her political career was not over yet, Mrs Gandhi tried to establish unity talks between the two branches of the Congress. However, she was ready to accept unity only on her own terms. In practice, in the words of Y. B. Chavan, she was ready to accept only those "who were prepared to prostrate before her in surrender" (cited in Mirchandani 1980, 85). Whether when Chavan rejoined Mrs Gandhi's party in 1981 he was "prepared to prostrate before her" remains a matter of speculation. Anyway, unity talks failed, also because Sanjay and his Youth Congress—which had stepped into the vacuum left by the defection of most Congress stalwarts—actively campaigned against such a move.

In March 1979 the Congress Working Committee (I) (CWC) authorised the Youth Congress (I) to enrol members and gave it more freedom regarding the management of its own funds, thus restoring its status as it was before 1977, when, in the wake of a wave of resentment among congressmen, Sanjay's political machine had been severely limited in its autonomy.

This led to apprehension in the Congress (I) ranks. Apparently Mrs Gandhi even had to reassure Congress (I) MPs that Sanjay Gandhi would not have taken an active role in politics (Mirchandani 1980, 86). However, Mrs Gandhi's reassurances did not suffice. A few months later (June 1979), Devraj Urs was expelled from the party. It is likely that his decision to raise the issue of the role of Sanjay Gandhi in politics before the AICC (I) played a significant role. More generally, Urs was certainly aware of the growing weight that Sanjay Gandhi was assuming in most states of the Union and particularly in Karnataka, and he was probably not ready to "prostrate before him". On the other hand, when Mrs Gandhi was re-elected to the Lok Sabha from Chikmalagur in Karnataka, Urs, who had had a major role in the campaign, "came to be regarded within the Congress (I) hierarchy as next in importance only to Mrs Gandhi" (Raghavan and Manor 2009, 79). This was probably unacceptable to her.

In the meantime, the central government was falling apart. Deep infighting at central and state levels resulted in severe political instability. Morarji Desai lost his majority. The Jana Sangh and the Lok Dal components of the Janata Party embarked on a battle over the control of the state governments (Jaffrelot 2003, pt. II). Charan Singh finally managed to become prime minister even though, in what was a rather tragicomic development, had to ask for Mrs Gandhi's support, which she accorded and withdrew within two weeks. In August 1979, the President of the Republic Neelam Sanjiva Reddy dissolved the Parliament and called for fresh elections.

The General Elections of January 1980: The Context

In the days that followed Mrs Gandhi's withdrawal of support to Charan Singh's government, Jagjivan Ram, the leader of the truncated Janata Party, claimed that he controlled a majority in the Lok Sabha. However, Sanjiva Reddy decided instead to dissolve the Parliament and call fresh elections[12] to be held in the first week of January 1980. Contextually, he asked Charan Singh to head a caretaker government.

The prime minister faced a precarious economic situation. However, what appeared to be Charan Singh's priority was to please his constituency among the rich peasantry. In the process, he distributed large sums to farmers, while ignoring that the growth of budgetary deficits worsened the already critical price situation. In a few months he set up a National Agriculture Bank, established higher support prices for farm products than those recommended by the Agricultural Prices Commission, and, in a desperate attempt to win some sort of support among the middle class, he acquiesced to the request for higher wages and benefits for both public and private sector employees. In the meanwhile, public sector investments, which represented about 60 per cent of the country's capital formation (Weiner 1983a, 32) were stagnant, while industrial production came to a virtual halt because of shortages of most industrial inputs and severe infrastructural bottlenecks. International factors like the doubling of oil prices did not make the situation any better. In fact, in 1979 the Gross National Product declined by 4.8 per cent, while agricultural and industrial production fell by 15.5 and 1.4 per cent respectively (*Economic Survey 1981*).

More than any macroeconomic indicator, what had a decisive impact on the electorate was the deterioration of the living conditions in the countryside in the months immediately preceding the elections. In the first place, a severe drought affected seventeen states, the worst since the great famine of 1896–97, according to some newspaper reports (*Indian Express* 04 October 1979). "Quasi-famine conditions" occurred, particularly in the north (*Indian Express* 23 September 1979).

Second, the drought, combined with budgetary deficits and the second oil shock, led to heavy shortages of essential commodities and high inflationary pressures. It is sufficient to note that "in the *week* ending on December 15, 1979, wholesale prices went up by 1.5 points; compared with a year earlier, the index was higher by as much as 21.7 per cent" (Dasgupta 1980, 182). *India Today* called that of 1980 the "sugar and kerosene election" (01 January 1980).

Third, not surprisingly, the law and order situation was at least as bad as the economic one. Broadly speaking, three kinds of conflicts exploded during the Janata phase. First, the realignment of the political equilibria in the north Indian states that we have described above, resulted in an eruption of violence between intermediate-/lower- and upper-caste groups. Secondly, violence against Dalits—probably a backlash against the "awakening" of subaltern strata and of limited land redistribution during the emergency—by landowning caste groups increased enormously. According to Ramachandra Guha (2007, 535) 17,775 cases of atrocities against Dalits were reported between April 1977 and September 1978 as against 40,000 in the preceding ten years. In some cases the increased number of atrocities reported reflected both the growing awareness among Dalits of their rights and their determination not to be victimised any longer; in some others, it reflected the breakdown of the structure of social dominance, which allowed information to reach the national press and the state authorities (see Brass 1984a). However, it is hardly deniable that the security conditions of subaltern strata severely worsened during the last phase of the Janata rule. Further, much of the land that had been redistributed during the emergency had been re-appropriated by the original owner during 1977–79 (*Indian Express*, 29 November 1979). Third, especially in the north-east of the country, an "orgy of violence" (*Indian Express*, 23 December 1979) erupted between tribal and non tribal groups (most notably in Meghalaya—*Times of India*, 21 December 1979).

In the towns, the situation was not much better. Needless to say, the middle class was badly affected by the rising prices and by the increases of excise duties on a number of middle-class items envisaged by Charan Singh's budget.[13] Prolonged and frequent strikes disrupted life in most towns and cities. The textile workers' strike in Delhi lasted more than three months. Moreover, student unrest was spread throughout the country (see *The Hindu*, 24 October 1979). In Assam, the agitation against "foreigners" led by the students resulted in the imposition of a curfew and policemen were ordered to shoot on sight in many towns. Furthermore, the virtual blockade of economic activity in Assam led to a worsening of the oil crisis that affected the country, as one third of the domestic production of oil came from the state. Finally, communal violence, often but not exclusively between Hindus and Muslims,[14] reached new heights, both in the north and in the south of the country. In this respect, the decay of the Congress organisation created an organisational vacuum that was gradually filled by the RSS network (Brass 1981), which, by openly encouraging a confrontational approach with the Muslim community, contributed to generate communal strain. All these tensions were often exploited and eventually inflamed by political activists belonging to every party. The growth in importance and number of Sanjay Gandhi's Youth Congress (I) members certainly did not contribute to the containment of political violence (see Arun Shourie in *Indian Express*, 30 October 1979).

This was the situation when, on the eve of the election, the Soviet Union invaded Afghanistan, which added an international dimension to the already tense internal situation. Most electors must have felt that what the country needed was "a government that worked", which could replace the inept and self-destructive Janata coalition or what remained of it.

Coalition-building and Electoral Alliances

At the national level, the three-month-long coalition-making process resulted in three alliances, each centred around a "national" party. The first one was led by Charan Singh's Lok Dal. It was supported by Devraj Urs and his Congress (U), the Akali Dal, and the AIADMK. Both communist parties offered their support to this coalition, as explained by E. M. S. Namboodiripad, according to whom the "working classes" needed a Lok Dal-Congress (U) victory against Mrs Gandhi and the RSS (*Indian Express*, 30 September 1979). The fact that the leader of the coalition he was supporting thought that wages to landless labourers had to be "subsistence wages" (if they were to be paid at all) (Singh 1959, 168) did not disturb the communist leaders. The scant attention paid to ideological considerations in building electoral coalitions even by the most ideological among Indian parties reveals how, by the 1980s, political values and norms had been completely subverted.

In November 1979, one of the components of the coalition, Bahuguna's Congress for Democracy,[15] defected to the Congress (I) even though, according to Bahuguna himself only a few months earlier, this was made up of "the same people who [had] brought about the emergency and [had] indulged in excess rule there" (*Indian Express*, 22 November 1979). Bahuguna was followed by Brahmananda Reddy of the Congress (U) who was the President of the undivided Congress party at the time of the split in 1978 and was now ready to return to Mrs Gandhi's court.

Despite all this, the coalition's leaders tried to give an ideological foundation to their political formation, claiming to be "secular" and "democratic", in order to distinguish themselves from both the "communal" Janata Party and the "authoritarian" Mrs Gandhi. However, it is rather difficult to believe that people like Charan Singh, Raj Narain, and Madhu Limaye had defected from the Janata Party because of their "delayed discovery [...] of links between the Jana Sangh and the RSS" (*Indian Express*, 05 September 1979). Similarly, the democratic credentials of Charan Singh were somewhat eroded by the enactment by his caretaker government of the Presidential ordinance reintroducing preventive detention. In any case, the two major components of the coalition (the Lok Dal and the Congress (U)) could not find sufficient agreement to present a single election manifesto, even though they had triumphantly announced that they would have done so at the beginning of the electoral campaign. Indeed, confusion and defections continued till mid-December, less than a month before the election day.

The second coalition revolved around the truncated Janata Party headed by Jagjivan Ram and the Jana Sangh.[16] The party's process of self-destruction continued till the eve of the elections and indeed even later. The "double-membership controversy"[17] (see Jaffrelot 1996, 305) went on lacerating the Janata Party and would ultimately lead to the further break up of the party in April 1980, with the creation of the Bharatiya Janata Party (BJP).

The two biggest forces in the Janata Party—Jagjivan Ram and the Jana Sangh—undertook a bitter fight over the allocation of tickets. On the one hand, Ram used to threaten to defect to the Congress (I) if his men were not accommodated, while, at the same time, he successfully diverted the party's funds towards his own supporters (Manor 1983a). There were persistent rumours that Ram would join Mrs Gandhi shortly after the elections, which of course did not facilitate the relationship between him and the other components of the Janata Party. Indeed, that Jagjivan Ram seriously thought of defecting to the Congress (I) would be confirmed by a letter from Gopal Singh[18] to Mrs Gandhi in which the former mentioned Ram's intention to join the party if only the prime minister had invited him to do so.[19] On the other hand, the RSS network of activists was definitely not happy about supporting a Dalit candidate for the prime ministership. This "coalition" received the support of different parties in different parts of the Union. In Tamil Nadu, for example, the Janata made an alliance with the AIADMK, despite the fact that the latter was supporting the Lok Dal-Congress (U) government at the national level. In Maharashtra, given the negligible presence of the Lok Dal in the state, the Congress (U) found an agreement with the Janata Party.

Both "coalitions" were beset by internal problems and contradictions, especially at the state level (particularly in Uttar Pradesh and Bihar) thus revealing, on the one hand, their regional rather than national character and, on the other, their inability to coordinate themselves between different levels of the polity.

The third coalition was centred on Mrs Gandhi's Congress (I). We can speak of a coalition not so much because it was made up of a number of different parties, but because of the continuous influx of defectors into the party's fold. As soon as the elections were announced, politicians throughout India realised that, on the one hand, the electoral prospect of the parties which had been part of the Janata coalition were extremely poor; on the other, that Mrs Gandhi's popularity was far from having collapsed.[20] Mass migration towards the Congress (I) occurred in Maharashtra, where Sharad Pawar's parallel Congress could not prevent the drastic erosion of its support base among legislators and local notables. In Haryana, Bansi Lal and his followers, who had been expelled from the undivided Congress in the wake of the 1977 electoral defeat, were readmitted to the party. In Karnataka, Veerendra Patil, who had contested against Mrs Gandhi in 1978 in the Chikmagalur by-election, joined the Congress (I). In Rajasthan, the former chief minister Mohan Lal

Sukhadia joined the Congress (I), promising that he would have tried to convince as many members of the Congress (U) as possible to follow him. A similar promise was made by P. C. Sethi in Madhya Pradesh, a promise that was actually followed by mass defections to the Congress (I).

Parallel to the politics of "open doors" announced by Mrs Gandhi herself (*Indian Express*, 13 November 1979), there was an effort to reach a political understanding with other parties in those states where the Congress (I) was weaker. It was in such cases that the most bizarre coalitions took shape. In Kerala, the Congress (I), the Congress (U), and the Janata Party formed a coalition that could contest the dominance of the communist parties in the state. In Tamil Nadu, the Congress (I), after having held talks with both the DMK and the AIADMK, chose the former as a political ally, despite the fact that it was the latter that had supported Mrs Gandhi during the emergency and the fact that many members of the Congress (I), who had been Kamaraj's followers, resented the alliance with their "historical" enemy. In West Bengal, individual alliances were built with members of the Congress (U) and the Janata Party, in order to avoid splitting the anti-communist vote. In short, on the eve of the elections, the Congress (I) was a "hasty coalition of hard-core loyalists of the past and a large number of new joiners of a bandwagon" (Dasgupta 1981, 48).

In some cases, the members of the two groups coincided, as most of the "newcomers" had been part of the Congress before 1978. This situation, of course, provoked a wave of resentment among those Congressmen who had remained "loyal" during the turbulent years of the Janata phase. In addition, the Sanjay brigade was strong enough to become the largest faction in the upcoming Congress (I) Parliamentary Party (*Indian Express*, 30 December 1979). At the state level, factionalism came into the open even before the general elections (e.g. in Madhya Pradesh, Haryana and Maharashtra). However, in most cases, Congressmen pretended to be part of a cohesive party and acted accordingly.

In short, on the one hand Mrs Gandhi "made desperate alliances with former enemies, exploited caste loyalties, assiduously courted Muslims and spent huge sums of money to refurbish her party machine in rural areas". On the other, their adversaries' "criminal ineptitude in government over the past three years ha[d] virtually presented the country to her on a golden platter" (*India Today*, 01 January 1980).

The Electoral Campaign

Electoral alliances and seat adjustments only had the effect of limiting—but by no means of nullifying—the structural biases due to the First-Past-the-Post electoral system. Their effect on the parties' or the candidates' electoral fortunes were minimal. More than a competition between coalitions, the 1980 general election was presented as a contest between three personalities. All national parties made it clear that their respective leaders would have been the party's choice for the prime ministership. Indeed, as the results would show, the contest was limited to two of them, Mrs Gandhi and Charan Singh, and only in north India. As far as the third contestant was concerned, Jagjivan Ram, it was quite clear that he could not mobilise broad support even among his core constituency, namely the Dalits. In some cases, this was due to the resentment among them for the prominence given to Chamars (Ram's caste); in some others, voters belonging to the Scheduled Classes saw the Janata Party as dominated by the upper-caste members of the former Jana Sangh. Moreover, it is likely that the RSS activists—the only asset the Janata Party could count on—were not that keen on campaigning for a Dalit candidate for the prime ministership (*Hindustan Times*, 24 January 1980).

Charan Singh and his Lok Dal, on the other hand, were, among non-Jat voters, "largely indistinguishable from the Janata Party from which it had split in July, 1979" (Wallace 1980, 622) and were thus—quite rightly indeed—associated with the mismanagement of the political and economic situation of the last years. In fact, the bitter fight between the two parties, more than helping the electorate to distinguish between the two, had the effect of cementing the image of divisiveness of the ruling coalition. Given the fact that the dominant political culture at that time considered coalition governments a taboo, the divisiveness of the opposition and their probable inability to form a government if elected played an important role in determining the Congress (I)'s victory. Indeed, many voters must have felt that "voting for Mrs Gandhi's opponents was rather like buying a lottery ticket" (Manor 1983a, 100).

The absolute protagonist of the elections was thus Indira Gandhi. Her campaign was highly personalised. She travelled extensively throughout the country, reaching more than 300 constituencies, impressing the audience with the "royal quality" of her campaign and addressing about 1,500 meetings (Weiner 1983a, 37), which were usually attended by very large audiences. Indira Gandhi's personal message "overshadowed the publicity for her party's parliamentary candidate in each constituency"[21] (Wallace 1980, 619). Indeed, the decisive factor in the 1980 general election was a combination of Mrs Gandhi's personal popularity with the feeling, quite widespread, that she was the only alternative to chaos.

As far as the themes of the campaign were concerned, these played an even smaller role than the electoral alliances. Indeed, as Nayantara Sahgal put it, there was only one, single "secular, socialist, progressive, democratic programme that every party claim[ed] as its own" (*Indian Express*, 18 September 1979). Thus, in a sense, the Congress (I) was playing at home, as all principal competitors chose to challenge it on a terrain set by Nehru many years before.

Election manifestos were released at the beginning of December. They were all quite similar. All promised to provide stability with change; all blamed the others for having caused instability; all promised one job per rural family; all appealed to weaker sections, women, pensioners, minorities, Dalits and adivasis. The main difference was between the Lok Dal's and Janata's promise of rural-oriented development as opposed to the Congress (I)'s more industrially-centred path. Moreover, Mrs Gandhi's party put more emphasis on the chaos brought about by the Janata Party and on the fact that the only hope for the country to exit this situation was Mrs Gandhi herself. In addition, while the Congress (I) clearly appealed to the urban middle class's desire for order and stability, the Lok Dal, perhaps believing that alienating this group would have automatically increased its support in the countryside, promised that the production of "luxury items" such as TV sets and refrigerators would be banned. Obviously, Mrs Gandhi's opponents highlighted the dangers for democracy that Mrs Gandhi represented (see the Janata Party, Congress (I), and Lok Dal Election Manifestos, 1980).

The chaotic law and order situation, the harsh economic conditions and the need for a "government that works"—as the principal slogan of the Congress (I) read—were arguably the themes that dominated the electoral campaign. The Lok Dal and the Janata Party were put on the defensive, while Mrs Gandhi could insist on the same theme irrespective of the audience in front of her. Indeed, the promise to provide stability and restore law and order assumed different meanings to different audiences. For Dalits, Muslims and tribals, it meant a promise of protection against landowners or Hindu chauvinists or both; for farmers, especially those belonging to upper-caste groups in the north, it meant a restoration of the protection from above which had guaranteed their dominance at the local level in the previous decades; for the urban middle class, it meant a battle against rising crime and chaos; for the business community, it meant the end of strikes and of the infrastructural bottlenecks that were paralysing the country. For all, it meant the betterment of the economic situation and the fight against inflation and shortages.

The theme on which both the Janata Party and the Lok Dal insisted was the authoritarian nature of Mrs Gandhi. They not only reminded the voters about the excesses of the emergency, but they warned them that if Mrs Gandhi had won, it was likely that a new emergency would have been imposed. However, the electorate's response to this warning was quite cold. It seems that rural voters either forgave Mrs Gandhi (especially after she had apologised for the excesses that had occurred) or did not blame her directly for what had happened during the emergency (Weiner 1983a, 39). In Amethi, (Sanjay Gandhi's constituency in Uttar Pradesh) even though people had not forgotten the abuses, when villagers were reminded that the Janata Party had restored freedom, many of them, very pragmatically, replied that "along with freedom, one also needs something to eat" (*Indian Express*, 19 December 1979).

To sum up, the electoral campaign was played on a terrain—the Nehruvian path—which was more congenial to Mrs Gandhi, who was able in addition to set the main theme of the campaign—the need for stability, given the disastrous economic and social situation inherited by the misgovernment of her adversaries. Election results in India are usually quite difficult to predict; but with hindsight, it is definitely not surprising that in January 1980 Mrs Gandhi swept the polls.

The Election Outcomes

In the first week of January 1980 about 86 million people chose Mrs Gandhi's party to take the country out of the difficult socio-economic situation.[22] The Congress (I) secured 351 seats and 42.7 per cent of the votes. Compared with the 1977 elections, the Congress (I) (which was at that time undivided) increased its share of votes by 8.2 percentage points, which resulted in a striking increase of 198 seats. The second (Lok Dal), third (CPI(M)) and fourth (Janata Party) largest parties acquired 41, 35, and 31 seats respectively. The Congress (U) virtually disappeared (getting 13 seats). Mrs Gandhi's party nearly repeated the 1971 performance, when it got 43.7 per cent of the votes and 352 seats.

In many respects, that of 1980 was a "national" election. The outcome was influenced by nation-wide trends, which diminished—but by no means nullified—the importance of local factors. It was in many senses both a personal and a negative victory for Mrs Gandhi. On the one hand, it cannot be denied that she was still very popular. This would be suggested by at least three factors. First, Mrs Gandhi won by a large margin in both her constituencies in Andhra Pradesh (Medak) and in Uttar Pradesh (Rae Bareilly, from where she had been badly rejected only a few years before); second, political unknowns like Jagdish Tytler or Kamal Nath won against local leaders just because they were closely associated with Mrs Gandhi's son; third, even where the Janata Party had governed rather well (as in Madhya Pradesh) (Weiner 1983a), the Congress (I) swept the polls. Moreover, regional parties, the AIADMK and the Akali Dal in particular, took "a big knock" (*Indian Express*, 08 January 1980) in the elections. The electorate apparently chose the strong centre that the Congress (I) had promised.

On the other hand, it is quite evident that the Indian voters, as one of the sharpest critics of Mrs Gandhi (Kuldip Nayar) put it, "were so fed up with the past that they did not mind taking risks with the future" (*Indian Express*, 09 January 1980). The combination of national economic problems affecting a national economic market with an election campaign based on the contest between personalities who were (Mrs Gandhi), aspired (Jagjivan Ram) or pretended to be (Charan Singh) national leaders resulted in a nation-wide trend that ultimately contributed to the Congress (I)'s resounding victory.

It is unquestionable that an Indira/anti-Janata wave had an impact throughout the country. However, if we look at the electoral results since 1971, it appears that a national trend can be found in five states only, all of which are located in the Hindi belt: Uttar Pradesh, Bihar, Rajasthan, Haryana and Himachal Pradesh. All these states followed a trend according to which the Congress (I)'s popularity severely declined between 1971 and 1977 and then recovered only partially in 1980 (Tab. 1). A sixth state (Maharashtra) followed a similar trend[23] and could therefore be added to the list. However, this was one of the states where the 1978 split had the biggest impact and electoral data are less likely to be comparable. In Madhya Pradesh, the Congress's share of votes declined between 1971 and 1977, but then it fully recovered its pre-emergency popularity and indeed increased it.[24] The same happened in Punjab.[25]

Table 1: Congress' share of votes in the Hindi belt 1971–80

State	*1971*	*1977*	*1980*
Uttar Pradesh	48.55%	24.99%	35.9%
Bihar	40.06%	22.9%	35.9%
Rajasthan	50.35%	30.56%	42.64%
Haryana	52.56%	17.95%	32.55%
Himachal Pradesh	75.79%	38.58%	52.08%

Source: *Election Commission of India—Statistical Report 1980.*

In the south, there was no discernible trend. In one state (Andhra Pradesh) the support for the Congress remained stable throughout the 1970s.[26] In Karnataka, Mrs Gandhi's party declined from 70.87 per cent of the votes in 1971 to 56.8 per cent in 1977 to 56.25 per cent in 1980. However, since Karnataka was the other state where a major split in the party occurred (Devraj Urs's Congress (U) got 16.69 per cent of the votes), it is difficult to assess the decline in the Congress (I)'s popularity. In any case, the party's dominance over Karnataka remained—for the time being—unchallenged. In Kerala, the "national" trend was reversed. The Congress's popularity increased from 1971 to 1977 (from 19.95 per cent to 29.12 per cent) and then slightly declined to 26.32 per cent in 1980. In Tamil Nadu, the party nearly tripled its share of the votes passing from 12.51 per cent in 1971 to 22.47 per cent in 1977 to 31.62 per cent in 1980.

An upward trend was witnessed in Gujarat too, where the Congress (I) increased its share of the votes from 44.85 per cent in 1971 to 46.92 per cent in 1977 to 54.84 per cent in 1980. In Orissa, the percentage of the votes for the party remained stable during the 1970s[27] and increased sharply in 1980 when it polled 56.07 per cent of the votes.[28] In West Bengal, there was a moderate increase in the share of the votes for the Congress (I),[29] which nevertheless remained a marginal force, if compared with the CPI(M)-led front, which, for the first time, polled more than 50 per cent of the votes. In the northeast, the Congress's share of votes declined everywhere.[30]

To sum up, although there was a nation-wide tendency in favour of the Congress (I) between 1977 and 1980, if we look at the data from a medium term perspective a clearly recognisable trend emerges only in the Hindi belt. For this reason it is at best improper to talk of a series of nation-wide "waves" (Rudolph and Rudolph 1987) that determined the outcome of the 1971, 1977 and 1980 elections. Rather, it would be more appropriate to qualify such waves as regional (i.e. the Hindi belt) and as in any case intertwined with local factors.

Therefore, Weiner's argument (1982, 341) according to which "the breakup of the Janata coalition in 1979 and the victory of Congress (I) in 1980 restored India to its *normal political state*" (emphasis mine), cannot be fully accepted. In the first place, as can be discerned from what we have noted above, the central element of the "normal political state" of the first decades since independence—Congress dominance in the Hindi heartland—was not restored. Indeed, the only reason why the Congress (I) was able to gain a majority of the seats in the region was the divisions between the opposition parties. Mrs Gandhi was able to conquer 145 seats (as against 2, in 1977). However, in four states (Bihar, Haryana, Rajasthan, and Uttar Pradesh), the share of the votes received by the Janata Party and the Lok Dal put together was either equal to or higher than that of the Congress (I). Weiner (1983a, 71) maintains that about one third of the seats won by Mrs Gandhi's party in the Hindi-speaking states would have gone to the opposition, had it been united.[31]

Second, the fact that the Congress (I)'s victory in 1980 (and the Janata's in 1977) was largely due to a rejection of the incumbent party marked a significant break with the past, when electoral victories were based on a positive support.

A second element that Weiner puts among the features of this restored normality is the electoral coalition that supported Mrs Gandhi—i.e. the extremes of the social order, "from Brahmins to ex-untouchables, from well-to-do businessmen and government bureaucrats to tribal agricultural labourers and Muslim weavers" (1982, 340). Middle strata, the argument continues, preferred opposition parties. Indeed, the politics of reservation pursued by the Janata-led governments in Uttar Pradesh and Bihar exacerbated the tension between upper and intermediate/backward castes, which reasonably gave their support in favour of the Congress (I) and the Lok Dal, respectively. In addition, it is likely that the deteriorating law and order situation, which resulted in an extremely high number of atrocities against Dalits, convinced many of the Scheduled Classes that Mrs Gandhi's party was the lesser of two evils. The same can be held valid for most of the tribals, as evidence from south Bihar seems to suggest. As far as Muslims were concerned, it is likely that they did not vote en bloc. Rather, some followed the advice of the Imam of the Jamia Masjid who supported Mrs Gandhi (*Indian Express*, 22 November 1979), while some others preferred opposition parties. Rudolph and Rudolph (1987, ch. 6) argue that by 1980 the "special relation" between the Congress and the Muslims had come to an end. However, evidence seems to suggest that a fairly significant part of the Muslims throughout the country did vote for the Congress (I) party. Thus, the "coalition of extremes" seems to be a fairly accurate portrait of the social base that supported the Congress (I) in the Hindi belt in the 1980 general election.

However, as pointed out by Manor (1984), Weiner's argument cannot be considered valid for the south. Indeed, Manor adds that Weiner's all-India generalisation is not really convincing for parts of the Hindi belt itself, such as Rajasthan, where the political strategy of the Janata Chief Minister Bhairon Singh Shekhawat aimed at winning the support of the lower strata might have altered the political equilibria in the state. Moreover, at the other extreme of the social order, the Janata Party enjoyed the support of many former maharajas.

In Gujarat, the composition of the electoral coalition that supported Mrs Gandhi's party had undergone significant changes in the second half of the 1970s. As shown by Wood (1984a) the state unit of the party was able to shift its power base from upper to disadvantaged groups, forming what is usually known as the KHAM alliance.[32]

In Maharashtra, in the aftermath of the split of the party, the sugar-Maratha lobby that had hitherto dominated the state's politics through the Congress party, divided its support between the two Congresses, thus favouring the rise of non-Marathas in the Congress (I) ranks (Lele 1990).

In Karnataka, Mrs Gandhi was able to cash in the results of the good administration of Devraj Urs, who had left the party only a few months before the elections. As argued by Raghavan and Manor (2009), the core of the Congress's support base was among the disadvantaged groups. In fact, it is likely that many voters did not even fully realise that a split in the party occurred and in any case many among Devraj Urs's supporters were unwilling to reject Mrs Gandhi after the Chief Minister himself had supported her for so many years.

In Andhra Pradesh, a sort of coalition of extremes comprising the dominant landowning castes (the Reddis and, to a lesser extent, the

Kammas) and the poorer sections of Andhra societies (mostly Scheduled Classes and Tribes) and the minorities assured the Congress (I) a stable base of support (Reddy 1989). Also, Andhra Pradesh was the state with the fewest political alternatives. Indeed, if there were one state where the "Congress system" (Kothari 1964) had survived, this was Andhra where the Congress (I) continued to include both the ruling party and various "pressure groups" that functioned as an internal opposition. In the east of the country the situation was still different.

In West Bengal, Mrs Gandhi was supported by the middle and upper class groups who opposed the CPI(M) as well as by the non-Bengalis (Kohli 1990a). While the reason behind the steep increase in the Congress's share of the votes in Orissa is not clear, it seems that a coalition of extremes—comprising the Brahman-Karan elite and the tribals of the inland regions (Mohanty 1990)—constituted the core of the party's social base in the state.

To sum up, although national electoral data may lead us to conclude that what determined the outcome of the 1971, 1977, and 1980 general elections was a series of "national waves", it is clear that such waves were regional (i.e. confined to the Hindi belt) and in any way deeply influenced by local factors. It is certainly true that a nation-wide trend in favour of the Congress (I) and its leader existed, but this, rather than determining the result of the elections, helped reinforce the state-level coalitions that supported the Congress (I). In practical terms, the pro-Indira/anti-Janata wave increased the number of Congress (I)'s supporters within those caste/class groups that supported the party in any given state. In particular, national concerns—the destabilising effect of an eventual victory of the forces opposing Mrs Gandhi being the most important among them—seems to have been particularly important in orienting the electoral choice of many "opinion leaders" (Manor 1983a), who were in many cases instrumental in influencing the electoral behaviour of the social groups to which they belonged.

The seventh general elections, although resulting in a stable government supported by a huge majority in the Lok Sabha, concealed the fragility of the entire political system. Not only were opposition parties in complete disarray and therefore not able to exercise their function as democratic watchmen, but the cornerstone of the political system—the Congress (I)—was restored to a dominant position in the Indian polity without, on the one hand, enjoying effective dominance at the grassroots level and, on the other hand, being equipped with the necessary institutional strength to manage the conflicts arousing from its extremely diverse and increasingly assertive social base.

January–June 1980: The Defectors Market

In January 1980, the electorate chose Mrs Gandhi and her party to take the country out of a difficult socio-economic situation. Having conquered two thirds of the seats in the Lower House, the Congress (I) was expected to form a government that could work smoothly and efficiently. However, Mrs Gandhi's party could not fulfil such expectations. On the one hand, as we have seen in chapter 1, the growing assertiveness and awareness of the electorate made governing India an objectively difficult task. On the other hand, as we shall see in the course of this chapter, the party itself lost any internal coherence it might have had in the 1970s, which resulted in a quasi-anarchic situation. Given that the Congress (I), from June 1980 ruled in a majority of the states, the instability of the party had serious repercussions on the whole country, which precipitated into a serious "crisis of governability" (Kohli 1990b).

A first cause of administrative inefficiency was the composition of the central Cabinet. Being that Mrs Gandhi did not trust most of the people in her party, her choices were in fact limited. Most of her colleagues in the Cabinet were "mainly men who are long on loyalty and short on original thinking and proven administrative ability" (*India Today*, 16 January 1980). Following cabinet reshuffles did not change the fact that "Mrs Gandhi ... preferred to stick to mediocrity for reasons of loyalty" (*Indian Express*, 20 October 1980).

Moreover, ministers were not actually in charge of their ministries. In some cases, their assigned responsibilities were not related to the ministry they officially headed. P. V. Narasimha Rao, for example, was made minister for foreign affairs despite the fact that he did not have any experience in the management of foreign relations. The person who took care of India's external relations was Mrs Gandhi herself, while Rao, according to a senior foreign official, handled "more domestic problems than foreign relations" (*India Today*, 1 August 1984). Indeed, important sections of the foreign ministry worked directly under the supervision of Mrs Gandhi (*India Today*, 1 August 1984). Rao was finally made home minister in August 1984, during the twelfth cabinet reshuffle in less than five years—this being a cause of administrative inefficiency in itself.

The various home ministers in turn—Zail Singh, Ramaswamy Venkataraman, P. C. Sethi—were superseded either by Mrs Gandhi herself or by whoever the prime minister entrusted with a given task. During Zail Singh's tenure of the Home Ministry, major administrative decisions were in fact taken by the Finance Secretariat (*Indian Express*, 27 August 1981), while the minister was simply informed about the measures adopted. Similar situations applied to most ministries. In fact, only three persons in the Cabinet—Pranab Mukherjee, R. Venkataraman and Narasimha Rao—were entrusted with all major decisions. Others, like Zail Singh or Buta Singh, were given important positions, but their responsibilities were more cosmetic than substantial. In certain cases, Mrs Gandhi relied upon the advice of people like L. K. Jha and C. Subramanian, who did not even have any official position (*Indian Express*, 04 October 1980).

Another major source of administrative inefficiency at the central level was the continuous process of reshuffling the Cabinet. In some cases, decisions were taken so rapidly and without prior notice that even senior ministers were "taken by surprise" (*Times of India*, 2 September 1982). In January 1982, for example, the Finance Minister R. Venkataraman was replaced by Pranab Mukherjee only a few weeks before the presentation of the budget. In other cases, decisions were taken so slowly that in October 1980—ten months after Mrs Gandhi's comeback—several important ministries like defence, industry, steel and mines, and labour, continued to be without full-time or permanent incumbents of Cabinet rank (*Indian Express*, 21 October 1980).

Important as central government inefficiency might have been, it was at the state level that the crisis of governability had the biggest impact on Indian society. The root of the problem lay in the pervasive factionalism of the Congress (I). As we have seen in chapter 1, the nature of Congress's factionalism changed during the 1970s. In particular, "traditional" factions—headed by powerful local leaders controlling a set of vote-banks—diminished in importance, while a series of new leaders whose legitimacy was based on the favour of the central leadership and/or on their ability to raise money for the party, gradually took control of the organisation.

In 1980, the picture was still different. As I. K. Gujral put it, the post-1980 Congress (I) was "a totally new product" (*Seminar*, October 1982, 29). The key features of this "new product" were two interrelated factors.

The first one was the rise of what was arguably the strongest faction in the party, namely, Sanjay Gandhi's Youth Congress. While factions had always had a localised power base, Sanjay Gandhi's one was a nation-wide phenomenon. It is certainly true that his followers were stronger and more numerous in certain states—Uttar Pradesh, Haryana and Punjab in particular—but it is equally true that his appeal transcended local considerations and aspired to build up a national base of support. This does not mean that Sanjay's factions in the states could ignore the local political and caste arithmatics. It means that the source of its power was coming from Delhi, rather than from the localities and that an "ideological" substratum Sanjay's political "philosophy"—linked all these factions across the country. Indeed, in 1980 Sanjay's followers were recognisable in virtually all states.

We have already seen how Sanjay's growing power had been a major source of discontent among Congressmen, after the party's defeat in 1977 and during the process of fragmentation of the party in 1978–79. The selection of the party candidates for the general elections in 1980 confirmed the power position reached by the prime minister's son, whose men rapidly filled the gap left by the outflow of Congressmen in the previous years. This was reflected in the high number of Sanjay's men to whom a Congress ticket was given. According to *India Today* "every second candidate in UP, Bihar, Haryana and Punjab [were] Sanjay's protégés" (01 January 1980). His loyalists were strong in Tamil Nadu and Karnataka too. About 70 of them—i.e. one fifth of the total—were elected to the Lok Sabha (*India Today*, 16 January 1980). Moreover, roughly 100 more MPs were well-known loyalists of the Gandhi family and were therefore prone to humour the prime minister's son. However, the prominence acquired by Sanjay's men at the central level did not arouse major problems in the party's circles. Things complicated when the central government announced the dissolution of nine Legislative Assemblies[33] in February 1980.[34]

As soon as the announcement was made, warring factions started bitter confrontations in order to get the highest possible number of tickets. In some cases, the state units of the party were so badly divided that they could not even present a final list to the Central Parliamentary Board, which was thus asked to finalise the list on its own. Even when an agreement could be found at the state level, the final word on the list was that of the party's High Command, which often made significant last-minute changes in order to accommodate Sanjay's men (e.g. *Indian Express*, 08 May 1980).

The state where the rise of Sanjay's brigade caused a major confrontation with the old guard was Uttar Pradesh. More than ten thousand nominations were filed for the 425-strong Legislative Assembly (*Indian Express*, 27 April 1980). A great majority of these were long-time congressmen who had been side-lined by Sanjay's meteoric rise (*Indian Express*, 26 May 1980). In at least 150 cases (*Indian Express*, 16 May 1980) disgruntled party-men openly contested the elections against the official party nominee. In many other cases, factional leaders who had been excluded from the distribution of the party tickets campaigned for rebels or even for opposition candidates. However, open defections seldom occurred, as it was evident to most observers that the Congress (I) would sweep the polls. One notable exception was Bahuguna's decision to resign from the party and from the Lok Sabha (*Times of India*, 20 May 1980). Among the reasons given, Bahuguna included Sanjay Gandhi's power in the party, its "undemocratic" functioning, and the "arbitrary" way in which the PCC(I) had been appointed and the list of candidates finalised. Probably even more critical in determining his choice to leave the party he had recently (re)joined, was the fact that the majority of his followers were denied a ticket (*Indian Express*, 20 May 1980).

Many "loyalists" who had stood by Mrs Gandhi during the Janata phase met the same fate. Although an AICC(I) circular to the state party chiefs had stated that those who had remained loyal to Mrs Gandhi "when she was in the wilderness" (cited in *Indian Express*, 04 January 1980) should have been given precedence over those who joined (or rejoined) the party shortly before or shortly after the general elections, this did not completely apply to Uttar Pradesh, where Sanjay Gandhi was powerful enough to impose his men even against his own party's (i.e. his mother's) guidelines. Out of 80 incumbent Congress (I) MLAs, 45 were denied a ticket. Political stalwarts like Kamalapati Tripathi and Narayan Dutt Tiwari—both loyal supporters of the Gandhi family—had to be content with the accommodation of only a few of their followers (*Indian Express*, 16 May 1980).

Finally, it is important to note that Sanjay's faction in UP was fully integrated into the political logic of the state and its caste arithmetic. It is certainly not a coincidence that most of Sanjay's supporters belonged to the Rajput caste cluster. Indeed, for the first time since independence, Brahmin candidates were relegated to second position, while Rajputs, with 115 candidates, became the single largest group (*Indian Express*, 16 May 1980).

Needless to say, Congress (I) workers were "up in arms" (*Indian Express*, 29 May 1980) in virtually every district of the state. Despite this, Sanjay Gandhi's party polled 37.65 per cent of the votes, conquering 309 seats. Out of these, 185 MLAs were elected for the first time and 60 were under 35 years old (*Indian Express*, 05 June 1980). Similarly, the new Cabinet was made up of 9 new faces out of 15 members who were sworn in a few days after the elections (*Times of India*, 10 June 1980). The Chief Minister Vishwanath Pratap Singh—a Rajput—was the Youth Congress (I)'s second choice, after Sanjay Gandhi himself (*Indian Express*, 08 June 1980). The old guard only had two options: either try to be elected on their own (as Bahuguna[35] and other 150 rebels did) or support the prime minister's son.

Even though UP was arguably the state where Sanjay's brigade was strongest, groups of his supporters could be found in all major Indian states. According to some newspaper reports, a proportion between 10 and 50 per cent of the Congress (I)'s candidates in every state was made up of Sanjay Gandhi's followers (*Indian Express*, 04 May 1980; 31 May 1980). As a consequence, state units of the Congress (I), already badly divided and, as we shall see shortly, constantly under pressure from waves of new entrants from other parties, were put under severe stress by Sanjay's factions. The fact that, in the words of Raj Krishna of the *Indian Express*, most of Sanjay's men were "intellectually blank and amoral musclemen, [who did] not see any political or ethical reason in the world why dissenters should not be blackmailed, slandered, silenced, economically ruined, preventively detained and even physically abused" (31 January 1980) certainly did not contribute to easing tensions within the party. One has only to think that two of the MLAs elected to the UP Vidhan Sabha[36] had hijacked an Indian Airlines plane to protest against Mrs Gandhi's arrest in 1978, to have an idea of both the extent of the erosion of democratic institutions that had occurred since independence, and of the kind of people who could be found among Sanjay's followers. Countrywide, in the 1980 state elections Sanjay Gandhi brought into politics more than 1,200 "history sheeters"[37] (interview with Prem Shankar Jha, Delhi, 02 December 2010). In any case, the old guard of the Congress (I) had no choice but to rally around Sanjay as well. This was made abundantly clear by Mrs Gandhi herself, when she publicly endorsed the representation given to the Youth Congress (I) (*Times of India*, 26 May 1980).

Despite its national character, Sanjay's "brigade" was not a homogenous group. Rather, the Youth Congress (I) was a copy of what the Congress party had been in the 1970s: at that time the Congress was made up of a series of regionally-based parties, with their set of local intra-party alliances and rivalries, held together by a towering personality (Mrs Gandhi) who professed a national political "philosophy" (socialism) expressed through a rather precise political programme (the 20-point Programme). The fact that Mrs Gandhi was a truly national leader professing a national political ideology was a fundamental element that, on the one hand, kept the party together and, on the other hand, conferred strength, legitimacy and protection from above to all "regional" Congress parties. At the state level, these "parties" were relatively coherent as far as their social bases were concerned (Chhibber and Petrocik 1990), despite being extremely factionalised.

Sanjay Gandhi's Youth Congress (I) worked in a similar way. The cornerstone of the Youth Congress (I) was a strong leader, professing an easy-to-understand political "philosophy" ("things must get done"), expressed through the 5-point Programme. The Youth Congress (I) was made up of many regional units, which enjoyed the support of relatively coherent social bases—although not necessarily corresponding to that of the mother organisation. All these units were given legitimacy, strength and protection from above. The main difference was that while in the Congress party of the 1970s three forms of legitimacy—dominance at the local level, ability to raise money for the party and protection from above—determined the political equilibrium within the party, in the Youth Congress (I) of the 1980s it was the latter element that played an overwhelmingly important role.

In the first days of June 1980 the election results were announced. The Congress (I) won in eight out of nine states in which elections were held. Only in Tamil Nadu did the Congress (I) lose—to the AIADMK. The results not only allowed many of Sanjay Gandhi's supporters to enter the Legislative Assemblies and the Cabinets of the states, but were a clear recognition of his power and of his political ability, at least at winning the elections.[38] He had been one of the major architects of the process for the selection of candidates and of the electoral campaign. A further recognition of Sanjay's power position was the reshuffling of the Congress (I) organisation, which followed the elections. He was made General Secretary of the party and some of his liutenants reached important positions within the organisation (*Indian Express*, 14 June 1980).

The situation changed radically on the morning of 23 June 1980, when Sanjay Gandhi died in an air crash. Buta Singh (then Union Minister for Agriculture) declared that Sanjay's death "was the biggest tragedy of [the] century, for the people of India" (*Indian Express*, 24 June 1980). Of course, those who had experienced, for example, the partition of the subcontinent in 1947 might have disagreed with Buta Singh's remarks. However, for those politicians who had built their political career exclusively upon their closeness to Sanjay, his death did represent a political tragedy.

At the central level, those who were closest to Sanjay Gandhi were Zail Singh, Abdul Ghani Khan Chowdhury, and A. P. Sharma. However, given that they were (rightly) reputed to be loyal supporters of Mrs Gandhi too (otherwise they would have not been included in the central Cabinet), their position was not significantly affected by Sanjay's death.

Similarly, MPs who had grown in influence thanks to Sanjay's backing (e.g. Jagdish Tytler, Kamal Nath, Madhav Rao Scindia), had to maintain a low profile for the rest of the legislative session, but their position was not completely compromised, especially because some of them managed to establish a good relationship with Rajiv Gandhi, after his entry into politics the following year. In general terms, at the central level, where Mrs Gandhi was less prone to accept factionalism and confusion, the consequences of the air crash were limited in their extent.

However, the death of the "most important decision-maker" in the party (*Indian Express*, 26 June 1980) did generate confusion in the Congress (I) ranks, especially because Sanjay Gandhi was the one who had been entrusted to take care of the party's "organisation" (*Indian Express*, 9 July 1980; Andersen 1982). As a consequence, profound changes were made to the party's power structure (*Indian Express*, 22 November 1980), especially after Rajiv Gandhi's entry into politics.

The situation in the states was quite different. Here Sanjay Gandhi had been given a free hand to build his base of supporters. The Youth Congress (I) units were left in a "confused state" (*Indian Express*, 09 July 1980) by their leader's death. Literally hundreds of young and inexperienced politicians without any kind of social support in their constituencies found themselves adrift and, to make things more complicated, were surrounded by powerful former or current legislators who had been sidelined and who had reluctantly accepted their fate only because they had not been able to oppose to the prime minister's son. Needless to say, the old guard struck back (*India Today*, 15 February 1981).

The first reaction of the Youth Congress (I) was to ask for an immediate replacement of their source of legitimation and protection, namely another leader who could fill Sanjay's shoes. Maneka Gandhi (Sanjay's widow) seemed to many the best option. However, Mrs Gandhi did not trust her completely. Indeed, within a few months, Maneka would be dramatically thrown out of Mrs Gandhi's house (*Hindustan Times*, 30 March 1982). Given Rajiv Gandhi's unwillingness (for the time being) to enter politics, most of Sanjay followers looked for a local source of protection, thus aligning with some local party boss. This in turn resulted in the collapse of the artificial unity of the Youth Congress (I).

It was in UP, where Sanjay's group had been strongest, that this process was most visible. The rivalries among Sanjay's followers in the state were well known even before his death. Moreover, Congress (I) stalwarts like Narayan Dutt Tiwari and Kamalapathi Tripathi, whose influence over UP politics had been severely reduced by the Sanjay brigade, were ready to take back the control of the party. After a phase in which V. P. Singh was put under severe stress by the pressures coming from Sanjay's former followers and part of the old guard led by Tripathi and his son (*Indian Express*, 24 October 1980), the chief minister managed to rearrange the political equilibria in his favour.

In the process, the Youth Congress (I) in the state split. One faction, led by Akbar Ahmed (once one of Sanjay Gandhi's favourites) moved closer to Maneka Gandhi. The other, led by Sanjay Singh, aligned with the chief minister. The former group openly challenged the ministerial wing of the Congress (I) in the state. It first collected signatures asking for the removal of V. P. Singh (*The Hindu*, 30 September 1981); then Ahmed organised a convention in Lucknow in March 1982—dubbed as an "anti-party activity" by Mrs Gandhi herself (*Times of India*, 28 March 1982)—during which a "Sanjay Gandhi's Five-point Forum" was set up (*Indian Express*, 29 March 1982). This eventually led to the emergence, in late 1982, of the Sanjay Vichar Manch, which, after the formation of Maneka Gandhi's own party, the Rashtriya Sanjay Manch, in April 1983

(*India Today*, 15 April 1983), continued to function as its youth wing. The party aimed at gathering Sanjay's followers throughout the country. In practical terms, it welcomed all disgruntled—and possibly young—Congressmen who declared themselves to be former Sanjay followers who wanted to pursue Sanjay Gandhi's "ideals". Although Maneka Gandhi never became a major threat to the Congress (I), it boosted factionalism in several states.

The second faction of the Youth Congress (I) in UP aligned with the chief minister. This was arguably the stronger one. V. P. Singh, managing to remain in charge of the chief ministership for over two years after Sanjay's death, retained control over the distribution of political patronage. On the other hand, in January 1982, he supervised the elections to the local bodies (mainly cooperatives and gram panchayats) in which more than 100,000 party functionaries were inducted (*Indian Express*, 15 January 1982). Moreover, V. P. Singh managed to win the support of part of the old guard, by reshuffling his cabinet in December 1980 and by obtaining Mrs Gandhi's backing.

In June 1982 V. P. Singh resigned from the Cabinet, officially because he had not been able to tackle effectively the problem of Dacoits (who had been a major source of lawlessness in the state and who had killed the chief minister's brother and nephew a few months before). His resignations sparked off intense factional fights which V. P. Singh's successor (Sripati Mishra, a Brahmin) was not able to handle. The incompetence of the chief minister combined with rampant factionalism resulted in the mismanagement of the situation and a virtual halt in both the implementation of development programmes and the distribution of patronage (*India Today*, 16 October 1984).

In short, in UP the group of Sanjay's followers—which had been able to impose its will before their leader's death—was completely side-lined in the process of realignment of the political equilibria in the state. In general, all those whose only source of legitimation had been their relation with Sanjay Gandhi, had to find a new one. In some cases, they looked for another leader who could offer them protection from above. In other cases, more stable sources were sought, like the control over patronage and collection of money for the party. V. P. Singh was able to manage the difficult political situation because he maintained control over the distribution of patronage and Mrs Gandhi's favour: two important sources of political legitimation. However, the chief minister's resignation led to a phase of intense political instability, which ultimately resulted in the explosion of factionalism and the consequent increase in the state government's inefficiency. As the general elections approached, Mrs Gandhi had to appoint Narayan Dutt Tiwari as chief minister and V. P. Singh as state party chief (*Times of India*, 04 August 1984) to supervise a major operation of distribution of state resources, in order to win the support of this electorally crucial state (*India Today*, 16 October 1984), which had been seriously misgoverned in previous years.

Most chief ministers managed to remain in power following Sanjay Gandhi's death. The only one who was removed a few months after Sanjay's death was Chenna Reddy in Andhra Pradesh (in October 1980). However, this had more to do with the internal political situation of Andhra than with the death of the prime minister's son.

Most of the chief ministers chose to increase the amount of money they could provide to the party as the quickest way to secure their position. Gundu Rao in Karnataka and Abdul Rehman Antulay in Maharashtra are the most notable examples of this kind of strategy. In different ways, both managed to centralise the collection of funds in their hands. The former strengthened the "civil servant Raj" (Manor 1984, 1625) that came into being in the state and successfully excluded legislators from access to political spoils. This, on the one hand, caused legislators to squeeze that little amount of political spoils that remained available to them, which in turn resulted in even less developmental funds being properly allocated; on the other, it led to even higher levels of corruption. Virtually all members of the cabinet were involved in some scandals during Gundu Rao's chief ministership. The allocation of cement through illegal means became so explicit that even Congress (I) members of the State Assembly Public Accounts Committee felt obliged to sign the report accusing the chief minister (Manor 1984, 1626).

Antulay was involved in a cement scandal too. An article by Arun Shourie in the *Indian Express* (31 August 1981; see also Shourie 1983) in the summer of 1981, revealed that the Maharashtra chief minister orchestrated what was arguably hitherto the biggest scam in the allocation of public goods. Antulay collected a huge amount of money through a number of private trusts—the most famous being named after the prime minister herself, the Indira Gandhi Prishtan Trust—from private industrialists in exchange for a bigger allocation of cement quotas. This guaranteed he remained in power. Indeed, he was only removed when the

Bombay High Court upheld the charges against him in February 1982 (*The Hindu*, 13 January 1982). Until then, he was not removed from the chief ministership, despite the discontent among the powerful Maratha lobby (which, as we have seen, had been significantly reduced in the number of both legislators and cabinet ministers) and the overlapping farmers' agitation which had its epicentre in Maharashtra (*Indian Express*, 18 November 1980; on the farmers' movements see Brass 1995).

Antulay and Gundu Rao adopted very different techniques to reach the same goal. While the latter centralised control over legal and illegal sources of money and political spoils, the former shared such sources with some of his legislators. As a consequence, when they were removed from the chief ministership, Gundu Rao rapidly lost influence and power within the party (*India Today*, 30 September 1984); Antulay, on the contrary, maintained significant authority over the party in Maharashtra (*Indian Express*, 21 January 1982; *India Today*, 15 October 1983; 16 March 1984).

Other chief ministers throughout the country adopted similar strategies. The good relationship between the Chief Minister of Madhya Pradesh, Arjun Singh, and the Union Carbide chairman, Warren Anderson—who was allegedly allowed to flee the country shortly after the Bhopal tragedy thanks to an order of the Chief Minister himself (*The Hindu*, 10 June 2010)—was probably based on something more concrete than personal friendship. The Chief Minister of Rajasthan, Jagannath Pahadia, had to be removed in the summer of 1981 "because his government's incompetence and corrupt ways had become too much even by the prevailing permissive standards" (Malhotra 1989, 246). More examples could easily be provided.

To sum up, Sanjay Gandhi's death led to a reconfiguration of the political equilibria in virtually all states, especially those where the Congress (I) was ruling. In most cases, incompetent chief ministers, lacking their own local support bases, had to increase the amount of money that they could provide to the party in order to stay in power. So did many legislators who feared being side-lined after their mentor's death. This was seen as the only way to rapidly find a new, local mentor who could provide them with political protection. In the process, fewer and fewer resources were distributed in the constituencies. The pyramidal system of corruption that had come into being in the early 1970s reached new heights.[39]

The process of political realignment in the wake of Sanjay Gandhi's death intertwined with a massive process of defections and counter-defections that affected the entire party system. This resulted, in most cases, in a blurring of the lines between the political parties and their support bases, which rendered the link between voters and their representatives even feebler.

The Congress (I) in the States

We have already mentioned how, in the wake of Mrs Gandhi's defeat in 1977, the Congress was affected by a haemorrhage of party-men. More defections occurred following the party split in January 1978 and Devraj Urs's decision to leave the newly born Congress (I) in 1979. Before the 1980 general elections, when many politicians sensed that the responsibilities for the disastrous economic, social and political situation were attributed to the Janata Party, many former Congressmen re-joined Mrs Gandhi's party, along with a series of politicians from other parties, eager to join the bandwagon. The same thing happened, on an even larger scale, following the Congress (I)'s massive victory in January 1980 and the announcement that the elections to the legislative assemblies of nine states were to be held in a few months (*Indian Express*, 11 January, 22 January, 9 March, 27 April, and 8 May 1980; *Times of India*, 24 January and 1 February 1980).

To make a long story short, the massive process of defections and counter-defections which affected the entire party system between 1977 and 1980 caused not only a multiplication of the factions within the Congress (I), but also the social bases supporting the party in virtually every state to blur and to lose coherence.[40] The realignment of the political equilibria following Sanjay Gandhi's death expedited this process. This in turn led to a significant change in the nature of factionalism. The faction bosses stopped representing anything but themselves. Region, caste, and specific economic interests—the major sources of "traditional" factionalism—were now represented by a plurality of actors in a plurality of parties. Moreover, effective dominance at the local level was often in contrast with another extremely important source of political legitimation, namely protection from the Congress (I) high command. Mrs Gandhi was extremely wary of powerful party leaders at the local level, as they potentially represented a threat to her power position.

The confused political situation in most states and the intense factional fights led, in many cases, to the inability by legislators to attend to their constituencies' needs. This was due not only to the fact that trying to resist the attacks of dissident factions became the principal political activity of those in power, but also to the absence of any coordination between different levels of the polity and of the administration, as rapid shifts in the power structures at the top brought about major changes in both the civil service and in the local institutions like cooperatives, rural banks, state corporations et cetera. In short, the Congress (I) party lost its ability to govern and to distribute patronage effectively.

Two examples (Maharashtra and Andhra Pradesh) will illustrate this point. The political situation in Maharashtra on the eve of the general elections in 1980 was quite confused. The split of the Congress in 1978 had resulted in two rather strong parties: one led by Mrs Gandhi's lieutenants A. R. Antulay and Shankarrao Bhavrao Chavan; and another led by the two Maratha bosses Yashwantrao Balwantrao Chavan and Sharad Pawar. To oversimplify things, the Congress (I) represented the "new" guard, made up not only of Sanjay's loyalists, but also by a group of young, educated non-Marathas who had entered politics recently, plus a certain number of Maratha leaders who decided not to abandon Mrs Gandhi. Chavan and Pawar's party, on the other hand, included many of the old guard who had resented the entry into politics of the new—and often non-Maratha—generations.

Things became further complicated after the state elections in March 1978. The Congress (I) won 62 seats,[41] the Congress 69,[42] and the Janata Party 99.[43] The two Congresses, despite Y. B. Chavan and Pawar's reluctance, chose to form a coalition government. Such an unstable situation lasted till the summer, when Pawar, with some of his followers, quit the Congress and formed a brand new party, the Parallel Congress, which allied with the Janata Party and formed a coalition government headed by Sharad Pawar himself. Therefore, the two Congresses were opposing the Parallel Congress-Janata coalition. Many legislators of the two Congresses thought that the two parties could merge, despite Y. B. Chavan's resistance. Indeed, by August 1979 many members of the Congress—most of whom represented the Maratha-sugar lobby of western Maharashtra—had defected to the Congress (I). These defections "ensured the spectacular success of the Congress (I)" in the 1980 elections (Lele 1990, 191). In the meantime, Devraj Urs quit the party and, together with

Sharad Pawar's Parallel Congress and Y. B. Chavan's Congress, formed the Congress (U). Mrs Gandhi's victory brought even more people into the Congress (I)'s fold, while at the same time, those who could not tolerate the growing influence of Sanjay's men left Mrs Gandhi's party (in some cases for the second or third time in a few months) and joined the Congress (U) (*Indian Express*, 22 January 1980), which was still in power in the state. The imposition of the President's Rule in February 1980 and the call for fresh elections led to an intensification of this two-way process.

The selection of candidates put the Congress (I) under severe stress. The local Youth Congress (I) asked for as many as 100 nominees (*Indian Express*, 8 April 1980); Vasantdada Patil and Ramrao Adik, two powerful Maratha bosses, felt threatened but, at the same time, enough of their followers were accommodated—including Patil's wife, Shalini Patil—to convince them not to leave the party (*Indian Express*, 4 May 1980); over 100 Congress (I) rebels actively campaigned against the official party nominee and in some cases left the party (*The Hindu*, 8 May 1980); Antulay, who was very close to the Delhi circles, managed to get as many as 150 seats for his followers (*India Today*, 16 May 1980), which was also reflected in the doubling of the number of Muslim representatives in the Legislative Assembly (*Indian Express*, 6 June 1980); the powerful Maratha lobby, although represented by people like Patil, S. B. Chavan, and Adik, was nevertheless frustrated by the sharp reduction in the proportion of seats allocated to the community—from the "normal" 80 per cent to about 30 per cent (*Indian Express*, 21 May 1980). This, of course, reinforced the Congress (U)'s attraction. The fact that the final list of candidates was decided by Kamal Nath (*India Today*, 16 May 1980), a well-known Sanjay loyalist who knew little about state politics, did not ease the tensions within the party. The situation was so confusing that—as in many other states—the Congress (I) Legislature party[44] had to officially ask Mrs Gandhi to choose a chief minister herself (*Indian Express*, 07 June 1980).

Sanjay's death brought about a realignment of the factions in the state. Jayant Lele (1990) sees the political conflict in Maharashtra in the first half of the 1980s as one between the "elite pluralists" and the "populists". The major component of the former was the Maratha lobby, while the bulk of the latter was made up of Antulay's followers. The populists, Lele argues, made an attempt to tilt the political balance against the elite pluralists, who managed to resist the attack. However, things were more complicated than that.

In the first place, the Maratha lobby was far from being a unified force. As we have seen, it was split between a number of different faction leaders belonging to at least three different parties—the Congress (U), the Congress (I) and, to a lesser extent, the Janata Party. Furthermore, Sharad Joshi's farmers' movement—although officially apolitical—could count on a solid base of support in all parties. Moreover, in some cases, powerful Maratha legislators had followers among MLAs belonging to different parties. Sharad Pawar, for example, had a considerable following in the Congress (I) Legislature party, despite being the leader of the opposition (*Indian Express*, 13 January 1982). Similarly, Y. B. Chavan could count on a solid base of support in the Congress (I) even before officially joining the party in June 1981. Moreover, the very day that he wrote to Mrs Gandhi expressing his desire to join her party, 37 Congress (U) office bearers resigned in support of the move (*The Hindu*, 10 June 1981) and expressed their desire to follow Y. B. Chavan. Furthermore, other Maratha leaders, like Mrs Premila Chavan, rapidly shifted their allegiance according to the personal favours they received, apparently irrespective of any other consideration (*Indian Express*, 26 October 1980; 10 January, 18 April 1981) and not distinguishing at all between the "elite pluralists" and the "populists".

Secondly, the "populists" were at least as divided as the Maratha lobby. The 80-odd members of the Youth Congress (I) faction, who had strongly supported the nomination of Antulay as the chief minister, at first tried to act in a somewhat coordinated manner in order to secure their position, shifting their loyalty in order to find a mentor who could provide them with the protection that Sanjay Gandhi used to guarantee. For example, when Antulay understood that his position was not unchallenged in the wake of Sanjay's death, he established contacts with part of the old guard that had supported Mrs Chavan's confirmation as the Maharashtra Pradesh Congress (I) Committee chief (*Indian Express*, 25 July 1980). However, given that Mrs Chavan, as any other party boss in the state, was changing her system of alliances at least as rapidly, the Youth Congress (I) lobby ceased to act as such quite soon, as individual alliances prevailed. As we have already mentioned, Antulay, skilfully exploiting his position as chief minister, managed, on the one hand, to "create alternative channels of patronage for the newcomers" (Lele 1990, 194)—more traditional sources like the *zilla parishad*[45] and the cooperatives were firmly in the hands of the old guard—while, at the same time, he side-lined those among the newcomers who did not align with him; on the other, he successfully established contacts with part of the Maratha-sugar lobby, in order to secure his position (*The Hindu*, 20 September 1981).

To further complicate things, the central leadership of the party actively intervened in the state's politics. Not only did Mrs Gandhi act as the final arbiter in all major decisions, but central ministers led factions directly from the centre, thus developing a network of factional alliances between different levels of the party and polity (*India Today*, 15 February 1981). In some cases, central ministers were even included in the PCC(I)s (*Indian Express*, 18 April 1981). Furthermore, central ministers from other states were sent to mediate among different factions (see, for example, Narasimha Rao's mission to Bombay in September 1981 (*The Hindu*, 19 September 1981), or V. P. Singh's in August 1984 (*India Today*, 15 August 1984)).

The choice of an inept chief minister like Babasaheb Bhosale to replace Antulay (in the wake of the Bombay High Court's verdict) certainly did not contribute to simplifying the situation. In fact, the new chief minister could not even count on a small group of supporters in the Legislature party. Indeed, most politicians in the state were taken by surprise by Mrs Gandhi's choice (*Indian Express*, 21 January 1982; see also *India Today*, 15 April 1982). Factional leaders started conspiring against Bhosale from the very first day of his government (*Hindustan Times*, 1 April 1982). Occasional truces, usually following Mrs Gandhi's intervention against dissidents, or the expulsion of some of them for anti-party activities in other states, or following a cabinet reshuffle/expansion, did not last long.

In February 1983, when Bhosale's position had become untenable, Mrs Gandhi finally decided to let the Congress (I) Legislature Party choose its own chief minister. Vasantdada Patil, an exponent of the sugar-Maratha lobby, became the new chief minister. However, Mrs Gandhi imposed Ramrao Adik (Patil's arch enemy) as deputy chief minister, so that a delicate equilibrium had to be found. The task was not easy considering that a meeting of disgruntled party members was held simultaneously with the swearing-in ceremony (India Today, 16 February 1983).

Although Patil was able to hold his position till the end of the legislature, destructive factionalism did not stop. In fact, every time the administration had to take a decision involving the distribution of any kind of state resource, factionalism increased to new heights. The overall result was that in many cases patronage was not distributed at all, as no agreement could be found (*India Today*, 15 November 1984).

To sum up, in the first half of the 1980s, the politics of Maharashtra underwent a process of change and confusion. On the one hand, the political dominance of the Maratha-sugar lobby was seriously challenged. This was possible, despite the fact that the socio-economic dominance of the community was by no means under discussion, because the split in 1978 had created a political vacuum that was rapidly filled by a younger generation of politicians, who were backed by Sanjay Gandhi. However, when it became clear that being part of Congress (I) led by a member of the Gandhi family was still the best political asset for gaining power, many who had left Mrs Gandhi in the late 1970s or earlier rejoined her party. In the process, many who had been part of the Janata Party chose to jump on Mrs Gandhi's bandwagon. At the same time, those who feared the return of powerful party bosses either enlarged the ranks of the Congress (I) dissidents, or defected to the opposition, or looked for a new political patron. Sanjay Gandhi's death sped up this process and led to a reconsideration of the political equilibrium in the state. The overall result was that the party social base blurred and overlapped with that of the other congresses or other opposition parties in the state. Within the Congress (I) party many conflicting social groups represented by a plurality of actors multiplied their claims for a share of power, thus leading to the virtual paralysis of the state's administration.

This occurred not only because the chief minister and his supporters had to spend more time trying to defend themselves from the attacks and flying to Delhi to discuss even minor issues with the party high command; but also because the continuous changes at the top of the administration and the numberless reshuffles of the Cabinet were followed by major shake-ups of the state's administrative machinery.

A similar situation developed in several other states. In Andhra Pradesh, for example, four chief ministers were removed between Mrs Gandhi's comeback in January 1980 and the Congress (I)'s defeat in the state elections in January 1983: Marri Chenna Reddy (March 1978–October 1980), Tanguturi Anjaiah (October 1980–February 1982), Bhavanam Venkatarami Reddy (February–September 1982), and Kotla Vijaya Bhaskara Reddy (September 1982–January 1983). In the process, factionalism reached ridiculous proportions. T. Anjaiah's Cabinet rose to the record number of 63 members (the central government was made up of 49 members and UP's cabinet of 20 (*Indian Express*, 4 December 1980)), while the Andhra PCC(I) became larger than the Legislative Council and the Legislative assemblies of Haryana and Himanchal Pradesh put together. There were factions named after every former chief minister, and after every major caste or regional group (*Times of India*, 5 September 1982); there were "factions within factions" (*Hindustan Times*, 28 June 1982), and even a faction that called itself "the loyal dissidents" (*Times of India*, 8 November 1982).

Several elements that characterised the political situation in Maharashtra and many other states could be found in the politics of Andhra Pradesh: the appointment of non-entities as chief ministers without taking into consideration the local PCC(I) (*The Hindu*, 16 September 1981); the continuous intervention of the party high command in state affairs (e.g *Indian Express*, 25 November 1980; *Hindustan Times*, 17 February 1982) and the direct involvement of central ministers in the administration of the state (especially Bishma Narain Singh and Narasimha Rao)—"decisions [were] taken in New Delhi" (*Hindustan Times*, 7 April 1982) according to Anjiah himself; the development of factions between the centre and the state (*Indian Express*, 14 October 1980]; the blockade of the administrative machinery (*Indian Express*, 12 September 1980, 15 May 1981; *The Hindu*, 1 November 1981; *Times of India*, 05 September 1982), with the Cabinet not meeting for as long as three months (*Indian Express*, 22 September 1980); the failure in distributing resources—a mid-day meal scheme for school children pompously announced in September 1982, and supposed to be launched on 2 October 1982, was finally presented over a month later, simply because the administration failed to be ready on time (*Times of India*, 15 November 1982); and the rapid reconstitutions of alliances, even between former enemies (*Times of India*, 08 October 1982).

However, an important element distinguished Maharashtra and Andhra Pradesh. In the latter state, the support bases of the parties did not blur or overlap, or only to a minimum extent. Until January 1983, Andhra could be cited as one of the best examples available of the way the "Congress System" worked. The Congress (I) was the only credible party that could form a government and distribute patronage. Therefore, it continued to function as an umbrella organisation comprising both the ruling party and its "opposition", which came from the ranks of the party itself.

The main difference between Andhra's Congress in the 1960s and in the early 1980s was that in the former case, the organisational set up of the party was still capable of responding to the demands coming from below in a rather effective way (Weiner 1967, pt. III). The solutions found to the various agitations that marked the state's history (see Reddy 1989) clearly demonstrate the party's responsiveness to the demands coming from Andhra's society. In the 1980s, such responsiveness was completely lost. On the one hand, the Congress (I) party was not able to interpret the growing regional sentiments that marked Andhra's society. It is sufficient to note that the 1983 electoral campaign was based entirely on the need for a strong *central* government, at a time when the continuous interventions of the centre in the state were deeply resented. Rajiv Gandhi even managed to deepen these regional sentiments—when he humiliated Chief Minister Anjaiah who had come to welcome him at the airport (*The Hindu*, 3 February 1982).

Nandamuri Taraka Rama Rao's (NTR) resounding victory in January 1983 was due, to a significant extent, to his promise to defend the pride of the Telugu people. It was his newly formed Telugu Desam Party (TDP) that played upon—and ignited—such feelings. Along with the growing regional sentiments, the TDP also received most of the anti-Congress vote. In 1978, opposition parties had polled 51.28 per cent of the votes, plus 9.2 per cent that had gone to independent candidates (in most cases Congress rebels). In 1983, the TDP polled 48.6 per cent of the votes out of 59 per cent of the votes totalled by opposition parties (plus 9.19 per cent of the votes polled by independents). The Congress (I) polled 39.25 per cent in 1978 and 33.58 per cent in 1983.

The TDP, besides making inroads into the Congress (I) vote, collected the vote of the former Swatantra Party, the various Socialist parties and the Janata Party. Moreover, most of the leaders of all opposition parties barring the communists joined the TDP. In fact, a bipolar party system emerged in Andhra.

This would be confirmed by the caste composition of the support base that made NTR's victory possible. According to many observers, this was very different from that of the Congress. While the latter counted on a sort of "coalition of extremes" made up of the dominant caste of the Reddis plus the Scheduled Classes, Scheduled Tribes, the Muslims and other minorities, the TDP was supported by the other landed (and more and more entrepreneurial (Damodaran 2008, ch. 4)) caste, the Kammas—

NTR was a Kamma himself—and the bulk of the "backward classes" which were extremely divided, but united against the "special treatment" which the Congress party had reserved to the Scheduled Classes and Tribes (*Economic and Political Weekly*, 24 December 1983; Reddy 1989].

In short, the emergence of a bipolar system at state level resulted in a sharpening of the support bases of the two principal parties in the state. The abolition of the positions of 2,000 part-time village officials in January 1984, the adoption of a resolution abolishing the Congress (I)-dominated Legislative Council in March 1983 and, after Indira Gandhi's assassination, the major administrative reform of the local level bureaucracy (Tummala 1986, 386), on the one hand, undermined the dominance of the Congress (I) on the state's administration, and, on the other hand, sharpened the differences between the two parties.

However, Andhra was some sort of exception in India's political panorama of the 1980s. In general, the lines between the parties tended to blur rather than to diverge. Where the anti-Congress (I) front was made up of ideologically committed parties—as in West Bengal and Kerala, but also in Assam—differences remained important. However, in general terms, this was not the case in Andhra, especially because defections and counter-defections continued for the entire legislature. During the course of 1984, a few months before the general elections, the admittance of "newcomers" was made with even less consideration. Among those welcomed in the Congress (I) fold were Satyendra Narain Sinha, a powerful Jat leader from Bihar recently upstaged by the Janata Party President Chandrashekar and who had left the congress in 1969; Abdul Halim Khan, former UP minister and chief aide of H. N. Bahuguna; Pawan Dewan, former Janata minister in Madhya Pradesh; and so on. The open-door policy was adopted also in respect to the party hierarchy: the appointment of three new general secretaries in the course of 1984—A. K. Antony (who had contested against the party in the 1980 elections), Chand Ram (who was a Union minister in the Janata government), and Abdul Ghafoor (who joined the party very recently)—caused "considerable disquiet" in the Congress (I) ranks (*India Today*, 15 October 1984) and continued the process of the blurring of the lines between parties and social bases.

The confusion characterising the Congress (I) made it unable to distribute patronage. Extreme factionalism, combined with the blurring of the lines between parties and social bases, led, on the one hand, to a virtual halt of the states' administrative machineries, as deciding how to distribute patronage became increasingly difficult, to the point that, in many instances, no decision at all could be taken. On the other, it became objectively difficult to give a share of the cake to each faction, not only because the slow economic growth rates of the past decades made conciliating conflicting interests harder, but also because the incoherence of the social base of the party made this task even more difficult. Moreover, the "awakening" of Indian subaltern strata made them less prone to accept the fact that the great majority of the developmental resources allocated for anti-poverty programmes were intercepted before reaching the intended targets (Guhan 1980, 1979). More generally, interests in Indian society were crystallising rather than blurring (Manor 1983a). Such a crystallisation of interests would have required sharper not more blurred lines between different parties. As a consequence, the demand for political representation increased in intensity.

In the first half of the 1980s it became clear not only that the era of Congress dominance was about to end, but also that the way in which such a dominance had been acquired—through the distribution of patronage—was no longer practicable. Other ways to build political support had to be found. One response, as we shall see in chapter 3, was the appeal to regional feelings in various forms. Another, implemented at national level, was the attempt by the BJP to build up a "Hindu electorate", which had considerable success. Still another, was Mrs Gandhi's attempt to build up a national constituency, appealing to "national" social groups directly from the centre.

In the following section we will see how Rajiv Gandhi's entry into politics impacted on the Congress (I) and how the attempts to refurbish the organisation of the party failed. Indeed, from what we have seen above, it is clear that any attempt in this direction was doomed to fail.

Reform of the Congress (I): Rajiv Gandhi's Attempt

Rajiv Gandhi finally decided to enter politics, despite his own and his wife's reservations, in February 1981. He chose to contest election from Amethi, the constituency that had been his brother's. Those who had hoped that Rajiv's entry into politics would bring the Youth Congress (I) back to the centre of the political stage were left disappointed. Rajiv Gandhi's strategy towards the Congress (I) was twofold: in the first place, similarly to what had been his brother's strategy, he tried to build up his own base of supporters in the Youth Congress (I). However, this did not necessarily mean that those who had been part of Sanjay's coterie would automatically be included in Rajiv's "brigade". In fact, this was not the case. On the one hand, Rajiv personally disliked some of the people who had been Sanjay's close advisors. In particular, "Mr Clean", as the press began to call him to underline his extraneousness to turbid political practices, did not want to associate with political thugs. On the other hand, the political realignments that followed Sanjay's death and the break of the unity of the Sanjay factions in most states did not make the revival of the Youth Congress (I) an easy task anyway. The appointment of Ghulam Nabi Azad (who was very close to Rajiv Gandhi) as president of the Youth Congress (I) in November 1980 was interpreted by many as the first sign that Rajiv was not willing to provide Sanjay's friends with the protection they needed (*Indian Express*, 21 November 1980). In the following years, Rajiv Gandhi relied on his own men rather than on his brother's.

Secondly, Rajiv Gandhi did not concentrate his energy solely on the Youth Congress (I). In fact, he tried to reorganise the Congress (I) too. As far as the Youth Congress (I) was concerned, Rajiv's efforts did not point so much at filling the legislative assemblies of the country with his men;[46] rather, he considered the Youth Congress (I) not as a parallel and ultimately rival organisation, but as a laboratory where the younger generations could be trained before joining the party. He organised several training camps that were held throughout the country from September 1982. More than 25 camps were held in every state, preceding a six-week national camp that took place in Delhi in February 1983, where 150 carefully selected Youth Congress (I) members were trained to become the future national executives of the party (*India Today*, 15 March 1983). Similar camps were organised for all the organisations belonging to the Congress "Parivar"—the Congress (I) Sewa Dal, the National Students' Union of India, the Women's wing and the Congress (I) party itself (*India Today*, 15 September 1983). The Congress (I) suddenly "turned into a beehive of activity" (Singh 1990, 63).

Rajiv Gandhi also made an attempt to restore the Congress (I)'s ability to gather information from the grassroots and transmit it to the top. He selected 434 graduates throughout the country to work as Youth Congress (I) coordinators. Their task was to collect data from every district of the country about the implementation of the new 20-point programme,[47] and about corrupt candidates who were not popular in their constituencies (*India Today*, 15 September 1983). Needless to say, these coordinators were usually treated with hostility by the local branches of the party that, in previous years, had sent bogus reports to Delhi about the implementation of the central government programmes. The coordinators revealed how the reality was further from the picture that the PCC(I) chiefs and the chief ministers had portrayed. The data collected by Rajiv's coordinators and elaborated centrally thorough a computer located in the party's headquarter in Delhi, demonstrated how the Congress (I) was no longer able to distribute patronage, let alone to implement nation-wide programmes efficiently like the Integrated Rural Development Programme (IRDP) or the National Rural Employment Programme (NREP)[48] (*India Today*, 15 September 1983).

The new dynamism injected by Rajiv Gandhi involved the parent organisation too. Training camps were organised and five powerful committees (headed by Pranab Mukherjee, Narasimha Rao, Buta Singh, V. P. Singh, and Shiv Shankar) were set up to monitor the implementation of the central programmes and to question chief ministers about their governments' inefficiencies and about the party's prospects in the forthcoming elections. A great number of party instructors were trained and 372 of them were given the task of recruiting 20,000 members who in turn would have had to recruit a further million members.

All these activities, including a meeting of the AICC(I) in October 1983 in Bombay (the Committee had not gathered for almost three years), followed by the 77th plenary session of the Congress party in December 1983, were more cosmetic than substantial. As a matter of fact, Rajiv Gandhi was not recognised as a leader outside Delhi, not to speak of his lieutenants, who were in many cases treated with open hostility (*India Today*, 15 April 1984). Further, as the general elections approached, powerful party-men in most states became less and less tolerant of Rajiv's attempt to change things (*Indian Express*, 04 September 1984). This was especially due to the "institutionalisation" of the central intervention in the selection of candidates. The DCC(I), till then the first step in the preparation of the lists of candidates, was replaced by a set of "coordination committees" under the direct supervision of Rajiv Gandhi. The task of the committees was to send three names per constituency to be screened by the Central Parliamentary Board. This in turn would base its decision on the recommendations of the Youth Congress (I) coordinators (*India Today*, 15 October 1984).

All these attempts to renew the image of the party and to make it a tool for information gathering at local level needed the collaboration of the "traditional" party structure—DCCs, PCCs—in order to achieve the intended outcome. However, the party structure—not surprisingly—was not willing to work for the success of an operation whose ultimate objective was to bypass that very structure. Therefore, Rajiv Gandhi's attempt was in fact doomed to failure. It was based on the naïve conviction that a renewal of the party would have been welcomed, as it was evident to all that the bad shape of the party was seriously hindering its chances to win elections, as the results of the state elections in Andhra Pradesh and Karnataka in January 1983 showed (*India Today*, 16 January 1983). However, as the opposition to hold party elections by most chief ministers and party workers revealed (*Times of India*, 11 September 1982), nobody but Rajiv and his close associates seemed to be interested in the reorganisation of the party. Mrs Gandhi's assassination in October 1984 and the subsequent appointment of Rajiv Gandhi as prime minister put an end to any attempt to reform the Congress (I).

Declining Governability: The Deterioration of Law and Order

A particular example of the general inefficiency of the state governments was their inability to tackle a deteriorating law and order situation and to impede its further deterioration. We have already mentioned how, during the Janata phase, the security conditions of the population severely diminished, especially in the north. Indeed, the restoration of order was one of the main tasks that "a government that works" was expected to achieve.

Violence stems from a number of different reasons. Even though it is difficult to single out a specific reason why violence erupts, for merely analytical purposes, it is possible to list a set of reasons why disorder occurs, with particular reference to the situation in the early 1980s.

In the first place, regional issues occasionally resulted in widespread lawlessness. In the first half of the 1980s this happened in Punjab, Assam, and, to a much lesser extent, Andhra Pradesh.[49] In Punjab, the party of the Sikhs, the Akali Dal, had asked in 1973 for the implementation of a set of demands (the so-called Anandpur Resolution) concerning the share of the rivers crossing Punjab with neighbouring states, the end of the status of Chandigarh as a shared capital between Punjab and Haryana and the like. As we shall see in greater detail in chapter 4, these demands sparked off a prolonged conflict between the government and the leadership of the Sikhs that would eventually result in one of the bloodiest political conflicts of India's independent history. In Assam, the alteration of the demographic equilibrium due to massive immigration from Bangladesh and West Bengal reached a critical point. In Andhra Pradesh, widespread agitation followed NTR's dismissal by the Governor, Thakur Ram Lal, which was interpreted as yet another central interference in the state's affairs.

Secondly, political parties sometimes caused violence to break out. We have already mentioned that Sanjay's followers did not hesitate to resort to violent means. However, this was not limited to Youth Congress (I) members. Virtually every party resorted or threatened to resort to such means in order to achieve their political goals. A much-used technique was to deliberately create a situation where it was possible to accuse the state government of not being able to maintain law and order, as Congress (I) workers did in Andhra Pradesh in July 1984 (*The Hindu*, 30 July 1984). The same technique was used by the Congress (I) party in an attempt to delegitimise the newly elected state government in Jammu and Kashmir. Between September 1983 and February 1984, more than 40,000 Congress (I) workers were arrested and 1,500 people were injured in a series of incidents (*India Today*, 15 February 1984). At times, factional squabbles within the parties resulted in violent clashes that needed the intervention of the police. A particular form of political violence was that connected with various Naxalite groups that intensified their activities and spread outside West Bengal, reaching Andhra Pradesh, Bihar, and even Maharashtra.

Third, ethnic violence reached new heights. Broadly speaking three kinds of conflicts can be classified as ethnic—communal, caste, and tribal conflicts.[50] The principal manifestation of communal hatred in India is that between Hindus and Muslims, even though communal animosity is by no means limited to the two largest communities. Communalism in India has a long history (Bayly 1985). However, the phenomenon reached gigantic proportions in the early 1980s. According to official reports (MHA 1980–82) communal incidents increased from 196 in 1976 to 474 in 1982. With the explosion of communal conflicts in Assam and Punjab in 1983–4, the figure increased to 2185 (Torri 2007, 688).

While conflicts between members of different communities were more frequent in north Indian towns, the south was by no means free of communal violence.

This stemmed from a variety of reasons. In general terms, as showed by Varshney (2002), conflicts are more likely to occur when the two communities are not economically integrated. Indeed, if the two communities live in separate parts of the town and are engaged in different economic activities, violence erupts more easily. The riots in Biharsharif (Bihar) in May 1981 are a case in point (Engineer 1981).

Other, more contingent, factors contribute to the emergence of communal violence. The police seem to have a particularly important role. In most of the communal riots of the early 1980s, police forces were either directly involved in the explosion of violence (e.g. in Moradabad in August 1980 (*Indian Express*, 17 August 1980)), or participated in the looting and arsons (as in Biharsharif (*Indian Express*, 05 May 1981)), or were reluctant to intervene to restore law and order and the army had to be deployed in several instances.

Another factor that directly contributed to spread hatred was the network of communal organisations, in particular the RSS. Activists of such organisations often spread rumours that ignite the spirits of those affected by communal riots, "when conventional criteria of credibility and judgement seem suspended" (Hansen 1999, 204). For example, the RSS activists were apparently responsible for having spread the rumour that 200 Yadavs had been slaughtered by Muslims in Biharsharif, which obviously provoked an escalation of violence (Engineer 1981).

Other times, the leaders of these organisations made explosive declarations to the press. This was the case with the riots which occurred in Bombay in May 1984, in the aftermath of the declarations, widely reported by the Bombay Urdu weeklies, of Balasaheb Thackeray (leader of the Shiv Sena and founder of the Bombay-based Maha Sangh), who, according to these sources, insulted the prophet and compared the Muslims to a cancer to excise (*India Today*, 15 June 1984).

Still other times, communal riots followed the route of religious processions. In this respect, the early 1980s saw the emergence of a new phenomenon, the *yatras*. These were religious-cum-political processions organised on a national scale. The ultimate aim was to foster the construction of a Hindu electorate (Jaffrelot 1996). The RSS and its organisations, in particular the Vishwa Hindu Parishad (VHP), were engaged in the promotion of this form of political pilgrimage. In November 1983, the VHP promoted the *Ekatmata Yatra*. About sixty million people attended the *yatra* (Andersen and Damle 1987, 135) in 531 (out of 534) districts of the country. Incidents occurred throughout the country, especially in those areas which had been affected by communal tensions in the previous years, or where a significant number of Muslim families had achieved a relative degree of prosperity thanks to the remittances coming from the Gulf (*India Today*, 16 November 1983).

Finally, occasionally it was the Congress (I) itself that, for mere political reasons, sparked off the row of communal hatred. In Punjab, Sanjay Gandhi and Zail Singh's attempt to find a "Sikh leader who was more Sikh than the Akalis"[51] (interview with Mark Tully, Delhi, 10 December 2010), led to the "creation" and empowerment of Jarnail Singh Bhindranwale, who would eventually set up his own army and terrorise both heterodox Sikhs (Nirankaris) and Punjabi Hindus, until his death during Operation Bluestar in June 1984.

Tribal violence disrupted especially the north-east of the country. In Assam, violence erupted on a large scale in the last part of the 1970s. The agitation against "foreigners", i.e. illegal immigrants from Bangladesh and West Bengal, soon took a communal tone, as the majority of "foreigners" were Muslims. However, the mounting tension soon transformed what was a political conflict—Assamese feared being outnumbered by immigrants and therefore excluded from the control of state politics—into a "Hobbesian war of all against all" (*India Today*, 16 March 1983). In particular, the tribals of the hills played a major role in a number of violent episodes, including the most notorious one, in Nellie during the state elections in 1983. Other states of the north-east were affected by tribal "unrest". In Tripura, violence reached "unparalleled" levels (*Indian Express*, 11 June 1980). In Meghalaya the situation was equally dramatic (*Indian Express*, 31 May 1980).

Finally, caste disputes were perhaps the major source of violence in the 1980s, especially in the north, where, as we have seen, the politics of reservations pursued by the Janata governments in some states had exacerbated underlying tensions. In fact, Uttar Pradesh and Bihar were two of the most affected states, but caste-related violence was an all-India phenomenon. In virtually all cases, the roots of the conflicts were socio-economic tensions. In this respect, the "awakening" of the Indian subaltern strata—who were aware of their rights and, in general, more and more conscious that "their subhuman existence was not necessarily desirable (whatever the orthodox branches of Hinduism might say)" (Torri 2007, 683)—and the growing assertiveness of ascending social groups help explain most of the conflicts. Two examples will illustrate the point. In April 1981, two Dalits were shot dead by a group of Rajputs in Uttar Pradesh. In the shooting that followed, at least 28 people were injured. Apparently the Dalits (who were agricultural labourers in the Rajput's fields) were shot because they asked for their wages. When the landowner refused to pay them, they in turn refused to go home and even demanded that their wage should be in accordance with the minimum wage legislation (*Indian Express*, 3 April 1981). The second example is the lawlessness that characterised parts of Gujarat in October 1984. Two warring factions—made up of Patils and Kshatriyas, respectively—faced each other for no apparent reason. It is likely that the underlying reason was the resentment among Patils (a dominant landowning caste in Gujarat) of the newly acquired power of the Kshatriya (a lower-caste group in the state) that had been at the centre of the Congress (I) electoral strategy known as KHAM (*India Today*, 15 October 1984). Newspapers reported similar events on a daily basis. Of course, caste violence was not new in India. However, what was new was the scale of the phenomenon, which seemed to bring India back "into medieval times" (*Times of India*, 1 January 1983).

From what we have reported so far, it should be clear that all the above-mentioned factors were intertwined. The situation in Punjab, for example, originated from purely regional problems, but it soon took communal tones, which were in turn exploited by all political parties. Similarly, caste violence cannot be separated from other forms of social unrest. In Gujarat, for example, the two-month long students' agitation against the reservations accorded to Scheduled classes applicants for post-graduate courses was clearly something more than caste violence, as it interrelated with the youths' frustration due to high unemployment (*Times of India*, 05 February 1981). The Dacoits problem in UP was not simply a problem of criminality. On the contrary, the caste factor played a central role, as policemen belonging to different castes selectively repressed bands of Dacoits belonging to certain castes and not others (*The Hindu*, 3 December 1981). Tribal violence was strictly linked with Naxalite activities (*The Hindu*, 2 September 1981). The farmers' agitations which disrupted several states—in particular Maharshtra, Tamil Nadu,

Karnataka, Andhra Pradesh, and Uttar Pradesh—had an evident caste-cum-class dimension, not to mention the purely political aspect, as they were intimately linked to inter- and intra-party squabbles (Brass 1985). Finally, certain conflicts were exacerbated by an external dimension. The Pakistan intelligence services (ISI), for example, certainly had a role in providing Sikh terrorists with arms and logistical coordination (interview with Salmain Haider, Delhi, 24 January 2011). In Tamil Nadu, a bomb explosion in the airport of Madras in April 1984 expanded Sri Lanka's civil war beyond its borders.

To sum up, the law and order situation severely deteriorated in the first half of the 1980s. As we have seen, the eruption of violence stemmed from a very complex set of issues. However, if one common denominator could be found, this was the breakdown of the structure of dominance that had guaranteed the maintaining of order in the previous decades. The cornerstone of such a structure had been the Congress organisation that, through a set of effective (even though not necessarily democratic) tools, had been able to keep an acceptable law and order situation. However, the "awakening" of Indian society combined with the disintegration of the Congress organisation led to a "decline of the social order" (Frankel and Rao 1990), which made the perpetuation perpetration of the system simply impossible.

The deteriorating law and order situation had been a major factor in determining the outcome of the 1980 general elections. An important section of Indian society had "frozen" its demand for political representation, because it felt that the country needed a "government that work[ed]". For disadvantaged groups this meant, first of all, a government that could protect them. However, the Congress (I) was not able to restore order. Indeed, the situation worsened. Thus, not only was the Congress (I) increasingly unable to respond to the demand for political representation coming from Indian society, but it was not even able to guarantee acceptable security conditions to the population. Therefore, the Congress (I) began to lose its image as the protector of minorities. It is generally agreed that the Muslims did not vote en bloc for the Congress (I) even in January 1980 (Rudolph and Rudolph 1987, ch 6). The Scheduled Classes and Scheduled Tribes, although more "loyal" to Mrs Gandhi, started looking for political alternatives in order to satisfy their demand for political representation. A clear manifestation of such a pursuit of political alternatives was the formation of the Bahujan Samaj Party (BSP) in 1984 in UP.

For the middle class and the industrial bourgeoisie the desire for law and order was translated into a desire for a stop to urban unrest. However, prolonged student protests and strikes—to name just one example, the great Bombay textile strikes in 1982–83—disrupted Indian towns and cities throughout the first half of the 1980s, not to mention the frequent communal clashes.

The rich peasantry could no longer count on the Congress organisation to maintain the structure that sanctioned its dominance over the countryside. In order to maintain such dominance—a task increasingly difficult to achieve given the "awakening" of the subaltern strata—the rich peasantry resorted in most cases to violent means, which were not accepted by the victims as part of a "superior" social order, but were met with resistance and violent revenge.

Conclusion

The Congress (Indira) in the first half of the 1980s was nothing more than what its name suggested: a personal tool in the hands of its leader and a label under which politicians throughout the country could associate themselves with the prime minister, whose popularity remained relatively high.

The personalistic conception of the party became clear when, following Sanjay Gandhi's death, Rajiv was inducted into politics. From that moment, dynastic succession became the universally accepted rule, not only in the Congress, but in most other parties—e.g. in the National Conference in Jammu and Kashmir, the DMK in Tamil Nadu, and the Akali Dal in Punjab.

Parallel to the further personalisation of the party, there was a process of further centralisation. Mrs Gandhi was the final arbiter and the only authority that party-men across the country recognised. However, this power was more cosmetic than substantial. It is certainly true that Mrs Gandhi could change a chief minister at will; but it was equally true that legislators, through intense factional activity, were able to reverse her decisions, as the party high command could not control its state branches more than superficially. This, in fact, made the prime minister weaker (*Tehelka*, 15 May 1982). Therefore the Congress (I) in the first half of the 1980s was both increasingly centralised and increasingly weak.

More importantly the Congress (I) in the first half of the 1980s did not function as an effective instrument for the distribution of patronage at the local level and did not provide a government that worked, especially as far as the maintaining of order was concerned. Therefore, it lacked two of the principal reasons why it had been voted to power. Indeed, the Congress (I) performance in state elections since 1982 showed a declining trend. In Haryana and Himachal Pradesh in 1982 it ended up with less than half the seats but managed to form governments after "convincing" defectors from other parties. In Kerala and West Bengal, the party remained a marginal force. In 1983 things worsened for the ruling party when it lost its two bastions in the south—Andhra Pradesh and Karnataka. This was a particularly serious blow, as the two states had remained "loyal" to the Congress even in the elections that followed the lifting of the emergency in 1977. The Congress won the election for the municipality of Delhi and in Assam in 1983. The latter result, more than to the party's real strength, was due to the boycott of the elections by most parties in the state, which were protesting against the illegal immigration of "foreigners".[52] The victory in Delhi had, on the other hand, stemmed from a particular form of electoral strategy, that of appealing to the Hindu vote (Jaffrelot 1996) and thanks to the help of the RSS.[53] The good result of the Congress party in the Jammu region in Jammu and Kashmir was due to a similar strategy (*Economic and Political Weekly*, 2 July 1983).

The above-mentioned elements suggest that the Congress party—and indeed any other party—could not win elections the way it had done in the previous decades. In other words, it could not respond to the demand for political representation coming from large strata of Indian society. Such a demand was thus "de-frozen" and found expression not only in the increased levels of violence, but also in the emergence of new ways of political mobilisation, as we shall see in the next chapter. Mrs Gandhi, for her part, surely realised the ineffectiveness of her party as a vote-gathering machine. Indeed, after the electoral debacles in 1983 in Andhra Pradesh and Karnataka, she probably realised how the state of the Congress (I) had become an asset for the opposition. The only thing she could do was try to mobilise a national constituency from Delhi. Indeed, this is something similar to what she had tried to do in the early 1970s with the slogan "*garibi hatao!*" However, a qualitative change occurred in Mrs Gandhi's strategy. Emphasis was shifted from the rural to the urban world. At the same time new forms of political mobilisation emerged. This will be the subject of the next chapter.

3

POLITICAL MOBILISATION IN THE EARLY 1980s

Introduction

We saw in chapter 2 how the demand for political representation arising among larger and larger strata of the Indian electorate somehow "froze" during the January 1980 elections. Voters elected what promised to be a strong government that could take India out of social and economic instability. However, the inability of the Congress (I) to provide the country with "a government that worked"—especially as far as the law and order situation was concerned—resulted in a rapid "defrosting" of the demand for political representation. The ruling Congress (I) could not, in most cases, respond to this demand, given the virtual annihilation of its organisational machine and the growing awareness of the electorate. Moreover, the serious difficulties in distributing patronage at the state and local levels further reduced the Congress (I)'s ability to maintain a stable base of support, especially in the countryside. The blurring of the lines between most parties—and between their respective social bases—that we have described in chapter 2, further contributed to make unresponsiveness to the demand for political representation a structural feature of the political system.

One consequence of all this was that new forms of political mobilisation rapidly emerged. At the same time, political parties that successfully mobilised the electorate on the basis of these new forms of winning electoral support found it extremely difficult to keep their electoral support intact. Generally speaking—although each situation was peculiar in some respects—this was due to the fact that while it was relatively easy to win the support of sizeable strata of the electorate, given the high degree of unresponsiveness by the political system to the electorate's demand for political representation, the awareness and the political sophistication of the voters made the task of actually responding to this demand an extremely arduous endeavour, especially if parties expected to do so with the "traditional" political tools, namely patronage distribution and populist rhetoric.

This chapter will analyse three forms of political mobilisation that became relevant at the national level in the early 1980s. First, we will see how Mrs Gandhi mobilised a nation-wide constituency that had at its centre the urban middle class and the big industrialists. We will see how this strategy was implemented through a set of economic policies[1] and a series of more purely political initiatives. Second, we will see how the RSS network under the leadership of Balasaheb Deoras decided to undertake a set of initiatives aiming at building up a nation-wide Hindu electorate. I will also note how the RSS's and Mrs Gandhi's strategies converged to a certain extent. Third, we will analyse how growing discontent stemming from unresponsiveness to the demand for political representation was articulated in regional terms and how regional political formations aspired to become an alternative to national parties.

In the next section we will briefly deal with India's economic conditions in the early 1980s, in order to provide the necessary background against which Mrs Gandhi's economic policies were adopted and implemented.

The Indian Economy 1980–84: An Overview

In January, 1980 India was facing an extremely difficult economic situation. A severe drought, accompanied by political instability and unfavourable international circumstances (the doubling of oil prices being the most important factor), resulted in the decline in the Gross National Product of 4.8 per cent, a fall in agricultural and industrial production of 15.5 and 1.4 per cent, respectively, acute shortfalls of mass consumption commodities like kerosene or sugar,[2] heavy shortages of power, and a double-digit rate of inflation.[3] Not surprisingly, the law and order situation was at least as bad.

The new government, again not surprisingly, blamed the Janata Party's economic policies and in particular what the Indian Press called the "kulak budget", elaborated by Charan Singh in 1979. The latter had been able, first as deputy prime minister and later as finance minister, to please his "natural" constituency, i.e. the rich and middle peasantry (Byres 1988). During the two and a half years of the Janata Government, not only were investments in the agricultural sector elevated above investments in industry (Rudolph and Rudolph 1987, 329), but subsidies for fertilisers were increased from Rs 60 crore in 1976/77 to Rs 603 crore in 1979/80 (Joshi and Little 1994, 153), concessions were given to commercial banks to expand rural credit, taxes on various agricultural inputs (such as mechanical tillers, plastic PVC pipes for irrigation et cetera) were either reduced or abolished, and procurement prices for food grains were increased.[4]

On the other hand, the industrial sector and the middle class were less appeased by the Janata Party's economic policies. It was clear to the business community that a new path of development was about to be undertaken, one that would have reversed the Nerhuvian model of rapid industrialisation, to favour the rural world. The proposals for the Sixth Five-Year Plan included a reduction of the plan outlay for the industrial sector by four per cent, and an equal increase in the outlay for the agricultural sector (D6FYP).[5] The middle class was explicitly indicated by Charan Singh as the main target for mobilising additional resources through increased excise duties on items like tooth paste, soaps, biscuits, instant coffee etc. and increased direct taxation (both income and wealth taxes) (Bhattacharya 1979).

The Janata Party's economic policies tried to win the support of the most important (in numerical terms) social group in India: the poor. The electoral manifesto of the party for the 1977 elections stated that a "Gandhian" path of decentralised development would be the cornerstone of the party's anti-poverty strategy. Such a developmental strategy aimed at creating employment opportunities for the rural poor through heavy investment in the rural sector. In this respect, the Food-for-Work Programme and the peak in food grain production of 1978–79 can be seen as two of the achievements the party could be proud of (Dasgupta 1979, 400). However, the overall situation of the rural masses severely worsened during 1979. In particular, the drought, the subsequent inflation (wholesale prices rose by as much as 21.4 per cent in 1979–80

(*Economic Survey 1980*)) and the mismanagement of the situation affected the rural poor more than any other social group in India.

Therefore, the Janata Party's economic policies surely conquered the support of the middle and rich peasantry, but failed to maintain the broad electoral coalition which had allowed the party to come to power in 1977.

Needless to say, economic considerations can only partially explain the overwhelming success of the Congress (I) in the 1980 general elections.[6] However, it is arguable that the bad shape of the economy and the feeling among large strata of the electorate that Mrs Gandhi was the only alternative that could provide "a government that works",[7] necessary to set the economy back on the path of stability, played an important role in determining the results of the elections.

In this respect, it can hardly be denied that Mrs Gandhi kept her promises. Five years later the gloomy picture of the Indian economy had been replaced by a much more optimistic one. The GNP had increased by 5.42 per cent on average (*Economic Survey 1986*) and inflation was under control. India had taken off.[8] What used to be termed the "Hindu rate of growth" which had characterised the whole economic history of independent India was a thing of the past.[9]

The reasons for how India managed to enter the path of sustained growth and whether such growth was sustainable or not have been two of the major issues of debate: some emphasised the role of liberalisation measurers adopted by the government (Frankel 2005; Panagariya 2008); some underlined the role of a highly interventionist state in promoting growth as a state goal (Kohli 2006, Ghosh and Chandrashekar 2002); some others stressed how India's economic growth in the 1980s was the product of fiscal expansionism and was therefore not sustainable (Ahluwalia 2002); finally some scholars found the cause of India's economic growth in the "new" attitude of Mrs Gandhi's government towards the private sector (Rodrik and Subramanian 2004). Most of these scholars underlined the fact that, in 1980, India had a robust indigenous industrial sector and a huge, skilled workforce without which any attempt to undertake the path of growth would have been unfruitful.

This chapter will not take part in such debate. We will only suggest that it is likely that what occurred in Mrs Gandhi's views was an "ideological" turn (Raj Narain 2006). Many observers this author has spoken with in Delhi in late 2010–early 2011 shared the view that in the 1980s the prime minister did not want to repeat the rather unsuccessful economic performance of the 1970s. Thus, when she returned to power, Mrs Gandhi was probably willing to undertake a new path of development—and, as we shall see below, to change the nature of her national social base of support accordingly. This is also consistent with what Chaudhry et al. (2004) argued about the formulation of a strategy of "homegrown conditionality" for approaching the IMF, a strategy to which Mrs Gandhi gave the go-ahead.

In the next sections, we will attempt to delineate the kind of social base that Mrs Gandhi sought to build and to point out what groups were chosen as the principal allies in the process of growth and what others were, if not excluded, at least relegated to a secondary role. In order to do so, we will analyse the impact of economic policies on "national" social groups, "national" because their economic interests were affected by central government-controlled policies.

In particular, we will consider national economic policies in respect to four social groups that can be considered national, as far as their economic interests are concerned. Three of them roughly correspond to what Pranab Bardhan (1998) called the "dominant proprietary classes", namely industrial capitalists, rich farmers, and the middle class. The fourth group is made up of the Indian poor.

The Business Community

The Bombay stock market reacted positively at the proclamation of the results of the 1980 general elections (*Indian Express*, 9 January 1980). It was a clear sign that business circles were "extremely gratified" (*Economic and Political Weekly*, 26 January 1980) by the outcome. Indeed, the industrialists' gratification was justified. Indira Gandhi's government rapidly chose to change the traditional anti-capitalist approach (Guha 2007, 694),[10] to embrace what has been called a "pro-business" orientation (Rodrik and Subramanian 2004, 4). Growth became the principal state goal and industrial growth the "key-stone" (R. Venkataraman, Finance Minister, *Indian Express*, 29 February 1980) of the new strategy of development. In other words, the business community's and the state's goals converged: the government chose to "embrace ...Indian capital as the main ruling ally" (Kohli 2006, 1252).

Of course, Indian capitalists were not chosen as the main component in the political coalition being forged by the government because of their numerical strength. Their importance lay in the huge resources they were able to mobilise. In 1980, Congress (I) was far from being one of "the world's ... best-institutionalised political parties" (Rudolph and Rudolph 1987, 127) as it had been in the 1950s. Indeed, as we have seen in the previous chapters, the organisational structure of the party had been wiped away during the course of two splits (in 1969 and 1978) and because of the centralising policies of Mrs Gandhi (Manor 1983a; 1983b). Therefore, raising funds for the party was as difficult as it was important. An American scholar (Frankel 2005, 659 n83) estimated that the cost of state elections to the party exchequer was around $100,000,000 in the mid-1980s, at a time when the average per capita income was $350. The industrial sector was the only one that could provide the resources the party needed to function.

On the other hand, the business community needed the support of the government to prosper. This was even truer in a country like India where the government, beyond rhetoric, did in fact control "the commanding heights" of the economy (one just needs to consider that, after the nationalisation of six banks in the spring of 1980, the state controlled 91 per cent of the total bank deposits in the country (*Indian Express*, 1 July 1980)). The alliance between the government and the business community could therefore be founded upon solid common interests. Moreover, as we shall see in the next section, the policies favouring the industrial sector were matched by a set of measures which were aimed at winning the support of the Indian middle class—the second major ally in the government's economic strategy in the first half of the 1980s. The reciprocal advantages were clear: while the government gave important concessions to the extremely influential middle class, Indian industrialists could benefit from an expanding internal demand for industrial products and increased savings which were made available to them through the state-controlled banks (credit to the industrial sector more than doubled between 1979–80 and 1985–86; see RBI 2009, tab. 48).

The strategy favouring Indian capital was made up of two elements. First, the government sought to create a new economic environment in which the industrial sector could take advantage of the new developmental strategy. Such a new environment was not, as two scholars have argued (Rodrik and Subramanian 2004) brought about just by an "attitudinal" shift; rather, the new approach was accompanied by a set of policies that added consistency to the new stance of the government towards the private sector. Second, the government gave a series of fiscal concessions to the industrial sector in order to provide incentives to step up industrial production.

Within months from the 1980 general elections, the shift that occurred in government circles was clearly recognisable. The first sign that the new government intended to pursue a strategy that would not hinder the growth of the industrial sector was the fact that restrictions on imports were not tightened despite the acute crisis in the balance of payments of 1979–80 (Joshi and Little 1994, 59).[11] In April 1980 a new import-export policy was announced.[12] Export promotion was accompanied by a slightly more liberal import policy (in particular as far as industrial inputs were concerned) which, in any case, as specified by the finance minister himself, gave "due consideration" (*Indian Express*, 16 April 1980) to the protection of indigenous capabilities. The whole import-export policy was to be financed by the newly established Import-Export Bank (whose initial capital was set at Rs 200 crore).

Shortly afterward, the procedure for industrial licensing, including conversion, expansion and setting up of new units was centralised. In other words, the final word on any request by the business sector to expand or convert production would have been that of the economic committee of the cabinet. This, on the one hand, made the process of licensing quicker and more efficient; on the other, it channeled black money (often—if not always—necessary to obtain a licence) towards the central government.

In July, 1980 the Minister of State for Industry, Charanjit Chanana, presented a document to the Lok Sabha that constituted the basis upon which the industrial policy of the government was to be built in the following years. Apart from some very general socio-economic objectives, the statement on industrial policy contained a set of measures which removed some of the barriers which had hitherto hindered the growth of big business. Such a "rethinking on industrial policy" (*Economic and Political Weekly*, 20 September 1980) included the recognition of existing excess production capacity; the extension to all the nineteen industries coming under the Monopolies and Restricted Trade Practice Act (MRTP) and the Foreign Exchange Regulation Act (FERA) of the facility of automatic expansion by 25 per cent in a plan period; the introduction of incentives for 100 per cent export-oriented units; and other minor measures aimed at easing the process of maximisation of production. This set of "pragmatic policies" (*Indian Express*, 24 July 1980) was consistent with the new "philosophy" of the government, which was clearly enunciated by the prime minister herself two years later, when she remarked that the maintenance of "regulations whose only virtue [was] restriction on production [did] not make [them] socialists" (*Times of India*, 2 March 1982; the same argument had been made the previous year, see *The Hindu*, 15 February 1981). Such limited, internal liberalisation[13] was furthered few months later (October 1980) when the restrictions on the production of goods in excess of capacity by companies covered by the MRTP Act were completely removed, to the extent that goods were exported. The new economic environment was monitored by three powerful committees (headed by L. K. Jha, Abid Hussain, and M. Narasimham) whose composition was "well regarded by the Indian business community" (Kohli 2006, 1256).

Two more elements which contributed to create a more industry-friendly environment need to be pointed out. In the first place, the government made an enormous effort to bring an end to the infrastructural bottleneck which was largely responsible for the bad shape of the economy in 1980. The central outlay for sectors such as petroleum, coal, power generation, port development, transport et cetera had steadily increased (it reached 57.78 per cent of the total central annual plan allocation in 1984–85 (*Economic Survey 1986*)).[14] The heavy investments in the infrastructure sector resulted in an increase in all major sub-sectors: production of coal stepped up by an average of 7.2 per cent a year; generation of electricity increased by 8.5 per cent a year, while crude petroleum production rose by 19.8 per cent; the amount of goods handled by railways and ports grew by 4.1 and 6.3 per cent a year respectively (*Economic Survey*, various issues).

Secondly, Indira Gandhi's government tried to limit the loss of productivity due to undisciplined labour. Kohli (2006) argues that the taming of labour was one of the main components of the "pro-business" strategy of the government. However, if it is true that Mrs Gandhi imposed some "draconian" measures to deter strikes—the Essential Services Maintenance Act of 1981 being the most notorious example—results were disappointing (from the business sector's point of view). The number of man-days lost per year increased from 28.06 million in 1980–81 to 35.93 million in 1984–85 (*Economic Survey*, various issues).[15] Indeed, more than repressing labour, Indira Gandhi seemed to prefer some sort of corporatist solution to regulate industrial relations. In the government's view, workers and industrialists ought to collaborate to face the difficult economic situation. The government, on its part, offered to establish an apex body at the national level, tripartite committees for each industry and a task force for key industries for speedy settlement of industrial disciplines. Furthermore, wage boards and a central conciliation and adjudication machinery were activated (*The Hindu*, 3 March 1983).

However, strikes did not diminish. This was due to a variety of reasons. First, since the late 1970s, workers started to rely more on spontaneous actions than on concerted, union-led protests. When trade unions realised they were losing ground with respect to a new class of militant trade unionists (*Indian Express*, 8 December 1980) with no ideological or organisational affiliation (like Datta Samant in Bombay or Kuchelar in Madras), rivalries between them "became a feature of every industrial dispute" (Baru 1995, 119). As a consequence, while workers' bargaining power was severely weakened, their attitude became more militant. Second, harsh economic conditions, especially the high rate of inflation, did not help to soften the tense industrial relations situation. In this situation the government was neither ready to repress labour (for obvious political considerations) nor to appease it (because it needed the industrialists' support). It attempted to act as an arbiter but results were rather disappointing.

The government chose to prioritise broader economic and political considerations over the business community's interests in two other respects. The first one was the credit policy followed. This aimed at bringing prices under control, more than at providing cheap credit to the industrial sector. It is true that credit was largely made available to industrialists, but interest rates and tax on interest were kept at rather high levels (see Budget Speeches, 1980–84). The Federation of Indian Chamber of Commerce and Industry (FICCI) repeatedly complained about the credit policy of the government (e.g. *Hindustan Times*, 19 June 1980 or *Times of India*, 15 July 1982). The second provision which caused a strong reaction from the industrial lobby was the attempt by the government to have more influence on the private sector. In March 1984 the cabinet issued new guidelines relating to the conversion of loans granted by financial institutions into equity and appointment of nominee directors of financial institutions. The guidelines, especially as the powers of the nominee directors were concerned, were seen as an attempt by the government to keep intact its hold over the "commanding heights" of the economy, in a context where the business community expected further internal liberalisation.

The second element of the government's economic strategy towards the industrial sector consisted of a set of fiscal concessions. In general terms, the corporate sector highly benefited from the fiscal policy pursued by Mrs Gandhi's government. Concessions in direct taxes were given throughout the period under consideration. These included tax holidays for units established in free trade zones or backward areas, deductions of expenditure on research and development, and increased rates of depreciation. In addition to these provisions, the government provided several relief measures to specific industries which either had export potential (e.g. electronic industry) or were in a difficult financial situation (e.g. cloth and textile).[16]

Indirect taxation was the main instrument of resource mobilisation during the first half of the 1980s. Increases in excise duties were usually spread over a large number of items, so that no particular industry was penalised, with the exception of cement (which was liberalised in 1982). Reductions in excise duties, on the other hand, either favoured some specific industries (usually in the small-scale sector), or constituted a way to appease the middle class (see next section). Moreover, starting from 1982—declared the "Productivity Year" by the prime minister (*Times of India*, 15 January 1982)—indirect tax concessions were also used as incentives for those units which were able to expand production or their export potential. Custom duties, as we have already noted, were selectively increased to protect indigenous production or diminished to favour imports of industrial inputs.

Finally, two more measures are worth noting, as they show that Indira Gandhi's embrace of Indian capital as the ruling ally of her government was not complete and, in any case, subject to broader political and economic considerations. As the main problem of Indian developmental effort since independence has been the difficulty in raising additional resources, Indira Gandhi's government tried to avoid that highly profitable corporations did not pay any tax at all because of the high (and increasing) number of tax concessions available. In the budget for 1983–84, the finance minister decided that concessions could not absorb more than 70 per cent of the profits. The same logic was followed when tougher measures to fight tax evasion were enacted.

In conclusion, Indira Gandhi's economic strategy towards the industrial sector created a new economic environment in which the industrial sector could prosper and take the lead of the new developmental path the government had chosen to follow. Parallel to this, a set of tax concessions and (as we shall see shortly) incentives for savings tried to increase the amount of resources available for investment. The overall result of such a strategy matched the government's expectations: the secondary sector grew at an average rate of 5.76 per cent a year during the first half of the 1980s (*Economic Survey*, various issues).

The Middle Class

The second major component of the social base Indira Gandhi was seeking to build was the Indian middle class. Social scientists have always found it difficult to define this social group. In fact, many prefer to designate it in plural terms as the "middle classes". The Indian middle class is no exception. It is characterised by fundamental internal distinctions which cannot be ignored. First, a broad distinction can be drawn between urban and rural middle classes. Important economic differentiations contribute to further divide each group. Moreover, internal social hierarchies and differences such as caste, region, religion and language interact to "shape the middle class" (Fernandes 2006, xviii).

Despite difficulties in finding a definition which could take into account all these aspects, the middle class has been the object of extensive research. It has been defined as a group with relatively high income and non-manual occupation (Sridharan 2004), a structurally defined group (Bardhan 1998), a product of a discourse (Appadurai 1996), or as something ascertained by a combination of elements taken from the afore mentioned definitions, resulting in broad, dynamic and fluid understanding of the middle class (Fernandes 2006). Furthermore, Marxian (Ghanshyam Shah 1987), Paretian (Bhatia 1994), and empirical (S. M. Fakih quoted in Dubey 1992) definitions have been attempted. For our purposes, the broad definition used by D. L. Sheth (1999, 2508) is probably the most helpful. According to him the middle class is a highly diversified, "open-ended" entity whose members nevertheless share economic interests and lifestyles—and aspirations, one may add. In other words, subjective (i.e. the individual feeling of belonging to the middle class) and objective elements (i.e. ten or more years of schooling, ownership of certain assets like motor vehicle, TV, or non-agricultural land, residence in a "pucca house", white-collar jobs) define a blurred social group, whose importance cannot be overestimated.

Depending on the definition and on the methodological approach used, scholars have formulated many estimates of the size of the middle class. As far as the period under consideration is concerned, estimates range from 35–40 million people to almost 200 million (Dubey 1992). However, most observers agree on estimates varying between 10 and 20 per cent of the population. Another point of consensus regards the exponential growth, during the 1980s, of this sector of the population, however defined. Empirical evidence is usually used to support such a conclusion. Dubey (1992, 151), for example, shows the skyrocketing growth in consumption of typical middle class items such as refrigerators (+361 per cent), cars (+472.3 per cent), motor scooters (+1,102.8 per cent), and wristwatches (+145.4 per cent).[17] Similarly, the increase in domestic savings, appreciation of the Bombay Stock Market, or expansion of the advertisement sector, confirm the growing importance of the Indian middle class in both numerical and economic terms.

More than its size, what makes this group so important is the human and cultural capital possessed by its members, in the form of "education, skills and technical expertise" (Sridharan 2004, 408). The middle class counts "because it dominates the media, because its opinions are the ones that politicians have to hear, and because every election in Indian history has been determined by issues that were first raised by the middle class" (Priya Sahgal, quoted in Fernandes 2006, 173). The list could easily go on. Bureaucracy (both civil and military), public sector enterprises and political parties were dominated by middle class members. Their position allowed them to dispense jobs, state resources and patronage. Pranab Bardhan (1998) puts the middle class (which he calls "the professionals") among the three "dominant proprietary classes" that controlled the Indian state. In Gramscian terms, it is arguable that Indian middle class enjoyed a hegemonic position in Indian society (see Deshpande cited in Fernandes 2006). Therefore, every political party had to take into account the middle class's needs.

In this respect, Mrs Gandhi's party was in serious difficulties at the beginning of the 1980s. Myron Weiner (1982) argued that the urban middle classes were "either divided or opposed to Congress" in 1980,[18] as shown by evidence from Calcutta, Bombay and Madras, were the

Congress (I) lost a majority of seats. The middle class resentment against Mrs Gandhi's party stemmed from a set of reasons. First, the intelligentsia and a great part of the middle class had not forgiven Mrs Gandhi for the authoritarian regime that she had established a few years before. Second, many scholars (Fernandes 2006; Hansen 1999; Jaffrelot 1996) point out how an urban, upper-caste,[19] Hindu middle class started feeling more and more alienated from the late 1970s.[20] This feeling of alienation and political frustration was mainly due to a perception, quite common amongst middle class members, that Indian democracy was decaying because of the persisting appeasement (by the Congress party) of lower classes and castes. The feeling was reinforced by the "threat" represented by the "awakening" of Indian subaltern strata (Manor 1983a).[21] Third, middle class members were also threatened by growing unemployment (stemming from high birth rates and slow industrial growth). This problem was further aggravated by the competition of the "middle class aspirants" (Weiner 1982, 351). These could be members of disadvantaged communities who had benefited from affirmative action policies in the previous decades, or members of rural families who had invested part of the gains of the "green revolution" in the education of their sons. Fourth, the middle class had been the only social group (apart from the corporate sector) which had been taxed since independence. Therefore, there was a perception that the Congress's fiscal policies had resulted in an extraction of resources from the middle class members that had been used to finance the uplift not only of those living in poverty, but also of those groups that now threatened "the overall structure of inequality on which the privileged position of the middle classes ... had rested since the colonial period" (Frankel 1988, 227).

Mrs Gandhi's economic policies tried to reverse this trend. The government was facilitated by the anti-middle class economic policies of the Janata Party in 1977–79. The middle class had largely supported Morarji Desai's party in 1977 (Weiner 1978a), but the rural bias of the government had certainly convinced many that no national representative of the urban middle class existed in the late 1970s. Mrs Gandhi sought to fill this void.

The economic appeasement of the middle class was based on three main elements. First, the new economic strategy, which centred on industrial growth, constituted the only way out of the employment bottleneck that had frustrated the aspirations of young members of the middle class. Obviously, this was a medium-term strategy.

Secondly, the middle class was perhaps the main beneficiary of the fiscal policy of the government, as significant relief measurers were enacted in respect of both indirect and direct taxation. This, on the one hand, reinforced the industrial policy of the government, sustaining internal demand; on the other, it conceded some relief to tax-payers who had been badly affected by high inflation.[22] The Finance Minister, Venkataraman, made it abundantly clear that the anti-middle class stance of the previous government was to be reversed. "The entire thrust of Mr Venkataraman's [first Budget] speech was to undo what Charan Singh had done in his unpopular budget in March 1979" (*Indian Express*, 19 June 1980). Excise duties on many middle class items such as pressure cookers, soap, tooth paste, electric bulbs, TV sets and the like were reduced starting from the 1980–81 budget. In following years, goods typically purchased by this section of society were either exempted from excise duties or benefited from concessional rates. In other cases, middle-class consumers benefited from incentives on investments given to industries producing goods which could be purchased only by those who were better off—chinaware, mosaic tiles in 1982, cosmetics, toiletries and refrigerators in 1983, ceiling fans in 1984 and so on. The left-wing press called Mrs Gandhi's indirect taxation policy the "pressure cooker approach" (*Economic and Political Weekly*, 19 March 1983).

Direct taxation was restructured in a way to benefit income-tax payers in all slabs of income. The exemption limit for income-tax was raised from Rs 10,000 in 1979–80 to Rs 15,000 in 1984. This freed around two million people from the tax net (1.5 million in 1982 only (*Times of India*, 1 March 1981)). At the other extreme of the middle class, the wealth-tax exemption limit was raised from Rs 100,000 to Rs 150,000 in 1980 and further raised in 1984. Moreover, the value (up to Rs 50,000) of tools necessary to enable taxpayers to carry on their profession or vocation was excluded from wealth-tax. Other measures favoured the whole range of income earners: direct income-taxes were reduced by 10–15 per cent depending on the slab; the surcharge on income-tax was nearly halved (from 20 to 12.5 per cent); standard deduction entitlements were raised; exemptions from income-tax were granted to those retiring from work or buying a house; and civil servants and pensioners were either given fiscal concessions or granted higher salaries/pensions.

The third element of Mrs Gandhi's economic policy towards the middle class was the extensive series of incentives to stimulate savings.

Once again, measures in this respect were consistent with the growth-oriented path of development undertaken by the government. During the first half of the 1980s a number of schemes to stimulate savings were launched.[23] Income earners could therefore benefit from high interest rates and, in some cases, fiscal concessions on the income deriving from specified investments.

The overall result of this strategy, combined with a more purely political appeal to the middle class which we will outline below, was that this important social group was ready to re-establish a preferential relationship with the Congress (I) party. In 1985, *India Today* (16 December 1985) described the middle class as "Rajiv Gandhi's people" and as a group which was "relieved that the government no longer [tried] to tax everyone to distraction in the name of the poor, enamoured of a prime minister who [understood] the importance of colour TV".

Rich Farmers

Farmers form a social group which is even more heterogeneous than the Indian middle class. Not only caste, class and linguistic divisions characterise rural society, but in each state—if not in each district—agriculture has specific problems and needs. Yet, quite large sections of the peasantry share important economic interests. For the present purposes, what is crucial is to identify a group whose interests were profoundly affected by national economic policies, despite agriculture being in the constitutional domain of the states. Such a group is identifiable in peasant-proprietors of economically viable units (including tenants enjoying proprietorship rights). The actual amount of land which can be considered viable varies significantly according to the kind of crop cultivated, the quality of seeds employed, the type of irrigation and infrastructure available, et cetera. However, units of more than two hectares of land are usually considered economically viable. Moreover, such an amount of land was enough to take full advantage of the technology introduced by the green revolution in the 1960s (Torri 1974; Frankel 1971).

This social stratum has been identified in many ways. We will use the label "rich farmers" and this will include the whole spectrum of peasant proprietors owning more than two hectares of land. Thus, for the present purposes, Indian rural society can be divided into two groups, one constituted by landless labourers, and marginal and small owners (i.e. owning less than 1, and between 1 and 2 hectares respectively), the other made of middle and large farmers (i.e. owning between 2 and 4, and more than 4 hectares respectively)[24] producing most of the agricultural marketable surplus. According to Ali et al. (1981, tab. 2 and 5, 410–3) in 1975, the latter group constituted nearly 35 per cent of the rural agricultural population, controlled more than 80 per cent of agricultural land and produced more than three fourths of the crop output.

Two changes that occurred in the decades before 1980 need to be stressed in order to understand the national character of this social group. The first one is the centralisation of the decision-making process in regards to the rich farmers' economic interests. In the first two decades after independence the most important decisions which affected the rural world were taken at state level, as envisaged by the constitution. In particular, rich farmers were interested in blocking the effective implementation of the land reform. They were not so much interested in what happened in Delhi, where the other two "dominant proprietary classes" were free to direct national economic policies. Rudolph and Rudolph (1987, 51) call this tacit agreement the "Nehru settlement".

In the late 1970s the situation had completely changed. Land ceilings legislation had been effectively boycotted. The green revolution had brought immense change to the rural world. Rich farmers had been encouraged to invest (especially after the nationalisation of banks in 1969 which redirected credit towards agriculture (Torri 1975)) in the newly introduced state-sponsored technologies, and they had subsequently benefited from state assistance in terms of input subsidies and minimum support prices for their output. Therefore the key economic interests of rich farmers—by the late 1970s a "class-in-itself" and a "class-for-itself" (Byres 1981)—were no longer in the hands of the state governments; rather, it was the central government that decided what and how much to subsidy and it was the central cabinet that had the last word on procurement and minimum support prices, which were determined on recommendation of another central organ, the Agricultural Price Commission (APC).[25]

The second change which is necessary to point out is what has been called the "first democratic upsurge" (Yadav 1999, 2394), namely the rise of middle and lower castes in Indian politics, especially in the highly populated Hindi belt. In many cases, the most assertive groups were cultivating castes which had taken advantage of the green revolution.

"Crucially, economic gains had converted themselves into political ambition" (Guha 2007, 532). However, such ambition was thwarted by the fact that their growing economic power had not been translated into political influence (this has been suggested by Kaviraj (1988), Hasan (1989), Jaffrelot (2003)). The Janata Party had, to a certain extent, tried to respond to these grievances. But Mrs Gandhi's return in 1980 had in many cases restored the hold of elite groups on local and state level politics.[26] In some other cases—as in Maharashtra—the Congress (I), in the process of altering the power relations of state politics, had reduced the hold of powerful rural lobbies on politics.[27]

The overall effect of these changes was that rich farmers were divided despite common economic interests. In general terms, those groups with strong links—usually based on kin and caste—with the ruling party could still exploit the functioning of the "old" Congress system as described by Rajni Kothari (1964). However, two crucial features of this system could not work anymore. First, it was no longer possible for the Congress to pursue a strategy based on a "continuing accommodation of interests" (Kothari 1964, 1168) which had been the basis of the Congress political strategy in the first two decades after independence. In 1980 the context had profoundly changed: growing demand for developmental, state-administered resources, was paralleled by stagnating (if not shrinking) allocation of funds to the agricultural sector and growing prices of inputs (especially fertilisers). In this context a strong source of rural opposition to the Congress (I) arose in many parts of the country (Nadkarni 1987; Brass T. 1995). This opposition was in great part formed by rich farmers (Dhanagare 1995; Banaji 1995; Hasan 1995; Bardhan 1998) who were kept at the margin or excluded from the administration of state resources. For these groups the only way out of a deteriorating economic situation was to obtain higher support from the central government through higher procurement prices and higher subsidies for agricultural inputs—two forms of support less affected by caste and local factors. It is not surprising then that since the late 1970s mammoth farmers' demonstrations started taking place in Delhi, where these crucial economic decisions were taken;[28] and it is not surprising that the farmers' growing interests in national politics was matched by the growing number of MPs with a rural background (in 1952 only 22.5 per cent of the members of the Lok Sabha had such a background; in 1980 the percentage had increased to 39.3 per cent (LS, tab 3.3, 11)).

Secondly, the "awakening" (Manor 1983a) of part of the Indian electorate made vertical mobilisation increasingly difficult. Those once subaltern groups that had acquired significant economic power could not be mobilised any longer simply on the basis of a traditional social order, which was falling apart in many parts of the country, even in the heart of the Hindi belt itself (Frankel 1989). Instead, they demanded their share in the allocation of (shrinking) state resources.

To sum up, rich farmers in the 1980s, on the one hand, formed a truly national social group, as far as their economic interests were concerned. Yet, within this group, quite large strata of the rich peasantry all over the country—economically powerful but politically weak—were excluded or had limited access to state resources.

The situation was worsened (from the rich farmers' point of view) by the fact that Mrs Gandhi's government had no intention to alter the allocation of resources in favour of the rural world. After a phase in which agriculture had been the focus of India's developmental strategy (from the mid-1960s till the mid-1970s), now emphasis was being translated to the industrial sector. However, despite the rhetoric adopted by supporters of the farmers' movements, Indira Gandhi's economic policies in the 1980s cannot be called "anti-peasants" (Harkishan Singh Surjeet in *Seminar*, No. 267, November 1981, 14). On the other hand, they cannot be referred to as being totally pro-peasants either. Therefore the source of the farmers' opposition towards the central government, which was expressed in the nation-wide farmers' movements of the 1980s, was the result of the incapacity of the farmers to effectively use their power to impose a predominantly rural-oriented path of development which could fulfil their expectations; or, to use the words of the major ideologue of the farmers in the 1980s, Sharad Joshi, to make "Bharat" dominate "India".

In any case, Indira Gandhi's government took a set of steps to please rich farmers.[29] In fact, in 1980 "the dominance of the surplus-producing rich farmers in *all* political parties" was a "simple yet crucial fact of Indian political economy" (De Janvry and Subbarao 1986, 19) and therefore their demands could not be simply ignored. Indeed, one of the first moves of the new Cabinet was to expand the terms of reference of the APC, with a directive to take into account the prices of non-agricultural items used by farmers. Shortly afterwards, the Reserve Bank of India was asked to enlarge the scope of cash credit for fertiliser handling agencies and to remove obstacles in the norms for short-term crop loans to farmers. Therefore, only a few months after Mrs Gandhi's return, many thought that her aim was to "steal Charan Singh's thunder" (*Indian Express*, 19 July 1980) with heavy concessions to the farmers lobby. The feeling was reinforced when the Finance Minister, Venkataraman, exempted agricultural property from the ambit of wealth tax in his first budget. Other measures favouring rich peasants included the continuation of a credit policy that made significant resources available to farmers. Direct institutional credit to farmers increased from Rs 2,928 cr in 1979–80 to Rs 6,167 cr in 1984–85 (RBI *Handbook* 2009, tab. 57). The establishment of a National Bank for Agricultural and Rural Development in July 1982 and the mushrooming of rural regional banks were steps in the same direction for providing the farmers with the financial means they needed.

However, many measures adopted by Mrs Gandhi's government went in the opposite direction. In the first place, the overall allocation of resources to the agricultural sector[30] was decreased from 18 per cent of the total public sector outlay in 1980–81 to 14 per cent in 1984–85, which represents a decrease of 21 per cent. (*Budget Speech* and *Economic Survey*, various issues).

Secondly, the price policy followed by the government was not as favourable to the farmers as the increase in the procurement price of all major crops might suggest.[31] In fact, if one takes into consideration the rate of inflation (especially in the first two years of Mrs Gandhi's government), it is difficult not to conclude that increases in procurement prices were almost entirely absorbed by the increase in the level of prices. According to official reports (Mahendra Dev and Chandrasekhara Rao 2009, tab. 4) growth rates in minimum support prices for rice and wheat declined (in real terms) by 0.95 and 2.22 per cent respectively in the 1980s. Indeed, the term of trade between agricultural and manufactured products deteriorated starting from the late 1970s (*Times of India*, 20 December 1980; Mishra and Hazell 1996, A3; De Janvry and Subbarao 1986, 29). Farmers were particularly affected by the steep rise in the price of fertilisers (which was set by the central government).[32] These rose by 60 per cent in the first two years of Mrs Gandhi's government.[33] At the same time the cabinet reduced subsidies for fertilisers (from Rs 603 cr in 1979–80 to Rs 375 cr in 1981–82), even though in subsequent years subsidies reached the record amount of Rs 1,832 cr in 1984–85 (an election year). However, in more general terms the ratio of rural to urban per capita income deteriorated during the decade after 1980–81 (Nagaraj 2000, 2837).

Finally, Mrs Gandhi did not favour the writing off of farmers' debt (as proposed by some states) or the establishment of a nation-wide crop insurance scheme and, in order to keep the price of food grains as low as possible, she started importing wheat even though reserves were not in a critical situation.

In addition, it can be argued that given the reduced amount of resources made available to the states—tax concessions to the middle class and the industrial sector were in most cases financed through reductions in taxes collected by the state governments—these were not able to meet the expectations of the assertive and powerful rural lobby. Moreover, the declining ability of the Congress party to effectively distribute patronage severely affected the party's "popularity" in the countryside. In short, the "Nerhu settlement" had been broken.

The Poor

The last national social group which will be taken into consideration is constituted by the great majority of Indian people, namely the poor. Contrary to the other three groups, the Indian masses are not a powerful lobby or, to use Bardhan's terminology, poor people are not included in the dominant coalition which has ruled the country since independence. Yet, their importance in Indian politics is huge, basically because of their numerical strength and because, as many scholars have pointed out, voter turnout among the Indian poor is relatively high.

Many estimates of the incidence of poverty in India exist. According to the methodology employed, the number of people defined as poor in a given period varies. According to the World Bank (1999, Annex Table 1.1) those living below the poverty line[34] in 1980 were 45.31 per cent of the rural population and 35.65 of those living in town and cities.[35] Quite obviously, this is an extremely heterogeneous social group. Apart from the fundamental urban/rural distinction, many other elements differentiate the Indian poor internally—caste, gender, and language to name just a few. In addition, economic factors contribute to further divide this category. The Indian poor can be landless agricultural labourers, small or marginal farmers,[36] rural artisans, urban unemployed et cetera. Finally, within the poor, a fundamental distinction has existed since the late colonial period between the Scheduled Castes and Scheduled Tribes and the rest of the population. Despite all these differences, the Indian poor have a vital economic interest in common, namely to buy or produce enough food to survive. This makes the boundaries of this social category very fuzzy. A bad monsoon can significantly increase the number of people living below the poverty line. For this reason those on the brink of poverty should be assimilated to the poor more than to any other social group, at least as far as their primary economic interests are concerned.

The great majority of those living in poverty conditions are located in the countryside. They are prevalently landless labourers and marginal farming households. Their main source of income is the wage they receive, which varies significantly according to the number of days worked in a year or season. Therefore, weather affects the rural poor more than any other social group in India: a bad monsoon means less agricultural output, which means, on the one hand, fewer days of work and therefore lower incomes; on the other hand, it means higher prices of agricultural products and therefore still lower incomes (in real terms). Thus the prices of food, availability of work, and wage rates can be considered the main economic interests of the rural poor.

The Indian poor were political orphans in 1980. The emergency regime had alienated many of them from the Congress party, especially in the north, where the family planning effort—"a terrifying campaign of forced sterilization" (Frankel 2005, 563)—had been particularly cruel against the weaker sections of society, in the name of whom the emergency had been declared. On the other hand, the Janata Party had not been able to ameliorate their situation. In fact, the out-of-control rate of inflation in 1979–80 and the extremely high number of atrocities against the Scheduled and lower castes that occurred during 1977–79—17,775 cases were reported between April 1977 and September 1978 as against 40,000 in the preceding ten years (Guha 2007, 535)—convinced many of the rural poor that Mrs Gandhi's party was the lesser of two evils.

The Congress (I) strategy towards the poor was made of short- and medium-term elements. The former consisted of checking prices and assuring adequate provisions of food grains through the public distribution system. In order to achieve both objectives Mrs Gandhi did not hesitate to affect the interests of the business community and the rich farmers. The former resented the fact that the Reserve Bank of India kept interest rates artificially high in order to control the amount of liquidity in the system; the latter would have appreciated both higher procurement prices (which would have increased prices of agricultural goods in the fair price shops too) and higher market prices (kept low by the government through imports and the release of food reserves). The government was able to regain control of the price situation and food shortages did not constitute a serious problem.

The medium-term strategy was based on the hope that growth would have automatically ameliorated the living conditions of the poor and ultimately eradicated poverty—the "notorious" trickle-down effect. In the meantime, all that could be done—Mrs Gandhi loved to repeat that she had no "magic wand" (e.g. *Indian Express*, 07 December 1980)—was to contain poverty. Contrary to the 1950s, emphasis was not so much on structural policies—*in primis* land reform—but on specific programmes which targeted the weaker section of society or, as the government's rhetoric used to call them, the beneficiaries of the 20-point programme.[37] According to some observers the anti-poverty strategy endorsed by the government constituted a "radical departure from the past", as it gave up efforts to bring about social changes through "land reforms, progressive direct taxation, measures to restrain conspicuous consumption and control over monopoly" (*Economic and Political Weekly*, 28 March 1981). The best-known (and best-financed) programmes were the Integrated Rural Development Programme, the National Rural Employment Programme (which replaced the Food-for-Work Programme, particularly disliked by rich farmers), the Minimum Needs Programme, and the Rural Landless Employment Guarantee Programme.[38]

It is virtually impossible to reach a consensus about the effectiveness of these programmes. In particular, what is hard to evaluate is the amount of resources which reached the targets of anti-poverty programmes. Corruption, family or caste ties, connivance, negligence and simple mismanagement—bureaucracy in India "is not known for its ability to absorb the ethos of economic development and social change" (Kurian 1989, A-13)—contributed to direct significant resources towards the non-poor.

Arguably the most important anti-poverty program implemented in the early 1980s was the IRDP. This was initiated in 1978 and strengthened in 1980. The aim of the program was to provide to households standing below the poverty line with a series of productive assets that could help them to take up self-employment ventures. In more practical terms, the scheme was a subsidised credit scheme (Rath 1985).

According to the Government of India, after an initial phase in which the outcomes in terms of poverty reduction were relatively disappointing—after two years only about 40 per cent of the beneficiaries had crossed the poverty line (7FYP, Vol. 2, ch. 2)—the program was a complete success (Ministry of Agriculture, 1987; See also Subbarao 1985).

However, several scholarly works suggest that the impact of the program was rather limited. Jean Dreze, basing his conclusions on evidence collected in UP, points out how "the relatively privileged among the 'poor'—along with many non-poor—captured the lion's share of the benefits" (Dreze 1990). Similar conclusions were drawn by scholars working on other parts of India, e.g. Swaminathan on Tamil Nadu (1990) and Gopal and Ramulu on Andhra Pradesh (1989). Other studies conclude that exclusion of the poor from the beneficiaries was a structural feature of the IRDP all over India, with the partial exception of West Bengal (Rath 1985; Gaiha 2000; Dreze 1990).

Evidence suggests that the IRDP was the typical "clientelistic" program. More than addressing poverty and inequality, its importance lay in the opportunities for patronage distribution that it enabled. Indeed, political interference determined to a large extent the degree of success of the program. This was particularly evident in West Bengal, where the IRDP was significantly more successful than in other parts of India, mainly because the rural poor constituted the bulk of the ruling CPI(M)'s base of support (Dreze 1990; Swaminathan 1990).

Analogous considerations are valid for other anti-poverty initiatives. According to some empirical studies at the village level the number of non-poor benefiting from anti-poverty programmes ranged from 15 to 70 per cent of the total beneficiaries (Guhan 1980, 1979). Therefore it is not so important to evaluate the amount of resources invested,[39] also because the allocation of funds was by no means sufficient to assist all those who were in need (Rath 1985). For example, even a complete success of the IRDP would have covered not more than 75 million people (out of 230 million rural poor) (*Indian Express*, 03 October 80).[40] Thus, from our point of view, what is relevant is to evaluate whether anti-poverty measures adopted by the government resulted in a decline of the incidence of poverty and in an improvement—or at least not a worsening—of the living conditions of the rural poor. Evidence seems to suggest that poverty declined during the first half of the 1980s, thus continuing the positive trend initiated in the previous decade. According to the World Bank the incidence of rural poverty in India declined from 50.60 per cent in 1977–78 to 39.23 per cent in 1987–88 (World Bank 1999, Annex tab.

1.1). Other estimates do not vary significantly and in any case lead to the same conclusion (Minhas, Jain and Tendulkar 1991; Corbridge and Harris 2000; Rudolph and Rudolph 1987; Panagariya 2008).

Anti-poverty programmes were not the only steps taken by the government. Two more measures are worth noting. First, Indira Gandhi's government favoured the revision by the state governments of the minimum wages policy (*Indian Express*, 19 October 1983). During the 1980s, the wages of unskilled agricultural labourers increased by 4.6 per cent in real terms (World Bank 1999, tab. 1.2). Second, in 1981 the Cabinet issued new guidelines to the Reserve Bank of India in order to ensure that "an increasing share of priority sector credit is directed to weaker sections" (*Budget Speech*, 1981–82). The target of 40 per cent of net bank credit to the priority sector was exceeded by 1.3 percentage points (RBI 1985, 60).

In short, it is likely that the situation of the rural poor did not worsen in the first half of the 1980s. Poverty was not eradicated and indeed no effort was made in this direction. However, what the government wanted to achieve—checking the number of poor and making them feel that the government was taking care of them—was indeed achieved.

Mrs Gandhi's Political Strategy

The attempt to build up a large and nation-wide electoral coalition through a set of muddled economic policies—aimed at being "something to everyone" (Kohli 1990b, 4)—was paralleled by a more purely political strategy aimed at keeping and enlarging Mrs Gandhi's support base. This strategy targeted two of the above-mentioned national social groups. The first one, in complete continuity with her political strategy in the 1970s, was made up of the so-called "weaker sections". Needless to say, this was an extremely heterogeneous social group, which largely although not completely corresponded to what we have generically called "the poor" in the previous section. While "the poor" are an economically-defined social group, the "weaker sections" is a socio-political category which, by the early 1980s, was an integral part of Indian political discourse.

The weaker sections constituted a national social group because it was with this label that politicians belonging to all parties defined all groups who were economically, politically, and/or socially oppressed, and were therefore in need of special treatment and protection by the state.

Furthermore, the most important constituent parts of this heterogeneous social group—both in numerical and political terms—were three communities, which in turn can be seen as national social entities, namely the Scheduled Classes, the Scheduled Tribes and Muslims. Claiming that the former two are national groups does not imply that the internal differentiation within each group is underestimated; rather, it means that these are national labels which are used by the central and the state governments to outline policies targeted towards these social categories. In short, Scheduled Classes and Scheduled Tribes can be considered national social groups not only because they are the target of national policies, but also because there is a degree of self-identification in these national categories. As far as Muslims are concerned, their strong sense of identity—which transcends even national borders, one just needs to think about the concept of *Ummah*—make solidarities among the members of the community throughout India quite strong and politically important.[41] Moreover, what all three categories have in common is that, while peculiar socio-economic conditions may attend to people belonging to each of these categories living in different parts of India, one of the main reasons why they are "weak" is precisely because they belong to these very categories.

There is another very important constituent part of the so-called "weaker sections", namely women. Indeed, women in most cases constituted—and still do—the weakest of the weaker sections. However, no significant attempt was made by Mrs Gandhi to appeal to women nationally. Of course, she made sporadic attempts to win their support; however, it is hardly arguable that Mrs Gandhi was a feminist (Masani 1975). This does not mean that women did not support her. Indeed, they constituted one of Mrs Gandhi's key constituencies, although no significant attempt to mobilise them was made.

The second national social group whose support Mrs Gandhi attempted to win was that of the middle classes. We have already seen how D. L. Sheth's (1999) definition of the middle class—which comprises subjective and objective elements—let us consider this group as a national entity not only as far as its economic interests are concerned, but also because its members share a set of values, beliefs and aspirations, and, most importantly, the feeling of belonging to the group.

In the next two sections we will see how Mrs Gandhi tried to win the support of these groups and to what extent her attempts of enlarging her national social base of support were successful.

The Weaker Sections

Two arguments are generally made regarding Mrs Gandhi's political strategy in the 1980s. The first one is that "the rhetoric of socialism and *garibi hatao* [were] slowly being put on the back burner" (Kohli 2006, 1257), in favour of political flirtations with ethnic and religious appeals to the Hindu community. The second one is that populist rhetoric remained the only political tool at Mrs Gandhi's disposal (Rudholph and Rudolph 1987, ch. 5). Both arguments are only partially true.

The first argument reveals that something changed in the way in which Mrs Gandhi spoke to the electorate. However, it underestimates the extent of the deployment of the Congress rhetoric, which remained the central feature of the party's political message. The second argument, on the other hand, fails to appreciate the changes that occurred in Mrs Gandhi's political communication.

This section will show how the traditional Congress rhetoric remained the "official" political philosophy of the party, and indeed the only political strategy adopted to keep the support of an important part of the traditional support base of the Congress, namely the "weaker sections". It will also show how the lack of concrete policy initiatives to substantiate Mrs Gandhi's rhetoric resulted in an erosion of the Congress (I)'s social base, even though the prime minister's popularity among the weaker sections, although eroded, remained quite high.

We have already mentioned that the electoral campaign for the 1980 general elections was fought on the "Nehruvian path", with all major parties claiming to be socialist, secular and democratic. Of course, this was particularly true for Mrs Gandhi's party. The election manifesto, after an introduction that underlined the Janata Party's role in inaugurating an "era of instability at the centre" (CIM 1980, 2), was a summa of the Congress's traditional political philosophy. It elucidated the party's role in bringing the colonial regime to an end, its commitment to build a secular state and society in which all religious and ethnic groups could feel secure, and its promises to bring about significant changes in the living conditions of the weaker sections, in particular the Scheduled Classes and Tribes and the religious minorities. The final appeal of the manifesto gives an idea of how the party's rhetoric had not changed much since the early 1970s: "let us once more awaken that spirit of nationalism, forge the unity of purpose, strengthen that will and determination, which will enable us to take our people forward to socialism. Let us proceed with our unfinished revolution to end poverty and disparity, to afford social and economic justice to all our people" (CIM 1980, 33). In general terms, the manifesto integrated the main electoral theme—"elect a government that works"—with the traditional Congress rhetoric. Eradicating poverty, Mrs Gandhi used to say during the electoral campaign (e.g. *Indian Express*, 28 October 1979), would require a strong government, able to put an end to the chaos. Other elements of the Congress's traditional rhetoric like the attacks on big landlordism and big business found a place in the manifesto (CIM 1980, 19). The state elections manifestos released in following years—most of which were prepared and in some cases even presented in Delhi (e.g. for the Andhra Pradesh state elections (*India Today*, 1 January 1983))—were centred around the same kind of political discourse.

Dalits were the target of a lot of Mrs Gandhi's rhetoric and symbolical concessions. One of the first steps of the new government was to fulfil one of the promises made during the electoral campaign, namely to extend the policy for reserving seats in Parliament for the Scheduled Classes and the Scheduled Tribes (*Indian Express*, 19 January 1980). This was far from being a revolutionary provision, since reservations for Scheduled Classes and Scheduled Tribes were (and are) a central element of the political culture of all parties. Indeed, a year later, the Lok Sabha passed its second unanimous resolution of its history, proclaiming its firm commitment to the national policy of reservations (*Times of India*, 19 March 1981). Coherently, during the agitations in Gujarat in the wake of the enactment of a reservation policy for Scheduled Class post-graduate medical students, the central government strongly defended the provision. On their part, the opposition parties attacked the Congress (I)'s state government not on the policy itself, but because of its inability to maintain law and order (*Indian Express*, 26 February 1981).

Other highly symbolic provisions regarding the Dalits included the inclusion of Ambedkar's birthday among the central government's public holidays, the setting up of numberless commissions and programmes for the uplift of the Dalits, or the appointment of a Dalit as a Supreme Court judge in December 1980. In other cases, symbolic gestures came from Mrs Gandhi in person, as when she donated Rs 300 to a Dalit boy to buy a pair of trousers—a gesture which, not surprisingly, reached the national press (*Hindustan Times*, 1 April 1982).

However, as we have seen in chapter 2, the security conditions of the Dalits, especially in north India, deteriorated further, if possible, while their economic situation did not improve much. For all practical purposes, Mrs Gandhi's government did not make a serious bid to better the Dalits' living conditions significantly.

Other minorities traditionally considered to be part of Mrs Gandhi's national support base, were treated similarly—highly symbolic concessions were accompanied by highly rhetorical speeches. Mrs Gandhi, in particular, assiduously courted the Muslim community during the electoral campaign in late 1979. Thanks to Bahuguna's mediation, she could count on the backing of the imam of the Jamia Masjid in Delhi, who repeatedly invited Muslim voters to support Mrs Gandhi (*Indian Express*, 25 December 1979).[42] Mrs Gandhi continued to appeal to the Muslims—as "full and equal partners in national life" (*Indian Express*, 29 January 1981)—throughout her final term in office. However, as we shall see below, these rhetorical appeals became less and less frequent as the defence of the majority community began to have more and more importance in the prime minister's political strategy.

In more practical terms, Mrs Gandhi's promotion of the Muslims' interests was limited to two aspects, one more symbolic than substantial, the other manifestly connected with her party's interests. The first one was the enactment of the Aligarh Muslim University (AMU) (Amendment) Act, 1981. The AMU—a "symbol of Muslim life in India" (Graff 1990, 1779)—had been founded in 1875 by Syed Ahmed Khan and recognised as a Central University in 1920, through the enactment by the colonial government of the Aligarh Muslim University Act, which recognised the autonomy of the institution and ruled that its governing body would be exclusively composed by Muslims. After 1947 three amendments (in 1951, 1965 and 1972) progressively eroded both the autonomy and the "Muslimness" of the governing body. In other words, the AMU was among the victims of the process of centralisation which characterised many other formal and informal institutions in India. Muslims throughout the country had protested vehemently on each occasion, especially in 1972, when the most serious threats to the University's autonomy had been enacted. The 1981 amendment act recognised the minority status of the University—a promise which had been included in the Congress's electoral manifesto as early as 1971—and restored the autonomy of the institution. Needless to say, the consequences for the living conditions of Indian Muslims were far from revolutionary. However, it is certain that the amendment was truly appreciated by the community.

The second area in which Mrs Gandhi defended Muslims' interests concerned the immigrants from Bangladesh and West Bengal in the north-eastern state of Assam, many of whom were Muslims (and Congress (I) voters). The "foreigners" problem became a central issue in Assam politics in the late 1970s. The area had been subjected to high migratory waves, at least since the opening of the tea plantations by the British at the beginning of the nineteenth century. However, migratory flows dramatically increased in the post-independence period, in particular in the wake of the 1970 crisis in East Pakistan and the second Indo-Pakistan war. In the late 1960s and early 1970s millions of refugees crossed the border trying to escape violence and pogroms; in many cases they never returned to their home country. Estimates vary, but it is reasonable to fix the number of illegal immigrants who moved from East Pakistan/Bangladesh and settled in north-east India from 1947 to 1981 at three million (Weiner 1983b, 285–6), not to count the population increase due to these and previous migratory flows.

In 1979 the Janata Party Chief Minister, Golap Borbora, gave the police officer Hiranya Kumar Bhattacharya the task of individuating foreigners in the electoral rolls of the Mangaldoi district, where a by-election was about to be held. The number of foreigners found by Bhattacharya totalled 47,658 (*India Today*, 16 February 1983). The reactions to the publication of the officer's findings constitute the genesis of the agitations in Assam, which were led by two organisations, the All Assam Students' Union (AASU) and the All Assam Gana Sangram Parishad (AAGSP), an umbrella organisation grouping several local formations. The situation radicalised after the publication of the second part of Bhattacharya's investigation, which estimated the total number of foreigners in the electoral rolls of the state to be around 587,000,[43] out of approximately 8 million eligible voters (ECI Assam 1978). In 1980, protests reached such an extent that economic and political activities were brought to a virtual halt, curfew had to be imposed in several towns, and elections could not be held in twelve out of fourteen constituencies (*Indian Express*, 27 November 1979).

Following Mrs Gandhi's installation at the centre, several rounds of talks were held between the representatives of the AASU and AAGSP and the central government. However, a solution to the foreigners issue could not be found. The main bone of contention was the criterion which had to be used to determine who a foreigner was. The AASU demanded that all those who entered Assam after 1951 had to be excluded from the electoral rolls and eventually deported to Bangladesh or dispersed in other states of the Indian Union. The central government proposed to deport all those who entered the country after the formation of Bangladesh in March 1971 and to regularise all those who entered Assam before that date. After several rounds of negotiations—23 sessions between 1980 and 1982—the two factions reached an agreement, according to which citizenship would have been granted to those who entered Assam before 1961, while 1971 would have been taken as the cut-off date for deportation to Bangladesh.[44] The fate of the million people who had settled in Assam between 1961 and 1971—the majority of whom were Bengali Hindus who had fled the pogroms in East Pakistan in 1970–71 (Hazarika 2000, 30)—was left unresolved.

In the meantime the law and order situation severely deteriorated. Two Congress (I) governments (headed by Anwara Taimur and Keshab Gogoi) failed to restore normality and President's Rule had to be imposed (*Indian Express*, 19 March 1982). Ultimately, a solution was not found and the central government decided to hold fresh elections, on the basis of the unrevised electoral rolls[45] in February 1983, a decision which caused widespread violence throughout the state.

While the proximate issue was the exclusion from the electoral rolls of those who entered India illegally, the anti-foreigners agitation had deeper roots. For the Assamese urban middle class what was at stake was control over the state institutions which, in turn, were the key to the allocation of most middle class jobs. From the early 1970s, the Assamese middle class began to perceive the Bengali speakers as a threat to their quasi-monopoly over white collar jobs. Thanks to the propaganda by middle class leaders, supported by inflated figures about the number of Bengalis actually living in the state, the Assamese began to fear that Bengali speakers—both Hindus and Muslims—had reached a sufficiently high number to outnumber them at the elections. The figures spread by the various "nationalist" Assamese organisations set the number of illegal immigrants—thus excluding all Bengali speakers having Indian citizenship—at 34 per cent of the population of the state in 1971 (Baruah 1986, 1189), even though the actual number of all Bengali speakers was at most 33 per cent of the population (Weiner 1978b, 87). In any case, these figures ignited fear among the Assamese and led to violent reactions and widespread agitations.

In the first decades after independence, the Assamese urban middle class had aligned with the Bengali Muslims, who were overwhelmingly rural and thus not in competition with them. The Assamese in turn offered Bengali Muslims protection through the Congress party (which had won every single election since the formation of the state until 1978). The Bengali Hindus—the majority of whom lived in towns and cities—were kept at the margins of the white collar jobs market, but from the viewpoint of the Assamese they represented a latent threat and were seen as the vanguard of the 145 million Bengali speakers who surrounded Assam.

The split of the Congress party in 1978, the publication of Bhattacharya's and other demographic investigations, and the formation of a Janata-led coalition government in the state, altered the political equilibria and contributed to spread the perception that Bengali speakers were now "in a position to undermine Assamese rule" (Weiner 1983b, 286).[46]

Outside the urban world the situation was quite different. In the countryside, Bengali Muslims competed with Assamese cultivators for the control of increasingly scarce land (Hazarika 2000). Moreover, tribals in the state (who were overwhelmingly rural) entered into a very complicated system of local alliances, with no apparent discernible scheme.

Therefore, the foreigners issue was not rooted in Hindu-Muslim animosity. Indeed, ethnic solidarities were fluid and overlapping and changed according to the changing political and socio-economic situation. However, a set of factors contributed to communalise the situation. In the first place, although the AASU and AAGSP representatives did not officially distinguish between Bengali Hindus and Bengali Muslims, in practical terms the distinction was clear. Since in virtually all cases the immigrants did not have birth certificates, the main criterion for distinguishing between immigrants from East Pakistan/Bangladesh and from West Bengal was their religion. The former were illegal immigrants, while the latter had the constitutional right to settle wherever they wished within the Indian Union. Moreover, a faction within the AASU headed by Joy Nath Sharma (who was close to the RSS) further divided Bengali immigrants from East Pakistan/Bangladesh between "refugees" (i.e. Hindus) and "infiltrators" (i.e. Muslims) (*India Today*, 16 March 1983).[47] Although such a distinction was not officially accepted by the AASU, this idea was vehemently propagated by the RSS network, which had more than 130 *shakas*[48] in Assam (*India Today*, 16 March 1983).

Furthermore, Mrs Gandhi's electoral campaign deepened the fracture not only between Assamese and Bengalis, but also between Hindus and Muslims, by promising that the Congress (I), if elected, would have assumed its traditional role as protector of the minorities and by giving tickets to an extremely high number of Muslim candidates (*Indian Express*, 7 February 1983).

However, Mrs Gandhi's defence of the Muslims in Assam resulted in a complete failure to ensure the protection of the community, which was the main reason why it had supported her party en masse. In February 1983 the Congress (I) won 91 out of 126 seats in the Legislative Assembly,[49] almost exclusively thanks to the votes of the Bengali Muslims.[50]

We have already seen that the Assam problem cannot be dubbed as a conflict between Hindus and Muslims. In fact, it was more a "Hobbesian war of all against all" (*India Today*, 16 May 1983) that broke out after the state elections were announced. Nevertheless, the national (e.g. *Indian Express*, 22 February 1983) and the international press (e.g. *New York Times*, 21 February 1983), and the Congress (I) itself, presented the conflict as a particular bloody episode of the ongoing Hindu-Muslim guerrilla war,[51] in which the Muslims were identified as the victims (and, in many cases, actually were).[52] This allowed Mrs Gandhi to portray herself as the champion of the Assam Muslims *outside* the state in order to substantiate her credentials as the saviour of the community at the national level.

Immediately after her return to power, Mrs Gandhi made it abundantly clear that her government would not accept a solution to the foreigners' problem that would have compromised the integrity of the country and the interests of the minorities (i.e. Muslims) in the state (*Indian Express*, 2 July 1980). On one occasion, speaking at a public meeting in Moradabad (a Muslim majority district in UP), she even said that there were no foreigners at all in Assam, and that the immigrants were indeed "citizens of the country" (*Indian Express*, 26 May 1980). During the electoral campaign for the state elections in Jammu and Kashmir in spring 1983, at a public meeting—in the Kashmir valley—she not only told the audience that the country could not prosper if its 80 million Muslims remained an "inch" behind the others, but she recalled how the government responded to the Bengali immigrants' request to hold elections, so that the situation could be normalised (*Indian Express*, 22 May 1983). Numberless more examples could easily be provided.

To sum up, the Assam conflict was exploited by Mrs Gandhi on two levels. On the one hand, she explicitly appealed to the frightened

Muslims in the state in order to win their support in the 1983 state elections. However, she failed to protect the community since her decision to force the state elections resulted in the complete breakdown of the governance institutions in the state and in widespread violence which affected mostly, but by no means exclusively, the Muslim community. On the other, she presented herself at the national level as the protector of the Muslims of Assam and as the one who had defended their interests during the negotiation process. However, significantly enough, the negotiations with the Assamese organisations broke down on the issue of the immigrants who entered India between 1961 and 1971, a great majority of whom were Hindus, and who Mrs Gandhi was not willing to deport to Bangladesh or relocate elsewhere in India.

In more practical terms, nothing was done to respond to the most urgent demands of the 75.5 million Muslims of India (11.4 per cent of the population) (Census 1981). In particular, as reported by Gopal Singh (chairman of the High Power Panel for Minorities, Scheduled Caste, Scheduled Tribes and Weaker Section) to Mrs Gandhi, the leaders of the Muslim community were "unanimous" in identifying two problems as the most pressing ones: on the one hand, they felt that something had to be done "to instil in them the sense of security about their person and property"; on the other hand, it was reputed essential that a "fair proportion" of Muslims were inducted into the civil security services like the police and the various paramilitary forces (Gopal Singh Private Papers, D. O. No. Ch (HPP)/63/80 dated 19 December 1980, NMML). As we have seen in chapter 2, the deteriorating law and order situation and the increasing number of communal incidents between Hindus and Muslim throughout the country did little to reassure the Muslims about their persons and properties. Furthermore, Mrs Gandhi stopped rushing to the places where communal conflicts occurred. Mrs Gandhi visited Moradabad (which witnessed prolonged and particularly bloody communal riots in August 1980) only two months after the fact, when she dubbed the events as part of a strategy of the opposition to destabilise her government (Gill 1997, 307). Moreover, members of the police and of the paramilitary forces who were often responsible for the degeneration of communal squabbles were seldom punished. Indeed, the government's failure in protecting the Muslims—one of the principal reasons for their support of the Congress (I)—was virtually complete.

The demographic composition of the state's apparatuses, on the other hand, was far from reflecting the demographic composition of the society. In 1978, only 3 per cent of the Indian Administrative Service (IAS), 0.5 per cent of the central government's employees and 3 per cent of the Indian Police Service (IPS) officers were Muslims (*India Today*, 01 September 1980). In November 1983, there were only 5 Muslims with the rank of joint secretary or higher in the central secretariat, out of more than 300 officers. The same situation characterised the boards of nationalised banks and public corporations (*Economic and Political Weekly*, 3 November 1990). In April 1983, Mrs Gandhi even refused to meet a delegation of some Muslim MPs—most of whom belonged to her own party—who wanted to express their community's grievances on these matters. The only thing Mrs Gandhi did was to issue a directive in which she invited state administrators to give a fair representation to minorities in the police and other government services (*Economic and Political Weekly*, 27 August 1983). Needless to say, the directive remained on paper. Similarly, the AICC(I)'s commitment to "ensure the fullest participation of Muslims and other minority groups in all aspects of national life" (AICC 1983A), as the Resolution on Minorities adopted during the AICC(I) meeting in Bombay in October 1983 read, remained on paper too.

Other initiatives taken by Mrs Gandhi, although not explicitly anti-Muslim, could easily be interpreted as such. For example, the dismissal of the Farooq Abdullah in Jammu and Kashmir in July 1983 was certainly seen as an attempt by the central government not to let the only Muslim-majority state to choose its own chief minister; the non-condemnation of the Soviet invasion of Afghanistan—even though the prime minister apparently did so in private meetings with the Soviets (Natwar Singh, interview, Delhi, 20 January 2011)—was resented by part of the Muslim community; similarly, Mrs Gandhi's reference to "Gulf Money" as being behind the conversion of about a thousand Dalits to Islam in Tamil Nadu in early 1981 (cited in *Economic and Political Weekly*, 3 November 1990), certainly did not help to ease the already difficult Hindu-Muslim relations. Indeed, it looked like the prime minister was backing the theories of communal organisations like the VHP (*India Today*, 16 July 1981). In short, as A. G. Noorani put it, "the plight of the Muslims did not improve one bit by 15 years of Indira Gandhi's 'championship' of their rights" (*Economic and Political Weekly*, 3 November 1990).

Overall, it is not surprising that Muslims stopped voting en masse for the Congress (I). Press reports seems to suggest that in many state elections the community preferred opposition parties, as in Andhra Pradesh and Karnataka (*India Today*, 16 January 1983) or Delhi (*Times of India*, 16 February 1983). In other cases, evidence suggests that the Muslims did not vote en bloc any longer and in any case not for the Congress (I), especially in the north, where the community had been one of the principal victims of the emergency (Weiner 1983a; Rudolph and Rudolph 1987; *India Today*, 16 January 1984). In short, it was without doubt that Mrs Gandhi could not take the Muslims' support for granted any longer.

Mrs Gandhi's deployment of the traditional Congress rhetoric did not end there. The "weaker sections", irrespective of religious or caste differences, were the main target of the party's political strategy and "socialist" policies. A few months after coming back to power, the prime minister pompously announced the nationalisation of six banks. The declared objective was to direct more credit towards the "weaker sections" (*Indian Express*, 16 April 1980). However, the move, on the one hand, could not significantly alter the flows of credit, as the banks affected by the 1980 provision were not major institutions and were in bad financial conditions;[53] on the other hand, it did not result in widespread expression of enthusiasm across the country, as had been the case in 1969.

In January 1982, a "new" 20-point programme was launched. According to Mrs Gandhi, a "new" programme was necessary because most of the points of the "old" one had been fulfilled (*Indian Express*, 15 January 1982). The text of the new political manifesto of the party did not differ much from the one adopted in 1975, mainly because the aim was the same: portraying Mrs Gandhi as the champion of the weaker sections or, to put it in the terms of the party's official rhetoric "to give practical shape to Mahatma Gandhi's constructive programme" (*Times of India*, 6 November 1982).

Numberless committees for the implementation of the programme were set up. In one case, great publicity was given to the personal involvement of Mrs Gandhi herself in one such committee, which should have monitored and assured the speedy implementation of the twenty points (*Hindustan Times*, 17 June 1982). The degree of success in achieving the objectives of the programme became the main criterion for judging the performance of the Congress (I) state governments by the party high command (at least in theory). Congress (I) governments used to send enthusiastic reports to Delhi, invariably showing remarkable achievements. However, as Rajiv Gandhi's coordinators showed, most of these reports were bogus and they had the only objective, on the one hand, of sustaining Mrs Gandhi's rhetoric (*India Today*, 15 September 1983) and, on the other hand, of keeping the centre happy and possibly at a distance.

In short, "old slogans like the priority of the poor, secularism, national integration and non-alignment were, in fact, allowed to continue as surrogates for creative thinking" (Dasgupta 1981, 149–50). However, these old slogans were directed towards a profoundly and rapidly changing society and political system. The voters were more and more aware of their rights and of the fact that politicians had to deliver something in exchange for their votes. There was some kind of inverse relation between the rising expectations of the voters and the growing inability of the political system in general, and of the Congress (I) party in particular, to respond to these expectations. We have already seen how the ability to distribute patronage severely declined and, in some cases—as in Andhra Pradesh—reached a virtual halt. But even if the patronage distribution system had still worked, it would have been virtually impossible to accommodate every social group. This was partly due to the limited availability of material resources to distribute. But, more importantly, what was scarce was the political space necessary for the accommodation of new groups that demanded *direct* access to patronage resources.

Further, the effectiveness of the socialist and populist rhetoric of Mrs Gandhi was declining too. This was due, on the one hand, to the "disappointment by the weaker sections with the Indian state on which they had relied so much ... for ending their conditions of oppression and discrimination" (Kothari 1997, 442). Moreover, in the previous decades, the Congress rhetoric had permeated the political culture of the country to such an extent that no party dared to oppose a political programme based upon it. At the chief ministers' conference in April 1983, non-Congress (I) governments "were no less enthusiastic about the 20-point programme than their Congress (I) colleagues" (*The Hindu*, 5 April 1983). It is therefore quite natural that Mrs Gandhi's message on these themes was less effective than in the early 1970s, when she had been able to emerge as the only true representative of socialist ideas. On the other hand, the Congress (I) failed to instill in the weaker sections a sense of security and protection, which had been a key component of the success of the Congress party among these sectors of the population. In short, Mrs Gandhi's rhetoric became less and less effective in filling the gap left by the declining ability of her party to distribute patronage and the growing assertiveness of the electorate.

Her political strategy was more successful towards another "national" social group, namely the middle class. We have already seen how a set of economic policies specifically favoured this social group. In the next section we will see how these policies were reinforced by a set of political initiatives.

The Middle Class's Need for Political Representation

We have already mentioned how, by the early 1980s, the middle class had grown in number and economic and political importance. Indeed, it has been argued (Rajagopal 2011, 1011) that the emergency "separate[d] two different phases of the Indian middle class, the former being under the hegemony of the state, and the latter, increasingly assertive, but disenchanted with erstwhile forms of politics". In other words, the middle class "had begun to identify itself as a distinctive group with specific interests that needed political representation" (Fernandes 2006, 83). In this section we will see how Mrs Gandhi attempted to respond to this demand.

It is important to stress that the political strategy outlined below did not have an impact exclusively on the middle class; in fact this strategy had an impact on a much wider section of the electorate. However, it is arguable that it was the middle class that was particularly affected and/or pleased by the set of political initiatives spelled out below.

Another qualification is needed. What follows relies on the assumption that some sort of middle class "view of the world" exists. This does not mean that every single middle class member would react in the same manner to the same kind of political stimulus. However, in general terms, I believe that my assumption is grounded.

Three elements can be distinguished as the most important constituent parts of Mrs Gandhi's political strategy towards the middle class. First, the prime minister proclaimed herself as the strong leader that the country desperately needed. Second, the government tried to substantiate the modernisation dream of the middle class and to stimulate its sense of national pride. Finally, Mrs Gandhi actively promoted the interests of the upper castes, which constituted the bulk of the middle class.

Mrs Gandhi's strategy of self-proclamation as the saviour of the country proceeded at two levels. The first one was the continuous representation of India's unity and integrity as being constantly under threat. Indeed, it was a deliberate creation of fears that Mrs Gandhi pursued throughout her final term in office.

The need to vote for the Congress in order to strengthen national unity and integrity was the central theme of every single electoral campaign in the early 1980s. In the spring of 1982, for example, the Congress (I) released a common manifesto for four state elections[54] in which voters were warned that "international and external forces [were] fomenting movements to weaken the national fabric", while "obscurantist individuals and organisations" in the country were fanning communal passions, thus "propagating separatism" (CIM 1982).

In other circumstances, Mrs Gandhi was more precise about the nature of the threat. In Jammu and Kashmir, Mrs Gandhi based her electoral campaign on accusing Farooq Abdullah[55] of being a communalist, a separatist and of having links with the Pakistani army (e.g. *Indian Express*, 24 May 1983). In Andhra Pradesh in late 1982, Mrs Gandhi warned the electorate that voting for regional parties—i.e. NTR's Telugu Desam Party—would have compromised the integrity of the country. In Haryana and Himachal in 1982, the Congress (I) endlessly repeated that the Sikh menace in neighbouring Punjab was threatening the integrity of the country. In West Bengal in 1982, the threat was constituted by Assamese "separatism" (even though one of the slogans of the Assamese organisations was "save Assam to save India" (Hazarika 2000, 10)) and their anti-Bengali feelings. In short, the nature of the menace varied according to the regional context, but the message of the dangers to the unity and integrity of the country was propagated nationally and through national means, in particular advertisements in the national English press (e.g. *Hindustan Times*, 11 May 1982; *The Hindu*, 1 January 1983) and the government-controlled media.

Outside the electoral campaigns Mrs Gandhi usually emphasised the dangers coming from abroad. The prime minister regularly warned the nation that the international security conditions were very unstable. She put the armed forces on alert on several occasions, as generic threats coming from the sea (*Indian Express*, 22 January 1981), from the air (*The Hindu*, 30 October 1981) and, even more generally, from the "security environment around India" (*Times of India*, 6 October 1982), represented a "threat of war" (*Times of India*, 29 December 1983) for the country.

Sometimes Mrs Gandhi was more precise about the nature of the "foreign hand". In most cases, the "hand" was that of Pakistan, in particular after the US decided to supply Pakistan with a variety of modern military equipment, including F-16 aircrafts (*The Hindu*, 18 September

1981). A few months before the general elections in 1984, Rajiv Gandhi even predicted a war with Pakistan by the end of the year (Hardgrave 1985, 138). Significantly enough, in the 1970s, during Mrs Gandhi's leftist phase, it was the United States that in most cases stayed behind the "foreign hand". In the early 1980s, when ideological opposition to the United States had lost much of its appeal, the hand became in most cases that of Pakistan, which certainly was an "enemy" more in line with the middle class's view of the world.

Given this gloomy picture of India's security conditions, Mrs Gandhi operated at a second level in order to make its citizens, and in particular the middle class, feel safe. The government started a process of modernisation of its military equipment[56] (*The Hindu*, 2 November 1981), which at that time came almost exclusively from the Soviet Union. The military—and sections of the public opinion, in particular the middle class—did not want to lag behind Pakistan. Therefore, efforts were made to diversify India's military equipment, in order to equip the military with the most sophisticated arms available, namely those coming from Western countries (Salman Haider, interview, Delhi, 24 January 2011). Thus, India started buying arms from France (Mirage-2000 aircrafts), Germany (Type 209 and SK1500 submarines), Britain (Jaguar and Harriers aircrafts) and Israel (through which India accessed some US technology, despite restrictions officially envisaged) (Col. Mohan Kaktikar, interview, Delhi, 27 January 2011; *The Hindu*, 2 November 1981; *India Today*, 15 August 1983).[57] An additional "advantage" of this process of modernisation of India's military equipment was that kickbacks on foreign contracts constituted one of the main sources of funding for the party.[58]

In order to deal with the internal situation, Mrs Gandhi's government enacted a set of provisions which empowered the security apparatus with exceptional powers, especially in regards to preventive detentions (e.g. the National Security Act) and the management of strikes and protests (e.g. the Essential Services Maintenance Act). Moreover, the strengthening and the frequent deployment of paramilitary forces throughout the country (*Economic and Political Weekly*, 6 August 1983), the use and abuse of article 356 of the Constitution,[59] and the deployment of the army to deal with internal disturbances—Operation Blue Star being the most notorious example—are all examples of "strong" answers to the "threats" to national unity and integrity.

In short, Mrs Gandhi took a set of steps aiming at showing that India's response to the tense internal and international situation was strong and resolute. However, two points need to be stressed. First, Mrs Gandhi deliberately overestimated the dangers to India's unity coming from abroad. It is certainly true that the relations with its neighbours were not at ease. In Sri Lanka, the explosion of the civil war put relations with India under stress, especially because Mrs Gandhi openly espoused the Tamil cause in order to gain popularity in the South, after the two electoral defeats in Andhra and Karnataka in early 1983; Bangladesh resented the construction of barbed wire fencing on the Indian side of the border, which Mrs Gandhi had decided to build in order to better her electoral prospects in Assam and West Bengal; in Pakistan, along with well-known long-term problems, Mrs Gandhi's explicit support for the Movement for Restoration of Democracy—either because of a sudden espousal of the cause of democracy in the region or because of the desperate need for popularity at home—did not help to ease the tension between the two countries. However, India's military superiority was overwhelming.[60] According to military sources cited by *India Today*, Indian armed forces were made up of 1.1 million soldiers (the remaining South Asian armed forces combined totalled 687,025), 2,300 tanks (the rest of South Asia: 1,386), and 670 aircrafts (the rest of South Asia: 248) (1 October 1983). Moreover, the geopolitical situation made aggression by Pakistan or China extremely unlikely—the only two countries in the area that could reasonably be capable of posing a threat to India. Not only would the United States have presumably objected to such a move—the presence of Soviet forces in Afghanistan required strong military presence on the western border of Pakistan—but the Indo-Soviet military alliance was still in force, making any aggression to India a very remote possibility.

The internal situation was indeed more serious. However, it must be pointed out that, as we shall see in chapter 4, many of the problems—most notably in Assam, Punjab, and Jammu and Kashmir—had been caused or at least worsened by the mismanagement of centre-state relations by Mrs Gandhi's government itself. Some of Mrs Gandhi's sharpest critics even maintain that, especially in Punjab, she deliberately let the situation degenerate in order to give credibility to her "nation under siege" propaganda and in order to be legitimated to undertake a strong and spectacular action—Operation Bluestar—just before the general elections (Col. Mohan Kaktikar, interview, Delhi, 27 January 2011).

Second, the steps taken to face the dangerous situation portrayed by Mrs Gandhi, more than aiming at restoring law and order or at increasing the security conditions of Indian citizens, had the effect of showing the middle class that the government was responding adequately to the threats menacing India's unity and integrity. It is hardly arguable that allowing the police to arrest people without a charge and detaining them for up to a year[61] was a step made to deal with, say, the dacoits in UP; or that the deployment of paramilitary forces was a way to avoid communal disturbances (especially given the strong communal bias characterising many of these forces (e.g. in Moradabad—*Indian Express*, 26 May 1983)); or that the purchase of the Mirage-2000 aircrafts from France had an impact in ameliorating the security conditions of Scheduled Class agricultural labourers; and so on. On the contrary, it is arguable that the modernisation of the military equipment and the increasing allocation of funds to the army (*Budget Speech*, 1980–84) "fulfilled a deep-seated yearning in the educated Indian for greater military prowess as a defining aspect of India's search for "self-respect"[62] in the international community" (Varma 2007, 105).[63] The enactment of draconian laws, on the one hand, gave Mrs Gandhi "a free hand" in case her political position was threatened—as it had happened in 1974–75; on the other hand, it showed the middle class that the government was willing to deal firmly with chaos and lawlessness.

The Congress (I) officially embraced a political strategy based on the creation of fears as the main theme for the 1984 general election. At the AICC(I) session in Bombay and during the 77th plenary session of the Congress (I) party in Calcutta in late 1983 the party made a call "to all patriotic forces to grasp the gravity of the threat to India's existence as a nation" (AICC 1983b) and launched the slogan for the forthcoming electoral campaign: "*desh bachao*" or "save the country" (see also *India Today*, 1 November 1983).

According to some newspaper reports Mrs Gandhi's strategy worked to a certain extent. Romesh Thapar—certainly not a friend of the prime minister in the early 1980s—admitted that he had met a "number of well-meaning persons" in Delhi who had started thinking whether "a replacement of the ruling party at [that] juncture would not [have] increase[d] the confusion and disarray" (*Economic and Political Weekly*, 29 October 1983). The *Times of India* also recalled that many members of the intelligentsia knew from their experience of the Janata rule that "there [was] no alternative to her" (8 September 1982). Needless to say, the assassination of the prime minister in October 1984 made the

Congress (I)'s political message even more cynical and unscrupulous, as we shall see in greater detail below.

The second elements which contributed to enhance Mrs Gandhi's image among the middle class was the implementation of a set of initiatives that stimulated its national pride and need for "modernity".

Perhaps the most concrete steps towards the long-awaited "modernisation" of the country were the introduction of colour TV and the organisation of the Asian Games, also known as "Asiad", in late 1982. In fact, these were closely interrelated, as the former was introduced in order to broadcast the latter. The state-owned television, Doordarshan, began colour transmission on an experimental basis in November 1981. From that moment hectic efforts were made in order to ensure that the Games would be broadcast in colour and that the highest possible number of people could enjoy the spectacle. In particular, the government launched a "gift scheme" (*Times of India*, 22 October 1982), which allowed people to import under the open general licence—i.e. subject to nominal import duties—one colour TV set, before the beginning of the Games. Moreover, Indians residing abroad were allowed to send colour TV sets to their relatives, which came in sizeable numbers.

The Asian Games finally began in November 1982—on Mrs Gandhi's 65th birthday—and those who had managed to buy a colour TV set could follow the 9-hour daily colour telecast and, perhaps more importantly, make the neighbours extremely envious. The introduction of colour TV in India was followed by a national policy aimed at expanding TV coverage—regarded by Mrs Gandhi as "an essential instrument of national integration" (*Economic and Political Weekly*, 6 August 1983)—to 70 per cent of the population by the end of 1985. The plan, which was expected to cost more than Rs 232 crore, was complemented by an extremely liberal licence policy—a capacity of 11 million colour TV sets was licensed to virtually all those who requested it—"including a street food vendor in Delhi's Chandni Chowk" (*India Today*, 16 July 1984).

However, Mrs Gandhi's biggest policy success—from the middle class point of view—was the organisation of the Asian Games in late 1982. This was also Rajiv Gandhi's first important assignment after his entry into politics in 1981. To understand the importance of the event for the middle class, it will be sufficient to list some quotes from the *Times of India*:

"the big day all India has been waiting for so long dawns tomorrow as the biggest sport carnival ever to be staged in this country gets under way formally... When the games end, it will be, in a manner of speaking, a great dream realised... We are in the grip of a fever, the likes of which has not been known... An astounding achievement" (*Times of India*, 19 November 1982);

"It is common knowledge that India would not have been in a position to hold the 9th Asian Games in such a short time but for [Mrs Gandhi's] all-hearted support" (*Times of India*, 20 November 1982);

"the organisers of the ninth Asian Games had another success story to their credit today, when all the events got off a precise and punctual start" (*Times of India*, 22 November 1982);

"the Ninth Asian Games were undoubtedly the happening of the year... at least in this part of the hemisphere there has been nothing to equal the spectacle provided over the last fortnight in New Delhi... a marvellous achievement... dignity and self-respect demand that we hold [the games] at least more than once in a life time... The impact of the Asian Games on the Indian scene cannot be minimised" (*Times of India*, 7 December 1982).

Headlines and comments in other daily newspapers did not differ much, with the partial exception of the *Indian Express*, which was less enthusiastic about the Games, mainly because of the high cost of the infrastructures which had been built for the event (*Indian Express*, 17 November 1982). However, these were isolated voices.

The Asian Games put India at the centre of the world stage. For the first time India was opening itself to the world, to show that India was not anymore—or at least not exclusively—the country of famines and holy cows. Hosting such an important international event was indeed a "milestone" for India's middle class (Subash Agrawal, interview, Delhi, 17 November 2010).

The appearance of New Delhi was completely transformed[64] by the construction of "world-class infrastructures" (*Times of India*, 18 November 1982). Foreign guests—and affluent middle class members—could in addition find a series of Western commodities, which were made available through massive imports and reduced custom duties. The "excellent" (*Times of India*, 20 November 1982) live colour TV coverage, which was broadcasted worldwide, made Indians feel proud of the technological achievement reached by their country. Indeed, every effort was made so that the highest possible number of people watched the Games and felt proud of India and, of course, of its government.

Another aspect of Indira Gandhi's strategy to conquer the hearts of the middle class by stimulating their national pride was foreign policy.[65]

In particular, she relaunched the Non-Aligned Movement (NAM), which was extremely popular, as it was widely recognised as what had allowed India to play a great role in the international arena. In order to do so, Mrs Gandhi had to intervene in all three areas of the cold war international relations system: the USSR, the US, and the third world.

The Soviet Union remained India's most important economic and strategic partner. Brezhnev was warmly welcomed (*Indian Express*, 09 December 1980) during his visit to India shortly after Mrs Gandhi's comeback. However, the Soviet invasion of Afghanistan was deeply resented by Mrs Gandhi. It not only meant that the superpower game skirted the subcontinent, but that the US was somewhat pushed towards Pakistan—which, as we have seen, was provided with the best military equipment available.

Mrs Gandhi's visit to Moscow in September 1982 was portrayed as a diplomatic success (*Times of India*, 22 September 1982), although it was clear that relations were not as warm as they had been in the 1970s, also because of India's attempt to diversify their military equipment (Salman Haider, interview, Delhi, 24 January 2011). In fact, a sizeable part of the middle class had only reluctantly accepted India's tilt towards the Soviet Union after 1971 and was therefore convinced that a more "non-aligned" position had to be restored.

At the same time, relations with the United States significantly improved. In the first place, Ronald Reagan seemed to understand the concept of Non-Alignment far better than any of his predecessors. Indeed, the US "either with us or against us" approach to international relations during the coldest phase of the cold war had significantly contributed to the deterioration of Indo-US relations, which were then completely compromised in the wake of the 1971 crisis in East Pakistan. Ronald Reagan was apparently ready to accept that India could befriend the US and the USSR at the same time. The good personal relations between Mrs Gandhi and the US President certainly helped in the construction of a new phase in bilateral relations (*Times of India*, 31 July 1982).

Mrs Gandhi and Reagan met twice in the early 1980s. The first time was at the Economic Summit in Cancun in 1981, the second when Mrs Gandhi visited the US in the summer of 1982. The latter meeting was highly publicised in the Indian English press and dubbed as a huge success (*Times of India*, 4 August 1982) by the Indian government, which not only signed a set of agreements with the US—including a nuclear deal for the Tarapur power station (*Indian Express*, 29 July 1982)—but was treated with all possible honours by the president of the most powerful country in the world.

Similarly, the relations with other western powers—especially France and the United Kingdom—significantly improved. This was at least partially due to Mrs Gandhi's desire to recover her reputation in the West, after it had been severely damaged in the wake of the emergency (Guha 2007, 549). The 8-month long Festival of India held in London in 1982 was certainly part of such a strategy. Indians in the UK and at home certainly appreciated that their country was being celebrated in the capital of their former colonial master. Furthermore, New Delhi was chosen to host the Summit of the Heads of Government of the Commonwealth countries in late 1983, an event which once again improved India's status in the international arena (*India Today*, 15 December 1983).

Finally, Mrs Gandhi managed to assume the role of leader of the third world in general and of the NAM in particular. In March 1983, Delhi hosted the NAM Summit, which turned out to be the largest gathering of Heads of State and Government ever held. India's leadership of the movement was expected to restore the original balance between the two superpowers, which had been compromised in the previous years by Fidel Castro's presidency. Mrs Gandhi tried to do so, or at least the enthusiastic comments of most of the press reporting on the meeting portrayed it that way (*India Today*, 1 March 1983; *India Today*, 16 March 1983; *The Hindu*, 12 March 1983). Once again, middle class Indians were proud not only to be at the centre of the world stage, but also that "in its organisation, management, and presentation, the summit drew upon the widest range of skills and services, and applied them so effectively that even last year's Asiad '82 somehow seemed a lesser event" (*India Today*, 31 March 1983).

The third element constituting Mrs Gandhi's appeal to the middle class was made up of a set of policies and political messages promoting the interests and cultural values of the upper castes, which formed an overwhelming majority of the middle class.

Mrs Gandhi's defence of the upper castes—which, if seen in opposition to the lower castes, form a national social group—rested upon two elements, one socio-economic and one "cultural".

The socio-economic element was Mrs Gandhi's decision to ignore the report submitted by the Mandal Commission in 1980. The Commission had been instituted by the Janata Party government, to consider the possibility of promoting positive discrimination for socially and educationally backward groups. Mandal utilised eleven social, educational and economic indicators to establish which groups could be defined "backward". Among these, caste assumed a predominant role. The Commission submitted its report in December 1980. It estimated that the Other Backward Classes (OBCs)[66] amounted to 52 per cent of the population. The Commission recommended a 27 per cent quota of all services and public-sector undertakings under the central government and 27 per cent of all admissions to higher education institutions for these castes.[67]

At first, Mrs Gandhi's government tried to ignore the report. Then it said that it was impossible to identify who the backward classes were (*The Hindu*, 19 September 1981). When the government suddenly realised that the Commission had already identified 3,473 castes and communities, it said that the government did not agree with the criterion utilised (*Hindustan Times*, 1 May 1983). Finally, the home minister set up a commission of secretaries to look into the matter in greater detail (*The Hindu*, 7 April 1983). In short, nothing was done to implement the recommendations of the Commission.

The "cultural" element was the adoption of a strategy that defended the interests of the Hindus. This strategy can be dubbed as a soft—or subtle—approach to political Hinduism. Of course, the abandonment of secularism to assume the role of the champion of the Hindus had an impact that cannot be seen as limited to the upper-caste middle class. However, it is common knowledge that it was among these groups that the Hindu chauvinist organisations had found the most fertile soil for their propaganda (Jaffrelot 1996; Hansen 1999).

Mrs Gandhi's shift from "Nehruvian" neutrality to the promotion of the Hindu cause was so sharp that virtually all observers noticed it (e.g. Manor 1997; Malik 1988; Malhotra 1989, ch 17; Hasan 1990). Even those who interpret Mrs Gandhi's accommodation of the Hindu majority interests (along with the accommodation of the "militant minorities") as a way to "preserve India's national unity as a secular state" (Frankel 2005, 665), did not miss the shift in Mrs Gandhi's attitude towards the Hindu community.

Mrs Gandhi appealed to the Hindus in three ways. The first one was at the personal level. Starting from the late 1970s, Mrs Gandhi began to exercise her religiosity publicly. On the one hand, as suggested by some of her biographers (Frank 2001; Jayakar 1995), this must have been a reflection of her insecure personality and of a renewed religiosity that surfaced in Mrs Gandhi's maturity. On the other hand, such a public manifestation of her religiosity created a public image of the prime minister as a pious person (*Economic and Political Weekly*, 25 June 1983). *India Today* ironically remarked that "the number of the pilgrimages she ma[de] in a month vie[d] with that of her official engagements" (16 September 1980). The death of her younger son in June 1980 reinforced Mrs Gandhi's religiosity, leaving her even more prone to surround herself with astrologers and yogis[68] and to perform all kind of rituals (*India Today*, 1 June 1981).

A second level was strictly connected with electoral politics and was adopted in the states. Starting from mid-1982[69]—probably in the wake of the state elections in May, when it "rang a clear warning across 1 Safdarjung Road that the Congress (I) could no longer take election victory for granted" (*India Today*, 1 June 1982)—Mrs Gandhi began to borrow more and more words from the lexicon of political Hinduism, a strategy which was dubbed as "creative" by Satyanarayana, who was at that time an AICC(I) general secretary (cited in Manor 1997, 453).

The core of this strategy was to adopt a partisan approach in a number of local issues or debates, consistently in favour of the Hindu community.[70] For example, while in Bombay, she called for the revival of "the ideals of Chhatrapati Shivaji and others who always worked for the unity of [the] country" (*Times of India*, 9 November 1982); in Jammu, she said that the central government was against granting citizenship to those who fell under the Jammu and Kashmir Resettlement Bill[71] (*Times of India*, 4 October 1982); in north India, she repeatedly invoked measures to promote Hindi as a national language (e.g. *Indian Express*, 4 April 1981), while she prevented the UP Chief Minister, V. P. Singh, from promulgating an ordinance which would have made Urdu an official language of the state (*Indian Express*, 15 January 1982) and allowed her partymen in UP to do the same thing two years later (*Indian Express*, 24 March 1984); in Haryana, the condemnation of Sikh extremism in neighbouring Punjab was particularly strong and aggressive (e.g. *Hindustan Times*, 11 May 1982).

However, it was during the electoral campaigns that this strategy was implemented more systematically. The two best examples are the elections for the Municipality of Delhi in February 1983 and for the Jammu and Kashmir Legislative Assembly in June the same year. In the former case, Indira and Rajiv Gandhi's electoral campaign focused on a set of themes that were particularly relevant for the middle class, like the beautification of Delhi, the construction of infrastructures in the southern part of the city, and the success of the Asiad (*Indian Express*, 05 February 1983). Furthermore, the two Congress (I) leaders focused on the threats to national unity and integrity, in particular those coming from extremist Sikhs. It is widely believed that the local section of the RSS—whose leadership was made up of many Punjabi Hindus (Jaffrelot 1996)—actively helped the Congress (I) (*Economic and Political Weekly*, 4 June 1983; *Times of India*, 16 February 1983; *India Today*, 16 February 1983). This was due to at least two reasons. First, Hindus and, in particular, Punjabi Hindus were grateful to Mrs Gandhi for her confrontational approach towards extremist Sikhs. Secondly, the RSS activists resented the BJP's experiment with moderate politics, which had been inaugurated by L. K. Advani in 1980 (*India Today*, 16 January 1981) and which had even brought the party leadership to include some Muslims among the candidates. Moreover, there had been a serious power struggle between the RSS and the BJP, with the former asking for a 90:10 ratio in its favour in the selection of candidates, while the latter managed to impose a more balanced 50:50 ratio (*Hindustan Times*, 12 February 1983). The overall result was that many *swayamsevaks* (RSS volunteers) decided to support Mrs Gandhi's party. In fact, a voter in West Nizamuddin (a middle class neighbourhood in South Delhi) expressed his surprise that "Congress (I)" workers had visited him five times, while the BJP workers had never come. "In previous elections it [had] been the other way round" (*India Today*, 16 February 1983). Given the poor shape of the Congress (I)'s organisation and the extensive network of RSS-linked organisations in Delhi, it is extremely likely that those who visited voters in Nizamuddin and in other parts of the city were indeed RSS activists campaigning for the Congress (I).

In Jammu and Kashmir, the electoral campaign was fought on explicit communal terms by both "secular" opponents, namely the Congress (I) and the National Conference. Mrs Gandhi's campaign was monothematic. She accused Farooq Abdullah of backing communal organisations, fomenting secessionism, and of having links with Pakistani intelligence, thus putting the integrity of the country in jeopardy.[72] The Chief Minister of Punjab, Darbara Singh, was even invited to tour the state in order to explain Farooq's role in the agitations in Punjab (*Indian Express*, 2 June 1983). Further, the prime minister used to remind the people of

Jammu how Farooq's communal tilt had resulted in the neglect of their region[73]—thus implying that their economic and social backwardness stemmed from the fact that Jammu was a Hindu-majority region within a Muslim-majority state (*India Today*, 1 June 1983). Moreover, the Resettlement Bill was, according to the Congress (I), clear evidence that Farooq's plan was to "replace" the Hindus of the Jammu region with Muslims coming from across the border—an argument that was used by BJP and Congress (I) workers alike (*India Today*, 1 June 1983). Farooq Abdullah, on the other hand, played the card of "Islam in danger", sought the help of well-known fundamentalists like the *mir-waiz* Moulvi, and organised political meetings in the Jamia Masjid of Srinagar.[74] As if the situation was not tense enough, the electoral campaign, which "set a new record in viciousness" (Malhotra 1989, 278) was characterised by numerous episodes of violence, which inevitably took a communal tone.

The overall result was that there was a significant switch of support from the BJP (which failed to conquer a single seat in what had been one of its strongholds) to the Congress (I) (*Economic and Political Weekly*, 4 June 1983). The VHP workers explicitly boycotted BJP candidates, as they found the Congress (I) to be more in line with their political credo (*India Today*, 1 August 1983). At the same time, Farooq was able to acquire the vote of those who had traditionally supported the Jamaat-e-Islami (which did not get a single seat in the Assembly). Something similar had happened in Delhi, where Mrs Gandhi's party had been able to conquer a majority of seats, thus expelling the BJP from still another of its strongholds. In other states too—in particular Punjab, Haryana, Himachal Pradesh, and north India more generally—Mrs Gandhi's support among Hindus was enhanced by her defence of the community, especially against the Sikh "menace".

The third level of Mrs Gandhi's communal politics was national. In the first place, the echo of the state-level political strategy reached in many cases a nationwide audience. Secondly, the strategy of the creation of fears described above overlapped to a significant extent with the strategy of defending the Hindu community. As we have seen, the "foreign hand", turned out to be in most cases that of Pakistan. The internal "threats" to the country's integrity, on the other hand, invariably came from non-Hindu communities—most notably extremist Sikhs in Punjab. Therefore, what Mrs Gandhi was conveying through her constant references to the menaces to the country's unity was a political message that was in many ways identical—in substance—to that of the Hindu right. The idea of India being surrounded by enemies (i.e. Pakistan and, to a lesser extent, Bangladesh and Sri Lanka) actively engaged in destabilising the country through the support to a series of "anti-national" minorities sounded extremely similar to the RSS propaganda, which claimed that the Hindu community was "under siege" in its homeland. Third, Mrs Gandhi did not act firmly against a series of political initiatives, which put in serious question the secular credentials of her party and her government. For instance, she did not discourage the participation to the various *yatras* which the Sangh Parivar organised throughout the 1980s (Katju 2003, 39);[75] neither did she take action against a local section of her own party, which welcomed one of these religious cum political processions with a banner reading "the Congress (I) welcomes you" (*India Today*, 30 November 1983); nor did she dissociate herself from C. M. Stephen's[76] declarations that "the wavelength of Hindu culture and Congress culture [was] the same" (quoted in *Economic and Political Weekly*, 3 November 1990); and so on.

It is not surprising that the RSS—which was curiously spared the usual amount of criticism during the Bombay session of the AICC(I) in October 1983 (*India Today*, 1 November 1983)—actively supported Mrs Gandhi in the last years of her final terms. Not only did its workers either campaign for the Congress (I) or refuse to support the BJP candidates in Delhi and Jammu and Kashmir (*Economic and Political Weekly*, 25 June 1983), but it provided its support at the national level too (Andersen and Damle 1987, 234).

It must be stressed that Mrs Gandhi's defence of the Hindus was never explicit. Rather it was a soft—or subtle—form of majoritarianism. In fact, her defence of the Hindu community coexisted with the traditional Congress rhetoric towards the minorities, condemnation of all communal organisations, generic appeals to religious harmony, and self-proclamations as the only truly secular force in the country.

The three elements constituting Mrs Gandhi's political strategy towards the middle class—the self proclamation as the strong leader that the country needed, the stimulation of national pride, and the defence of the Hindu community in general and of the upper castes in particular—converged in the electoral campaign for the general elections in late 1984.

The campaign was constructed around the theme of the country under siege. We have seen how the slogan *desh bachao* (save the country) had been selected as the main focus of the Congress (I)'s campaign as early as 1983. Mrs Gandhi's assassination on 31 October 1984 obviously reinforced the party's message and made the leadership of the party feel justified to use the most opportunistic and explicitly communal forms of political mobilisation. It will be sufficient to give just one example to illustrate the point. In December 1984, in most English and vernacular newspapers there appeared a Congress (I) full-page advertisement which, after having rhetorically asked whether "the country's border [will] finally be moved to your doorstep", it described the so-called anti-national forces in this way:

> "They put a knife through the country and carve out a niche for their cynical, disgruntled ambition as public aspiration. They raise a flag and give this niche the name of a nation. They sow hatred and grow barbed wire fences, watered with human blood. But it's you who step out and bump into the fences and bleed while they cash your vote to buy their ticket to power".

The advertisement ended asking "Why should you feel uncomfortable riding in a taxi driven by a taxi driver from another state?" (reported in Manor 1997, 454). If the anti-Sikh message was not clear enough—many taxis in north India were driven by Sikhs—the Congress (I)'s posters showing two turbaned assassins gunning down Mrs Gandhi swept away the confusion.

Mrs Gandhi's Social Base in the 1980s

Mrs Gandhi's political strategy in the 1980s was deeply influenced by the two processes that had marked the two previous decades, namely the decay of the Congress organisation and the demand for political representation that arose among large strata of the society. In 1980 the voters had entrusted Mrs Gandhi and the Congress (I) with the objectively difficult task of putting an end to chaos and at the same time responding to their growing expectations. However, these could hardly be fulfilled in the ways they had been in previous decades, that is by a mix of patronage distribution and populist rhetoric. Moreover, Mrs Gandhi's party, as we have seen in chapter 2, lost its ability to distribute patronage to a significant extent. On the other hand, her political message did not differ much from that of "*garibi hatao*", which had, if not exhausted, at least severely consumed its political potential. Therefore both strategies of political mobilisation which had made possible Mrs Gandhi's coronation as the

"Empress of India"[77] in the 1970s could not be used any longer to enlarge the party's support base and build up political support for the government's actions.

Mrs Gandhi's strategy towards the middle class was more successful. This still was a relatively marginal force in numerical terms. However, it was from this social group that most of the "opinion leaders" (Manor 1983a, 98), who had an increasingly important role in influencing the political choices of a sizeable section of the rural electorate, came. The support of big business and kickbacks on foreign contracts ensured a huge availability of funds for the prime minister's party. On the other side, the remaining power of the landowning castes—who resented the declining ability of the Congress (I) to distribute patronage and the "anti-peasant" economic policies of the government on the one hand, and the fact that the abolition of poverty was nowhere in sight on the other—negatively affected the Congress (I)'s electoral fortunes.

The overall result was that election outcomes in the most important states after 1980 offered a mixed picture. Of course, state elections only partially reflect the electorate's opinion of the central government. However, Mrs Gandhi managed to personalise these elections to such an extent that it is arguable that, at least in some cases, these were referenda on her personal performance. Not only did she personally campaign, holding more public meetings than anyone else, but the entire political communication of the party was centred upon her person. Party posters invariably showed Mrs Gandhi's or her son's faces. Only in Jammu and Kashmir was another party member, Mufti Mohammed Sayed, allowed to show his face beside the prime minister's (*India Today*, 1 June 1983). Newspaper advertisements paid equally scant attention to the local units of the party and to local concerns. For example, in Himachal Pradesh, voters could read this kind of political advertisement:

> "fourty-two [sic] lac Himachalis express their deep sense of gratitude towards their beloved prime minister, Smt. Indira Gandhi for always evincing special interest in the speedy development of their Pradesh ...Honest and hardworking people of Himachal Pradesh today rededicate themselves to the sacred task of implementation of Smt. Indira Gandhi's New 20-Point Economic Programme in all earnest" (*Hindustan Times*, 15 April 1982).

In 1982, the Congress (I) obtained a narrow victory in Himachal Pradesh, managed to form a coalition government in Kerala, and doubled the number of seats in West Bengal, where it nevertheless remained a marginal force (in terms of seats), if compared with the Left Front. In Haryana, although the Congress (I) conquered the largest number of seats, it was the Lok Dal who had managed to form a majority. However, the governor of the state, Ganpatrao Devji Tapase, swore in Bhajan Lal as chief minister, mainly because of the strong pressures coming from the central government, which managed to "convince" some independent candidates to support a Congress (I) Cabinet (*India Today*, 1 June 1982). Overall, out of 443 seats contested by the party in 1982, only 132 Congress (I) members became legislators. In terms of the percentage of votes, the Congress (I)'s share (compared with the Lok Sabha elections in 1980) declined in Kerala, West Bengal and Himachal Pradesh, while it increased in Haryana.[78]

The following year, two other important states went to polls, namely Andhra Pradesh and Karnataka. Both states had uninterruptedly been governed by the Congress party since their formation in the 1950s. Even in the 1977 general elections this part of south India had supported Mrs Gandhi. In early 1983, both states turned their back on the prime minister. In Andhra Pradesh the newly born Telugu Desam Party (TDP) led by NTR swept the polls. In neighbouring Karnataka, the Janata Party conquered the majority of seats, although polling 7 per cent less than Mrs Gandhi's party. The Congress (I)'s share of votes declined by about 16 per cent in Karnataka and by about 23 per cent in Andhra Pradesh. Of course, regional factors played a big role. The mismanagement of Gundu Rao's government in Karnataka (Raghavan and Manor 2009) and the continuing interferences by the central government in the political life of Andhra—four chief ministers had been removed in the previous three years—and the humiliating treatment by Rajiv Gandhi of the then Chief Minister T. Anjiah (*Hindustan Times*, 24 February 1982), negatively impacted on the Congress (I)'s electoral prospects. In both cases what became apparent was that Mrs Gandhi's charisma—who tirelessly campaigned for her party, perhaps like never before (*The Hindu*, 3 January 1983)—was not enough to win elections any longer.

In the Delhi and Jammu and Kashmir elections, the Congress (I) party performed fairly well. However, as we have seen above, the results had been influenced by the "unusual" political strategy of the party and by the fact that Mrs Gandhi had been supported by the RSS network.

To sum up, in the early 1980s, in continuity with her political strategy in the 1970s, Mrs Gandhi attempted to build a national social base of support which could cut across regional, caste, and, to a lesser extent, religious and class divisions. Whereas in the 1970s such a strategy had focused mainly on the rural world and among disadvantaged social groups—peasants benefiting from the Green Revolution and "weaker sections" hoping that the prime minister would abolish poverty and would protect them—in the early 1980s the emphasis was shifted towards the urban world. In particular, the middle class and big business were chosen as major allies. According to an opinion poll launched by *India Today* in sixteen cities across India, the prime minister's popularity increased during her last term in office (1 January 1984). The traditional Congress rhetoric, on the other hand, still portrayed the prime minister as the champion of the poor and of the minorities, but the effectiveness of this political message was fading, while the ability of her party to ensure protection to the weaker sections severely declined.

It is likely that Mrs Gandhi was not fully aware of this trend. Not only was she still able to attract large crowds at her public speeches (e.g. *Hindustan Times*, 12 May 1982), but there was a widespread feeling in the government that Mrs Gandhi's personal popularity was still intact (Vasant Sathe, interview, Delhi, 11 December 2010) and that she could still win elections on her own. It is likely that bogus reports from local units of the Congress (I) about the implementation of centrally sponsored programmes and the virtual halt to the flow of information reaching the top of the party made Mrs Gandhi underestimate the erosion of her and her party's popularity. Anyway, there was little she could do. Her personality was still the main asset the party could count on. But larger and larger strata of the electorate were not willing to believe any longer that the simple "domination of Indira" (Wadley 2002) would automatically guarantee them a significant betterment of their living conditions. The spectre of the coalition government was haunting India (see also *Seminar* No. 298, June 1984).

The Rise of Political Hinduism

In the early 1980s another form of building up political support at the national level began to become important. Although still in an embryonic form, Mrs Gandhi's final term witnessed the emergence of a national Hindu electorate.[79] As shown by Christophe Jaffrelot (1996), the Jana Sangh had tried to build up a national "Hindu vote" since its inception in the early 1950s. However, the regional concentration of the RSS network in the north of India, the division of the Hindu community along caste, regional and religious (sects) lines, and the Nehruvian consensus on secularism—still in the late 1970s the "untouchability" of communal politics had been used as a pretext to break up the Janata coalition—had hitherto hindered the emergence of a nation-wide Hindu constituency. All this changed in the early 1980s.[80]

The main actor in the construction of a Hindu vote was one of the RSS's organisations, namely the Vishwa Hindu Parishad (VHP). This had been founded in the 1960s with the objective of protecting the Hindus, spreading the ethical and spiritual values of Hinduism, and establishing and strengthening links with Hindus abroad (Andersen and Damle 1987, 133). The results had been rather disappointing. However, its network had grown significantly and, in 1981, the VHP had more than 3,000 units in 437 districts throughout the country (Jaffrelot 1996, 200). In the early 1980s, the RSS chief, Balasaheb Deoras, entrusted the VHP with the task of building a national Hindu electorate.

A turning point was the conversion of about a thousand Dalits to Islam in February 1981 in Meenakshipuram in Tamil Nadu. "No other incident has given such a fillip to Hindu communalism or done so much damage to the cause of communal harmony" (Gill 1997, 309). The conversions had a big echo in the local and national press. Even newspapers not close to the RSS's positions referred to an alleged conspiracy architected in the Gulf countries to promote mass conversions to Islam in India, aiming at reversing the numerical proportion between Hindus and Muslims (*Times of India*, 21 March 1981). The *Indian Express* even published a report according to which this would happen within a couple of centuries (Jaffrelot 1996, 342). "From now on, the underlying theme of all public discussions among militant Hindus was 'Hindu society under siege'" (Jaffrelot 1996, 342). The "besiegers", depending on the context, were the Muslims (allegedly funded by "Gulf money"), Christian missionaries aiming at converting as many Dalits as possible, but also extremist Sikhs, and (Muslim) "infiltrators" from Bangladesh.

The VHP took the lead in the defence of the Hindus. First, it organised a set of conferences on the theme, especially in the south of India; second, it fiercely condemned untouchability and organised a set of symbolic banquets, during which Dalits and caste Hindus dined together. Conferences and banquets were attended by politicians belonging to virtually any political party (*India Today*, 01 November 1981). Third, the VHP expanded its network of welfare organisations. Fourth, it promoted a set of "reconversion" campaigns, especially in Rajasthan and among Christians and Tribals. Finally, the VHP was deeply reformed at the organisational level. Between 1982 and 1984 a Central Margdarshak Mandal (a committee of spiritual guides) and a Sadhu Sansad (a parliament of sadhus, later to be called Dharma Sansad) were created and functioned as a powerful visibility platform for spiritual leaders, who spread the RSS credo. In 1984, the Bajrang Dal—a sort of armed wing of the VHP—was established with the aim of recruiting lower-caste Hindus to be taught "how to be bold" (Jaffrelot 1996, 363).

The fulcrum of the VHP's strategy was to promote a sense of solidarity among the Hindus. In order to do so, the RSS organised a set of gigantic religious-cum-political processions. The first one—called *Ekatamata Yatra*, roughly translatable as "pilgrimage of one-soulness"—took place in late 1983. Three main processions started in Haridwar (in present Uttarakhand), Kathmandu, and Gangasagar (West Bengal), converged in Nagpur (Maharashtra)—where the RSS headquarters is located—before reaching their final destinations in Kanyakumari (India's southernmost point), Rameshwaram (Tamil Nadu) and Somanath (Gujarat), respectively. At least 47 smaller processions (which followed local pilgrimage routes) joined the larger ones at important pilgrimage centres throughout India. In total, about sixty million people attended the processions (Andersen and Damle 1987, 135), especially in the areas that had been affected by communal tension in the previous months (above all in Punjab, Assam, and UP) (*India Today*, 16 November 1983).

The whole exercise aimed at promoting "national integration", where the "nation" was constituted by the Hindus. The way in which the processions were conceived suggested a coincidence between spiritual and geographical India. Indeed, the "pilgrimage was effectively transformed into a ritual of national integration" (Van deer Veer 1994, 124), through a "physical" connection of local, state, and national pilgrimage centres. Each procession was led by a *ratha* (the processional Hindu chariot, traditionally used during festivals). Each *ratha* carried the images of Bharat Mata (Mother India), which was a "nationalist" version of the mother goddess worshipped in various forms in many parts of India. The chariots carried huge pots filled with the water from the Ganges and smaller pots filled with the waters from local sacred rivers and lakes, symbolising the connection among all sacred waters of the country. The "unity" of the waters became a symbol of "national" (i.e. Hindu) unity. More than 1.5 million small bottles of sacred water were sold along the routes (Andersen and Damle 1987, 135). In short, the *Ekatamata Yatra* "made very effective use of an existing ritual repertoire on the mother goddess, on the sacredness of the Ganges water, and on Lord Rama, transforming this repertoire to communicate the message of Hindu unity" (Van der Veer 1994, 125–6). Any reference to issues that could cause divisions along the lines of sect or caste was carefully avoided. The whole campaign focused on those rare "national" Hindu symbols, like the Ganges and the cow. The VHP even "invented" new "national" rituals and symbols.

Shortly before Mrs Gandhi's assassination, the "Committee of Sacrifice to Liberate Ram's Birthplace" was set up. This was a long-standing demand of the RSS and similar Hindu organisations. According to them, the Mughals had demolished a temple and erected a mosque (the Babri Masjid) on the spot where Lord Rama was born in Ayodhya (UP). India's institutions had taken the issue very seriously and had closed the venue to both Hindus and Muslims. In September 1984, a procession left Bihar heading to Ayodhya with the objective of "liberating" Ram's birthplace. Afterward, the procession would have headed towards Delhi, to ask the central government to allow the Hindus to access the site's premises, but the assassination of the prime minister obviously made the VHP change its plans. However, the committee was in fact an "all-Hindu" body, where people belonging to antagonist sects or different castes gathered (Van der Veer 1987, 295). The Babri Masjid would be eventually destroyed on 6 December 1992.

To sum up, the RSS network in the early 1980s adopted a strategy focused on the construction of a "national" Hindu constituency, which could be politically mobilised. Indeed, the themes on which the RSS based its propaganda coincided to a large extent with those on which Mrs Gandhi and her party based theirs. Both highlighted the dangers which threatened their respective constituencies—the Hindus, and the whole country respectively, both referred to as "the nation"—which were constantly portrayed as being under siege—by the Muslims, extremist Sikhs and the Christian missionaries in one case, and by a foreign hand or anti-national minorities in the other—the two "besiegers" largely coinciding in substance. Both attempted to promote national integration and unity, the only difference being the definition given to the word "national". In short, two of the most important informal institutions of the country propagated the same type of political propaganda. Thus the two messages not only reinforced one another, but each created the conditions for the success of the other. It is definitely not surprising that the RSS activists actively supported Mrs Gandhi's party on several occasions rather than the "moderate" BJP.

The Rise of the Regional Alternatives

Finally, a third way of building up political support became relevant at the national level in the early 1980s. The promoters were a set of regional parties. These were political formations that were relevant in only one state of the Indian Union. Accordingly, their political appeal was based on a set of themes that were specific to that particular state, while their social bases reflected the local caste and class arithmetic. In other words, they were "non-aggregative" (Palshikar 2004) political formations, thus standing in stark contrast with the "catch-all" ambitions of all national political parties.

Regionalism and regional parties were nothing new. We have seen in chapter 1 how regional and national politics started to diverge from the late 1960s, especially after the de-linking of national and state elections in 1971. Some regional parties emerged during the last phase of colonial rule, like the Akali Dal in Punjab (founded in the 1920s) and the Jammu and Kashmir National Conference (founded in the 1930s), or shortly after the obtainment of independence, like the Dravida Munnetra Kazhagam (DMK) in Tamil Nadu (founded in 1949). Indeed, the Congress party itself was more a constellation of regional parties that accepted to abide to a central authority, rather than a homogenous national party (Chhibber and Petrocik 1990). This was true not only during the heyday of the so-called Syndicate—which was made up of regional party bosses—but also during Mrs Gandhi's prime ministership in the 1970s. In fact, although Nehru's daughter centralised the party to a significant extent, the loosening of the Congress's organisation resulted in the regional units of the party diverging and acting rather independently (Manor 1978).

However, during Mrs Gandhi's final term, quantitative and qualitative changes occurred. In the first place, the number of regional parties which either won state assembly elections or became the main opposition party or assumed central importance in the politics of a given state—thus furthering the process of multiplication of competitive party systems at the state level (Sridharan 2002)—significantly increased. In previous decades, regional parties were politically relevant in Tamil Nadu, Punjab, and, to a lesser extent, Jammu and Kashmir. In the early 1980s they came to power in Tamil Nadu (AIADMK) in 1980, in Andhra Pradesh (TDP) in 1983, and Jammu and Kashmir (National Conference) in 1983. In two other states, they were the principal opposition party (the Akali Dal in Punjab), or assumed such an importance that their election to power was clearly in sight (the Assam Gana Parishad in Assam, which eventually came to power in 1985). Further, the Janata Party in Karnataka and the CPI(M) in West Bengal and Kerala, although claiming to be national parties, in fact appealed to regional sentiments and behaved as regional political formations for all practical purposes. The former came to power in January 1983, while the latter, having been elected in 1977 and re-elected in 1982, was in the process of laying the foundations of its 30-year long dominance of West Bengal politics. The importance of the regional parties continued to grow in the second half of the 1980s and, by the early 1990s, they were a fundamental element of Indian politics (Brass 1997, tab. 3.4).

Several factors contributed to the growing importance of regional parties. We have already mentioned that Mrs Gandhi introduced a structural element that favoured the divergence of state and national political arenas, namely the de-linking of parliamentary and legislative assembly elections in 1971. Furthermore, almost three decades of common political, administrative and linguistic history had made the states homogenised and self-defined polities.

Particularly important were Mrs Gandhi's centralising policies, not only towards the states vis-à-vis the centre, but also towards the regional units of her own party. In the 1950s, the local units of the Congress party had been able to champion the demand for state reorganisation along linguistic lines, notwithstanding the opposition of the party high command. During the 1970s the state units of the Congress party lost the necessary autonomy to raise regional issues in front of the central party. As a consequence, being that the Congress was in power in many states, not only were regional demands largely ignored, but the whole set of federal institutions—whose functioning had been guaranteed by the Congress system (see chapter 4)—started crumbling.

Indeed, even if the state units of the party had been "allowed" to champion regional demands, the Congress (I) could not function any longer as a mechanism for conflict management and problem solving, mainly because of the severe decay which had occurred in the previous decades and because of rampant factionalism. For example, the concern expressed by the Assamese about immigration from Bangladesh and West Bengal was not raised by the local unit of the Congress, despite the fact that it was the dominant party in the state and that the Assamese middle class had been a key sector of its constituency. The demand for political representation of the Assamese led to the birth of a series of local organisations, which eventually became a regional party and ultimately conquered power in the state (in 1985). Indeed, it would have been rather difficult for the Congress (I) to represent their concerns anyway. The demand for the expulsion of Bengalis from the state collided with other demands coming not only from within Assam, but from throughout India. The expulsion of the immigrants, for example, would have caused severe resentment among the Muslims, but also among Bengalis in West Bengal, while the deportation of Hindus to Bangladesh would have had serious consequences among Hindus throughout the country. Similarly, in Punjab, a solution to the political impasse could not be found, also because of destructive factionalism within the party and across different levels of the polity.[81]

In other cases, Mrs Gandhi's "responsibility" in the emergence of regional parties was more direct. In Andhra Pradesh, for example, the emergence of the Telugu Desam Party would have not been so terrific, had it not been for Mrs Gandhi's continuous removal of chief ministers and Rajiv Gandhi's insulting behaviour towards one of them.

In still other cases, regional parties were reinforced by the Congress (I)'s attempt to weaken those very parties. In Punjab, for example, Sanjay Gandhi's attempt to divide the Akali Dal ultimately led to Operation Bluestar, and caused the Sikhs of Punjab to close ranks around the Akali Dal itself (Tully and Jacob 1985), which conquered power—for the first time on its own—in 1987. Something similar happened in Jammu and Kashmir, where Farooq Abdullah's popularity increased following his removal from power in July 1984 in what was a constitutionally dubious move orchestrated by the Congress (I) party. Something similar happened in Sikkim.

However, growing regional consciousness was not only a negative reaction to Mrs Gandhi's mismanagement of centre-state relations. It was also a response of an increasingly assertive electorate to the failure of the Indian state to address many of the people's problems. The failure by both national alternatives—the Janata Party in the late 1970s and the Congress party in the early 1980s—to assure social stability and acceptable living and security conditions and the lack of any other national alternative must have made many voters look for political representation at other levels of the polity, first and foremost at the state level, which, as we have already recalled, were gradually becoming the "natural" unit of Indian politics.

The fact that the national state had failed in taking care of a sizeable part of the electorate could be easily exploited as a tool for political mobilisation along religious, casteist, linguistic, regional or sub-regional lines, or, more often, a combination of these. It was exactly along these lines that most of the regional parties constructed their constituencies. Indeed, the key feature of the regional parties' way of building up political support was radically different from the national parties'. All-India parties attempted to be "catch-all" political formations, thus challenging the Congress on its own field. Regional parties, on the contrary, aimed at winning the support of carefully selected and relatively narrow constituencies, which needed "exclusive" political representation.

Articulating grievances in regional terms—selectively "activating" one or more of the locally available identities of the people—proved to be a successful way of channelling growing discontent. Perhaps the best example of this way of building up political support was the Telugu Desam Party in Andhra Pradesh. Its leader, NTR, built his 1983 electoral campaign on the claim that Telugu people were being neglected—and humiliated—by the central government. The solution to all their problems, NTR seemed to promise, was to elect a government that would take decisions in Hyderabad rather than in Delhi. There was also another dimension. The domination of the Congress party had coincided with the domination of the Reddys on state politics and on the "excessive" accommodation of the Scheduled Classes and Scheduled Tribes. Other increasingly assertive groups—most notably the Kammas, to which NTR himself belonged, but also the Rajus, Kapus and Velamas, plus sections of the OBCs—which had been kept at the margins of the structure of power in the state, obviously resented such an exclusion,[82] especially because it was perceived as "externally" imposed, and thus not reflecting the local socio-economic fabric.

NTR was able to exploit all these grievances to win a considerable amount of support. However, the political awareness of the people of

Andhra which had contributed to his ascent to power was equally important in determining his descent a few years later, when voters realised that merely governing from Hyderabad did not necessarily guarantee a good performance of the government or a significant betterment of their living conditions. Something similar happened in Assam and in Punjab. Along with new forms of building political support, new ways of keeping that electoral support intact were desperately needed.

Secondly, the growing importance of the regional parties resulted in a qualitative change of political regionalism in the early 1980s. Even though their focus was on their respective states' politics, regional parties began to influence national politics to a significant extent. In the wake of the "southern tornado" (*India Today*, 16 January 1983) that brought to power NTR in Andhra Pradesh and Ramakrishna Hegde in Karnataka in January 1983, regional parties began to get organised at the national level. They moved at two levels. On the one hand, they began to coordinate their demands to the centre, especially as far as centre-state relations were concerned (*India Today*, 01 April 1983). I will deal in greater detail with this matter in chapter 4.

On the other hand, they tried to build a political alternative to the Congress (I) at the national level. The initiative was taken by NTR. In May 1983, he invited opposition leaders—most of whom belonged to regional parties—for a meeting in Vijayawada. What the TDP leader had in mind was not so much an alliance in the form of the defunct Janata Party. Rather, his aim was twofold. On the one hand, the Vijayawanada meeting sought to put the basis for a nation-wide arrangement to avoid splitting the anti-Congress vote (*Indian Express*, 24 May 1983), which could eventually develop into a confederation of regional parties (*Indian Express*, 27 May 1983). To use a more contemporary language, this was the first time that a "third front" was theorised. On the other hand, regional parties tried to coordinate their strategy in regards to specific issues. Indeed, for the first time since independence, fourteen opposition parties were able to sit together and issue a joint statement, in which they sharply criticised Mrs Gandhi's government and asked for a revision of the terms on which centre-state relations were based (*India Today*, 16 June 1983). Moreover, regional parties promised to help each other in case the central government took hostile initiatives against any of the state governments headed by one of them (*Indian Express*, 29 May 1983). Needless to say Mrs Gandhi reacted angrily to the Vijayanawada meeting, dubbing the move as a way to weaken national integrity and comparing regionalism with communalism and other threats to the country's unity.

Other meetings followed. In autumn 1983, Farooq Abdullah—who had recently won the Jammu and Kashmir state elections—hosted a conclave of seventeen opposition parties. Significantly, the newly formed National Democratic Alliance—which was made up of the Lok Dal and the BJP—did not attend the meeting, mainly because the "National" alliance strongly disagreed with one of Farooq's regional policies, namely the enactment of the resettlement act. Probably too enthusiastically, Bahuguna described the meeting as a "metamorphosis in the entire political scene" (*India Today*, 16 October 1983). The symptoms of such a metamorphosis were the realisation that opposition unity did not necessarily mean the creation of a "monolithic entity" encompassing contradictory ideologies and incompatible leaders. What the leaders of regional parties had in mind—NTR and Farooq Abdullah above all—was an "umbrella type concept of opposition unity" (*India Today*, 16 October 1983), which could not only oppose the Congress (I), but also discuss specific issues of common interest and look at national problems from a different—i.e. regional—perspective.

A few months later, another meeting was held in Bangalore, where a set of minor regional parties asked NTR and Farooq Abdullah to lead a "Union" of regional parties on the basis of a common "minimum" programme (*Indian Express*, 2 January 1984). The same month, opposition parties met once again in Calcutta (*India Today*, 16 February 1984), issuing another joint statement.

The importance of these meetings lay more in Mrs Gandhi's angry reactions, rather than on their effectiveness in building a national confederation of regional parties. Indeed, it is likely that NTR's and Farooq Abdullah's dismissals in 1984 had much to do with Mrs Gandhi's attempt to nip the regional alternative in the bud. However, the regional parties' combined electoral strength was probably enough to make the Congress (I) fall short of an absolute majority in the forthcoming elections. Given the sharp confrontational approach towards regional parties adopted by Mrs Gandhi, it would have been extremely difficult for her party to build a coalition with any of these, barring perhaps the AIADMK.

The prime minister's aggressive behaviour towards regional parties—all dubbed as "anti-national forces" which sought to destroy the unity of the country (e.g *Economic and Political Weekly*, 7 July 1984)—on the one hand, at least partially counterbalanced the blurring of the lines dividing parties, thus limiting defections and the further disintegration of her party (Manor 1997); on the other hand, it further polarised the electorate. The national and regional levels began to stand on opposite sides of the political spectrum. Indeed, rather than on a left-right axis—where the Congress (I) still occupied most of the space at the centre—the 1984 elections were about to be fought on the national-regional axis. Only Mrs Gandhi's assassination made the "national" overwhelmingly—but momentarily—prevail over the "regional".

Conclusion

Mrs Gandhi's final term witnessed the emergence of new ways of building up political support. To begin with, Mrs Gandhi tried to enlarge her national base of support by including the middle class and the big industrialists. Whereas in the 1970s it had been the rural world that had constituted the bulk of Mrs Gandhi's national constituency, in the early 1980s the emphasis was shifted towards the urban sector. In fact, since then, every Indian government, with the partial exception of V. P. Singh's brief premiership, has put the middle class and the big industrialists at the centre of its political strategy (Maiorano 2014a). The net result has been that if there is one sector of the population whose standard of living has increased significantly in the last thirty years, it is the middle class. The big industrialists, on the other hand, have built profound and sordid links with the entire political class, as the continuous emergence of scams in recent years clearly demonstrates. The market-oriented reforms of the 1990s cemented the alliance among the middle class, the industrial sector and the political class.

Secondly, the Hindutva project of the RSS, although not completely successful, managed to acquire not only political legitimacy—in this respect Indira and Rajiv Gandhi's contribution must not be underestimated—but resulted in its parliamentary representative, the BJP, becoming one of the two cornerstones of today's national bipolar party system. There is little doubt that without the Ramjanmabhoomi agitation the BJP—which, after the disastrous 1984 elections, abandoned its experiment with moderate politics—would have not been able to reach this position. Moreover, although in the south of India the Hindu politics never managed to kindle the kind of public sentiment that it did in the north, it nevertheless allowed the BJP to penetrate areas which had hitherto been out of its reach. The destruction of the mosque in Ayodhya in December 1992 and the Gujarat pogroms in 2002—to cite only the two most notorious examples—constitute the main "collateral" effects of this way of building up political support.

Third, although regional parties failed in their project of constituting a national alternative to all-India parties, the main issue on their agenda—a betterment of the terms of the relationship between the centre and the states—in fact met with success. Moreover, the regional parties managed to reach a central place in the national party system. As a matter of fact, since 1989, no party has been able to form a government at the centre without the support of regional parties (until 2014). This, on the one hand, resulted in a complete restructuring of centre-state relations and, on the other hand, enormously enhanced small parties' bargaining power, thus introducing a crucially important structural element in India's party system. As a result of these changes, power flew from the central government to the states, and from the prime minister's office to other institutions of the state, including the Parlaiment, that today plays a much more central role than it used to during the heyday of the "Indira system".

Two concluding points need to be stressed. First, these forms of political mobilisation would constitute the most important ways of winning electoral support for the following thirty years. These new forms of political mobilisation were rather successful ways of responding to the demand for political representation coming from below. The increasing importance of non-Congress actors was a manifestation of the fact that the political and the party system were re-aligning towards a configuration much more in line with the changes that had occurred within India's society. In other words, the overall result of these changes was a restructuring of India's party system, from one dominated by the Congress party to the present multi-party one. Indira Gandhi tried to prevent this from occurring. As we shall see in the next chapter, she did not hesitate to use the institutions of the state (including the military) to prevent the emergence of a multi-party system; however, she was only able to slow down, rather than to stop, the process.

In any case these new forms of political mobilisation proved to be rather unstable ways to win political support. Winning elections was much easier than re-winning them. The 1980s saw the emergence of the "iron law of Indian politics" (Nandy 1988, 14), according to which after a brief honeymoon, the relationship between the electorate and the government goes through a severe crisis, which in most cases ends with a divorce in the following elections.[83] The performance of the incumbents began to be a—if not *the*—central element in determining the election outcomes. Vertical mobilisation founded on both the traditional social hierarchy and the patronage distribution system was a less and less important tool for maintaining electoral support. In other words, the declining ability of most parties to distribute patronage and the growing political sophistication of the electorate combined to determine a dramatic decline of the effectiveness of political clientelism and populist rhetoric in influencing the electoral outcomes. As a consequence, ruling parties—both at the centre and in most states—found it increasingly difficult to be re-elected. The main reason behind this high degree of electoral volatility was that the new forms of political mobilisation were not accompanied by new forms of politics that could significantly impact on the electorate's living conditions.

Second, the process of change of the political system that I described in this chapter paralleled a structural change in Indian politics. The 1980s can be seen as a transitional phase between a Delhi-centred and a state-centred political system. Yogendra Yadav and Suhas Palshikar (2003) have convincingly argued that since the 1990s, the fundamental unit of Indian politics became the states, rather than the nation. The factors which explain the shift, according to the two scholars, are the different impact of the three "Ms"—Mandal, Mandir and Market—on different states, the internal political and administrative homogenisation within most states which occurred in the past 50 years, and the fact that the developmental effort of the Indian state had made the states the loci of the most important political decisions in the eye of the common citizen (Yadav and Palshikar 2003, 32–33). One may add, as suggested by Prem Shankar Jha (*Tehelka*, 10 September 2011), that the political economy of corruption which came into being after the ban on corporate donations to political parties in 1970, developed at the state rather than at the national level, thus making the states the loci where political clientelism was built.

What I said in this chapter constitutes the "pre-history" of this structural change of India's polity. All three "Ms" originated in the early 1980s. The "Market" was a result of Indira Gandhi's pact with the big business and the middle class and of the first, timid process of liberalisation of India's economy. The "Mandir" was a process that started with the *yatras* of the early 1980s and that acquired legitimacy also thanks to Mrs Gandhi's ambiguous approach to Hindu politics. The "Mandalisation" of India's politics, although buried by Indira Gandhi's government, found fertile soil on the much more regionalised polity that Mrs Gandhi left behind.

4

INSTITUTIONS

POLITICISATION, EROSION, AND INFORMALISATION

Introduction[1]

W. H. Morris-Jones (1985), writing shortly after Indira Gandhi's assassination, argued that "each institutional element of the political system has lost something of its earlier integrity and therefore of its capacity to make its independent and distinctive contribution to the interaction of the parts" (246). Indeed, in 1984 the question "will the state wither away?" (Rajni Kothari, *Illustrated Weelky of India*, 8 June 1984) was certainly posed more frequently than ever before. This was not only due to the constant repetition by the Congress (I) that national unity and integrity was in danger. Indeed, these fears have always been greatly exaggerated (Manor 2001). However, it is undeniable that a severe process of deinstitutionalisation occurred during Mrs Gandhi's rule. In fact, arguably no institution (except the prime minister's office) was stronger in the 1980s than it was the 1960s.

This chapter is dedicated to the severe institutional crisis of the early 1980s. Its main aim is to put such a crisis into a broader perspective in order to understand, along with the proximate elements which determined the coming to a head of the institutional crisis, its deeper causes. The chapter will seek to do so in two ways. On the one hand, it will attempt to draw attention not only to very important discontinuities that marked the passage from Nehru's era to his daughter's, but also to some important lines of continuity. As will be clear, this is by no means a way to downplay Mrs Gandhi's role in determining the severe breakup of governmental institutions or to deny that "changes of attitude among the rulers had signal consequences" (Kaviraj 1984, 235) on India's institutional framework. Rather, it simply means that these discontinuities will be read in parallel with some important lines of continuity, which will be highlighted.

On the other hand, we will try to qualify the term "deinstitutionalisation", in light of some evidence from the early 1980s. In doing so we will differentiate among three sub-processes that affected Indian institutions and which eventually resulted in the severe institutional crisis of the early 1980s. First, we will describe a process of politicisation of institutions. Our attention will focus on the bureaucracy, the judiciary, the presidency and the Parliament. Second, we will look at the erosion of the quality of Indian democracy and of the Constitution. Third, we will analyse the process of "informalisation" of federal institutions and Mrs Gandhi's attempts in the early 1980s to maintain such a framework despite the profound changes that had occurred in the political system.

Two further specifications are in order. The first one deals with the meaning of the term "institution" in the context of this chapter. We will use the term to indicate the formal institutions of the state. We have already dealt with the most important among India's informal institutions, namely the Congress party (chapter 2); it is now important to look at the ways in which the messy situation within the ruling party was reflected in the functioning of formal institutions.

Second, the chapter is solidly grounded in the belief that "the way in which parliamentary democracy works depends, more than we may like to admit, on the balance of powers between political parties" (Morris-Jones 1957, 113). In fact, Mrs Gandhi's desperate attempts to force the maintenance of an "artificial" one-party-dominant system can arguably be seen as the root of the breakdown of the institutional set up of the early 1980s.

Politicisation of Institutions: the Bureaucracy

It is common knowledge that, throughout her career, Mrs Gandhi heavily relied on the bureaucratic apparatus in order to "get things done". From the prime minister's point of view, bureaucrats were more trustworthy than most of her party colleagues, whose political ambitions were perceived as a constant threat to Mrs Gandhi's power position and, from the mid-1970s on, to her dynastic ambitions. Moreover, the bureaucracy carried out (although in an increasingly ineffective way) a fundamental role that, as we have seen in chapter 2, the Congress party was less and less able to perform, namely gathering information and making it available for the political leadership.

The Indian bureaucratic apparatus is a huge administrative machine. In 1989, it employed 18.5 million civil servants (Potter 1994, tab. 4.1) and is divided into numberless branches. The most important division, from our point of view, is that between the Indian Administrative Service (IAS) and the rest of the bureaucracy. The former is an all-India service[2] and represents the highest echelon of the bureaucracy. The IAS is made up of state cadres who are eligible to work for the central government. Even when serving at the state level and therefore under the control of the state governments, the IAS members are governed by rules set by the central government. Therefore, the IAS can be seen as the tool of the centre for administering both its own apparatus and its peripheries. Given the point of view adopted in this study, it is on the relations between the IAS and the prime minister that we will focus.

The IAS is the only formal institution of the state that survived—formally and in substance—the end of the colonial regime.[3] In fact, the IAS is the direct heir of the colonial Indian Civil Service (ICS). Indeed, it has been argued that the IAS has not changed much since the colonial period, at least as far as its organising principle is concerned (Potter 1994). However, an important change did take place. Politicians came to exercise an overwhelming influence on the working of the bureaucracy[4] which transformed it from a supposedly neutral administrative tool, into a political weapon in the hands of the ruling parties.

The importance of political loyalty as an internal organising principle of the bureaucracy emerged in the early 1970s. Removing poverty, Mrs Gandhi used to say, required a "committed bureaucracy". In principle, the commitment was towards the Directive Principles of the Constitution, which, at least in theory, were the source of inspiration for Mrs Gandhi's battle on poverty. In practice, in the prime minister's view, bureaucrats had to be committed to her. Loyalty to the ruling party gradually became a—if not the—central element in determining the career prospects of civil servants, especially as far as the most senior positions were concerned.

The years from 1975 to 1980 marked a fundamental break in the IAS's history for several reasons. First, we have already mentioned that hardly any civil servant resigned during the emergency (Guha 2007, 535), while abject decisions were duly implemented. More importantly, the more a civil servant showed himself ready to implement whatever the high command—i.e. Indira and Sanjay Gandhi—ordered, the more he/she was to be rewarded. A notable example is the then vice-chairman of the Delhi Development Authority, Jagmohan, who, thanks to his "services" in the "beautification" of Delhi and "family planning" campaigns—two of the programmes ideated by Sanjay Gandhi—became, after Mrs Gandhi's return to power in 1980, Lt. Governor of Delhi (1980–81), then Lt. Governor of Goa, Daman and Diu (1981–82) and, Governor of Jammu and Kashmir (1984–89).[5] Numberless other examples could be easily provided.

Second, the high number of "political" transfers and the concentration of power in the hands of those bureaucrats who were close to the Gandhi family—along with the concerns due to the suppression of the democratic rule in 1975–77—spread a climate of fear throughout the public administration. Therefore, even those bureaucrats who were not eager to pander to the political establishment, in fact in most cases obeyed out of fear (*The Hindu*, 20 September 1981).

Third, the climate of fear of the emergency became a witch-hunting climate (S. K. Mishra, interview, Delhi, 21 December 2010) during the Janata phase (1977–79). Bureaucrats who had been close to the Gandhi family were in most cases transferred or put on leave or even had their salaries suspended. The same happened to those who were perceived to be close to the Congress party. In still other cases, officers were transferred just because they were not close enough to the new ruling party and room had to be made for those who were. In particular, it was the Jana Sangh who managed to "recruit" many of its followers into the IAS ranks (Naresh Chandra, interview, Delhi, 14 December 2010), but also Charan Singh made every effort during his brief prime ministership to change the composition of the IAS as much as he could (*Indian Express*, 7 September 1979; 21 November 1979). Apparently Mrs Gandhi's concept of a "committed bureaucracy" made inroads among her opponents too.

Fourth, the witch-hunting did not end with the collapse of the Janata government. In fact, it started again with rejuvenated vigour after Mrs Gandhi's return to power in 1980. The first victims were those whose position had been strengthened during the Janata phase, thanks to their political connections. Then came those who, in line with one of the basic principles of any bureaucratic apparatus i.e. political neutrality, had consented to collaborate with the Janata government. Then, those who were close to senior politicians who had chosen not to follow Mrs Gandhi in the new Congress (I) had to be side-lined, especially to make room for Sanjay's friends and collaborators (*Indian Express*, 4 June 1980; Singh 1982, 83). After the latter's death, the top of the administration was reshuffled once again—a "de-Sanjaysation" took place (*Indian Express*, 10 August 1981)—in order to make it more in line with the changed political circumstances. In short, what emerged was a "spoil system" (*Indian Express*, 4 March 1980).

The overall result of these developments was that the subjugation of the bureaucracy to the political system became the accepted norm which regulated the administrative apparatus. This had several important consequences. First, the bureaucracy stopped being a reliable source of information for the central government. When the Director General Civil Aviation wrote to the Secretary Civil Aviation informing him that Sanjay Gandhi was violating air safety regulations, the former was asked to proceed on leave (*Indian Express*, 1 July 1980). Episodes like this reinforced the well-founded belief that the only information which could be transmitted to the top was that which was thought to be good news for the political leadership. It is worthy to recall here that, as we have seen in chapter 2, the Congress (I) had stopped functioning as an information-gathering tool. Therefore, the subjugation of the bureaucracy to political power further reduced the flow of information reaching the higher echelons of the central government.

Second, not only did information become less and less available to the political leadership, but the reliability of this information was more and more questionable. This stemmed from two sets of reasons. On the one hand, this was due to the development of vertical chains linking bureaucrats in the states to politicians at the centre. Indeed, this was nothing new. What was new was that, as we have seen in chapter 2, this was paralleled by an analogous trend within the Congress (I), namely the development of factionalism between different levels of the polity. Bureaucrats became an instrument in the hands of politicians to weaken factional enemies. Probably the clearest example of this was in Punjab. Before being elected to the presidency, Zail Singh used and abused his power as home minister to weaken his arch-rival Badal Singh. During the period of President's Rule in 1980, "mass transfers" of officers were ordered by the Centre, which let Zail Singh run the Punjab administration "by proxy" (*Indian Express*, 9 March 1980). As a consequence, bureaucrats began to base their communication with the Centre on local, political, and factional calculations. On the other hand, given that political and personal considerations became the key element in determining one's career prospects, ambitious bureaucrats did not hesitate to convey false information in order to strengthen their position and/or weaken their rivals (and eventually those of their political masters). For example, shortly before the Asian Games, the then sports secretary told Mrs Gandhi that no sport facilities existed close to the Delhi border. Indeed, such facilities did exist. They had been built in the previous years under the supervision of S. K. Mishra (who was very close to former Haryana Chief Minister and Union Defence Minister Bansi Lal). Mrs Gandhi eventually had to fly there by helicopter in order to verify whether such facilities existed or not (S. K. Mishra, interview, Delhi, 21 December 2010).

Third, the climate of fear pervading the administration resulted in the virtual halt of the administrative activity. Not only were actions which could be interpreted as hostile to the ruling family or to its close associates not taken, but officers, not knowing when and where they might have tread on the toes of someone who was politically connected, were afraid to take responsibility even in marginal cases (*Indian Express*, 6 January 1981). For example, in Madhya Pradesh in Winter 1982, a district collector was ordered to give up his charge for not withdrawing a case against a Congress (I) worker, who turned out to be part of the district's 20-Point Programme Implementation Committee and therefore somehow associated to Mrs Gandhi (*Hindustan Times*, 2 February 1982); in Jammu and Kashmir in Summer 1983, the Director of the State Doordarshan TV was dismissed immediately after he refused to broadcast the statement of a local Congress (I) worker about the supposed rigging of the state elections by the ruling National Conference (*India Today*, 16 August 1983). Many more examples can be found in all major national newspapers. Moreover, given that orders from politicians, especially if politically inconvenient, were given orally, and given that such orders were in many cases contradicted one another, officers were in the objectively difficult situation of not knowing which orders to follow and which to disregard (*Indian Express*, 3 January 1981).

Fourth, the growing influence of the politicians on the bureaucrats caused a defensive reaction. Officers at all levels began to look for protection. The easiest way to do so was to align with the ruling party. However, this was a short-term strategy that was likely to jeopardise future career prospects, since there were growing signals that the Congress (I) would not rule forever. Furthermore, the anarchic condition of the ruling Congress (I) made political alignment more risky than ever before, since power equilibria within the party changed rapidly and without following a discernible path. A wiser way to seek protection was, on the one hand, to adopt an approach of total submission to whatever party was ruling—a strategy which was adopted on a very large scale—and, on the other, to "unionise" on the basis of larger categories such as language, caste, religion and so on. In this way punitive transfers could be seen as being targeted against a particular community, which could act as a sort of internal lobby and limit to a certain extent the arbitrariness in the management of the administrative personnel.

Fifth, the submission of the bureaucracy to the will of politicians gradually transformed the bureaucratic apparatus into a fund-raising apparatus. We have already pointed out how politicians belonging to any party were virtually obliged to resort to black money to provide their parties with the financial resources they needed. One of the preferential channels through which this could be done was by filling the bureaucracy with civil servants who either willingly closed their eyes to corrupt practices or were willing to "supplement" their sources of income. Gundu Rao in Karnataka is perhaps one of the best examples of this kind of transformation of the bureaucratic apparatus into a fund-gathering machine (Raghavan and Manor 2009, pt. 2). The compression of the salaries of the higher echelons of the bureaucracy since 1950 as part of the "socialist" agenda and the increasing availability of expensive middle-class status symbols—e.g. colour TV, video-recorder—along with the declining appeal of the "idealistic" commitment to the nation-building effort, contributed to the endemic spread of corruption in the administration.

To sum up, one of the effects of the coming into being of a competitive party system at the central level, although for a very brief period of time, was the transformation of the bureaucratic apparatus into a personal instrument in the hands of powerful—and, in some cases, even not-so-powerful—politicians. Needless to say, this was particularly true for the prime minister (and her son), who was able to use the bureaucracy for personal and political ends.

The politicisation of the IAS was just the tip of the iceberg. Four examples will be provided in order to show the extent to which Mrs Gandhi managed to subject all kinds of centrally controlled state institutions. Shortly after 1980 elections, the newly appointed Lt. Governor of Delhi, Jagmohan, ordered the police to conduct an inspection of the *Indian Express*—the only national newspaper that had refused to submit to censorship during the emergency. Following the inspection, the editor was given 30 days to provide evidence why the building hosting the newspaper should not be confiscated (*Indian Express*, 12 March 1980). Eventually nothing came out of the inspection, but it surely sounded alarm bells for smaller newspapers, whose views were in contrast with the government.

We have already mentioned that H. N. Bahuguna, a powerful Brahmin leader with a strong following among Muslims in UP, joined the Congress (I) shortly before the 1980 general elections, but abandoned Mrs Gandhi's party a few months later. He also resigned from the Lok Sabha. Thus, a by-election for the Garwal constituency had to be held. However, pressures were exercised on the Election Commission that resulted in the indefinite postponement of the by-election (*The Hindu*, 15 November 1981), officially because, according to the UP (Congress (I)) state government, the maintaining of law and order could not be ensured. Curiously enough, the same kind of objections were not raised one year later, when elections in Assam were duly held despite the complete breakdown of law and order in the state, and despite numerous police reports, literally begging for a postponement of the elections (*India Today*, 1 May 1983). Bahuguna eventually managed to get elected to the Lok Sabha the following year.

In August 1983, the Governor of Andhra Pradesh, Ram Lal, dismissed the recently elected Chief Minister, N. T. Rama Rao (NTR), despite the fact that he enjoyed a comfortable majority in the State Assembly, and nominated the former Finance Minister, Bhaskara Rao, in his place.[6] The Congress (I) party supported the new government from "outside". A huge amount of money—between 20 and 30 million rupees (Tummala 1986, 391)—was allegedly sent by the Congress (I) high command to Andhra in order to "convince" some of NTR's followers to support the new chief minister. In order to "insulate" his legislators from temptations, NTR decided to bring all of them to Delhi to appeal to the President, Zail Singh. However, NTR was denied the right to set up a charter flight; train reservations were mysteriously cancelled (by the state owned Indian Railway) so that legislators had to be squeezed in regular, unreserved coaches; finally, the train journey, which normally took about 24 hours, lasted two and a half days.

Finally, Mrs Gandhi managed to transform the government-controlled media into a family-controlled media. News bulletins were particularly affected, where "all professional norms of news selection were cast aside to make room for a brazen personality cult" (*India Today*, 16 August 1983). Not only did Mrs Gandhi virtually monopolise the lead news on Doordarshan and All India Radio bulletins, but her son found more space in the headlines than any other minister in the Union government, not to speak of opposition leaders—N. T. Rama Ramo was even denied permission to broadcast from All India Radio (*India Today*, 16 August 1983). To give one example, on 22 July 1983 the bulletin began with Mrs Gandhi "dedicating" to the nation an atomic power project in Madras; however, that day the supreme court had refused a general stay on hanging; Nihangs had clashed with the police in Punjab; non-gazetted AP employees (who were on strike) accepted to talk with the state government unconditionally; and many top bureaucrats of the Union government were transferred (*India Today*, 16 August 1983).

In short, what emerged in the wake of the emergency was a "combination of US style 'spoils system' with the security of tenure of the mandarin system"—a disastrous mix indeed (Krishnan and Somanathan 2005, 299). The bureaucratic apparatus was subjected to the political system to a significant extent. As a consequence, it began to work according to distorted logics and rules, which seriously compromised its ability to function as one of the key institutions of a democratic polity, not to mention the consequences on efficiency and accountability.

Politicisation of Institutions: the Judiciary, the Parliament, and the Presidency

We will now turn our attention to the relation between the prime minister and three important formal institutions, namely the judiciary, the Parliament and the presidency. All of them were seriously affected by a process of politicisation. However, while the latter two had been subjected to the executive quite early in India's independent history, the judiciary had strenuously fought for its independence.

Mrs Gandhi's relations with the judiciary had been turbulent throughout her political career. In the wake of her left-turn in 1969, the prime minister included the judiciary in the list of those who had "vested interests" in maintaining the status quo and were thus hindering her projects of social transformation.[7] Indeed, the strained relationship between the executive[8] and the judiciary began in Nehru's years, when a vicious circle was established, in which "the parliament [could] pass a legislation, the courts [could] determine its constitutionality, the parliament [could] try to circumvent the courts by amending the constitution, the courts [could] pronounce that parliament [had] limited powers of amendment, parliament [could]...and so on and on" (Rudolph and Rudolph 2001, 187).

During Mrs Gandhi's years as prime minister the conflict intensified. The battle was fought, at least in theory, over two different interpretations of the Constitution. On the one hand, the government argued that the Directive Principles of State Policy[9]—supposedly the source of inspiration for Mrs Gandhi's developmental strategy—should have priority over the Fundamental Rights, and especially over the right to property. The judiciary, on the other hand, defended the supremacy of the Fundamental Rights.[10] In terms of policies, it meant that the implementation of the land reforms and other progressive measures was hindered by the Supreme Court's interpretation of the Constitution.[11] In institutional terms, the supremacy of the Directive Principles was translated into the unlimitedness of the amending power of the Parliament; on the contrary, the defence of the Fundamental Rights brought the Supreme Court to formulate the "basic structure" doctrine, enunciated for the first time in the Kesavananda case on 24 April 1973, according to which certain fundamental features of the Constitution could not be changed. The very next day, the government appointed Justice A. N. Ray as Chief Justice of India, superseding three more senior colleagues,[12] all of whom had been part of the majority that delivered the ruling (Justice Ray was on the minority that dissented).

The appointment of Justice Ray inaugurated a new phase in the relation between the government and the judiciary. Supersessions and transfers of the judges of the Supreme Court and of the state-level high courts became a more or less accepted tool in the hands of the central government to put pressure on the judiciary (Mehta 2005). While, as we have mentioned, the conflict between the executive and the judiciary had characterised independent India's institutional history since the very beginning, the intrusion of political considerations in the working of the Supreme Court and the high courts was a new thing. The new appointment policy was even candidly defended in Parliament, as a way to get a "committed judiciary" (Noorani 1994), which, the government used to say, along with a "committed bureaucracy", was a pre-condition for the proper implementation of anti-poverty initiatives. Needless to say, it was during the emergency—the proclamation of which stemmed from the on-going battle between the judiciary and the executive—that most of the abuses occurred.[13] Furthermore, a great many of the provisions included in the amendments of the constitution passed in 1975–77 aimed at curbing the judiciary's independence and power of judicial review.

The Janata phase, along with the restoration of the institutional equilibrium through the repeal of the most authoritarian pieces of legislation—first and foremost the 42nd Amendment of the Constitution—created the conditions for a temporary truce on the constitutional dispute between the judiciary and the executive. What turned out to be crucial from this point of view was the majority obtained by the non-Congress parties in the Rajya Sabha. It took almost five years for Mrs Gandhi to regain a nearly two-thirds majority in the Upper House, which was necessary for amending the constitution. Moreover, in Summer 1980, the Supreme Court in the Minerva Mills case reaffirmed the "basic structure" doctrine (*Indian Express*, 2 August 1980). Even though the government repeatedly said that it did not accept the doctrine (e.g. *Indian Express*, 2 October 1980), and despite the fact that the government actively sought to get the Supreme Court to review its ruling (*Hindustan Times*, 7 January 1981), in the post-emergency political conditions, it would have been quite difficult for Mrs Gandhi to pass through constitutional amendments which restored the unlimited amending power of Parliament.

This does not mean that the government-judiciary relations were at ease. The main bone of contention remained the transfer of high court judges and, more generally, the intrusion of politics into the functioning of the judiciary. Merely a week after Mrs Gandhi's return to power, the Law Minister, P. Shiv Shankar, told the Lok Sabha that the government was going to have "fresh look" at the policy of appointment of high court judges (*Times of India*, 15 January 1980). The Cabinet issued a press note[14] in early 1983 (*Indian Express*, 29 January 1983) in which the government explained the guidelines that were to be followed for the appointment of the judges. According to these guidelines, the chief justice and one-third of the judges were to be from outside the state. While, in principle, this would have fostered uniformity in the judicial process and limited the biases deriving from local pressures on judges who had spent most of their life in the same state, in actual terms the guidelines paved the way for the systematic humiliation and denigration of those judges that the government did not find "completely pliant and congenial".[15] This was particularly so from 1981 when the Supreme Court had ruled in the High Court Judges case that the consent of the judge to be transferred was not necessary. During the following five years, the government transferred thirty high court chief justices (Austin 1999, 532, n. 55).

Transfers were not the only weapons in the government's arsenal. Two other "popular" measures to put pressure on the judiciary were the undue delays in the confirmation of additional judges and in the appointment of judges to the Supreme Court and the high courts, and the granting of rewards to "committed" (to the ruling family) judges. For example, the judge who freed Mrs Gandhi in 1977, R. Dayal, was made Commissioner to Sick Mills in December 1980, with the status of Joint Secretary, a post carrying twice the salary of a temporary additional district judge (as he was in 1977) (*Indian Express*, 5 December 1980). Another example was the appointment of Baharul Islam, a former Congress member of the Rajya Sabha, to the Supreme Court in December 1980, despite the fact that he had already retired (*Indian Express*, 5 December 1980). Islam later contested a Lok Sabha seat on a Congress (I) ticket from Assam.

To sum up, Mrs Gandhi's relations with the judiciary in the early 1980s were in complete continuity with her earlier terms as prime minister. The judiciary's independence was seen as a potential restraint to her power. Therefore, she systematically sought to make the judiciary work on the base of political considerations, so that, in the last resort, it would be subjected to the executive. Indeed, it was Mrs Gandhi herself who explained to the Chief Justice of India, Yeshwant Vishnu Chandrachud, the logic underpinning the appointment of Supreme Court judges: "I am a political leader. I have to carry my people with me. I cannot displease my own people. My difficulties are political difficulties" (Mrs Gandhi, quoted in Noorani 1994, 111).

Mrs Gandhi was successful only to a certain extent. Indeed, at the time of her death, "an uneasy truce over transfers" (Austin 1999, 532) and over constitutional supremacy had been reached. The conflict would resurface after the collapse of the one-party-dominant system after 1989, this time with the Supreme Court acting from a much stronger position (Rudolph and Rudolph 2001).

Let us now turn our attention to the Parliament and the presidency. Their relationship with the government has generally been heavily unbalanced in favour of the latter. This was true during Nehru's years and even more so during Mrs Gandhi's terms. I noted in chapter 1 that the proclamation of the emergency regime made apparent the state of fragility of India's institutions. This was especially evident for the Parliament and the presidency, which were supposed to work as constitutional restraints to the executive's attempts to abuse its power. Such fragility stemmed from the high degree of politicisation to which these institutions had been subjected since the early 1950s, and especially after Mrs Gandhi's appointment as prime minister. As the emergency clearly demonstrated, both institutions, on the one hand, functioned following political rather than constitutional considerations and, on the other hand, were not capable of exercising any degree of autonomy. In turn, this way of functioning of these institutions led to their political irrelevancy.

While the presidency is somehow bound to be a relatively[16] marginal institution in parliamentary democracies, the Parliament is supposed to be the centre of the country's political life. However, the way the Parliament works is heavily influenced by the configuration of the party system. Therefore, paradoxically enough, the firm control of the Lok Sabha enjoyed by all prime ministers till 1989—with the exception of Charan Singh, and, to a lesser extent, Morarji Desai—created the conditions for the Parliament to play a marginal role in India's democratic life. At the same time, it paved the way for the concentration of power in the executive's hands. The Parliament came to play a merely procedural role, with the possible exception of those rare moments in which either there was a minority government (in 1969, after the Congress split) or there were two different majorities in the two Houses (as in 1969 and after Mrs Gandhi's return in 1980).

Mrs Gandhi came to see the Parliament as "something to be tolerated" (*Indian Express*, 26 November 1980). Several examples show the scant respect that Mrs Gandhi paid to the Parliament. First, throughout her last term in office, Mrs Gandhi resorted to legislation by ordinance on a regular basis, thus excluding the Parliament from the policy-making process (*Indian Express*, 13 November 1980). Second, she explicitly refused to discuss certain public issues (e.g. the Bihar Press Bill) in the Parliament (*Times of India*, 15 October 1982). Third, the government began to modify tariffs and state-controlled prices not only without informing the

Parliament, but immediately before the beginning of the Budget Session (*Indian Express*, 16 January 1981; *Hindustan Times*, 22 February 1982). Fourth, the partisanship of the Lok Sabha speaker Balram Jakhar, led to some rather bizarre interpretations of the procedural regulations of the Lower House, like when Zail Singh explicitly praised Adolf Hitler but the references were expunged from the records (*Indian Express*, 27 March 1982). Fifth, Mrs Gandhi stopped showing up in the Lok Sabha to report about her official visits abroad, as when she returned from the United States in Summer 1982 and the External Affairs Minister, Narasimha Rao, who had remained in India taking care of domestic affairs, was sent to report to the Parliament (*Times of India*, 14 August 1982). Quite naturally, the MPs began to consider themselves more as administrative clerks than as legislators. Many of them did not bother to show up, not even when they had put up questions for oral reply (*India Today*, 16 March 1983). In fact, parliamentary sessions became shorter and shorter (*Hindustan Times*, 1 May 1982). Many more examples could easily be provided.

Let us now turn to the presidency. Before 1989, the President of India played a significant role only twice (Manor 2005). The first one occurred in 1951, when President Rajendra Prasad asserted himself in an attempt to block legislation on Hindu personal law (Austin 1996, 140). The second one occurred in July 1979, when President Neelam Sanjiva Reddy discretionally refused to give Jagjivan Ram the opportunity to form a parliamentary majority and called instead for fresh elections. Apart from these instances, the role of the presidents has been largely ceremonial, with the partial exception of President Zail Singh who came very close to dismissing Rajiv Gandhi's government for "irresponsibility and corruption" (Manor 1994, 121).

However, presidents usually kept a low profile and avoided public controversies. In many cases, especially during Indira Gandhi's premierships, this was translated into complete subservience to the prime minister. The most striking example occurred in 1975, when President Fakhruddin Ahmed consented—although reluctantly—to sign the proclamation of the emergency, even though the Cabinet had not been informed before. Similarly, during the emergency he did not object to any of the draconian legislative measurers adopted by the government. The same can be said about the Parliament, which not only ratified the proclamation of emergency and the subsequent extension of the Parliament's life,[17] but acceded to subverting the democratic character of the constitution by passing a whole set of authoritarian amendments.

In the early 1980s the situation did not change much. The relation between Sanjiva Reddy and Mrs Gandhi was usually cordial, despite past animosity.[18] The president consented to sign whatever piece of legislation or ordinance that was brought before him, including the much-discussed dissolution of nine state assemblies, and the National Security Ordinance.

The election of Zail Singh to the presidency in 1982 made relations with the prime minister even smoother. The latter was universally reputed to be one of the most loyal politicians to the Gandhi family, as well as one of the most inept—in March 1982, shortly before being elected to the highest office in the country, he praised Adolf Hitler's achievements before the Lok Sabha (*Indian Express*, 25 March 1982). The president came to play a mere administrative role. In fact, when in late March 1984 Mrs Gandhi carried out a major reshuffle of governors, Zail Singh came to know about the changes only when his secretariat brought him the files for signatures (*India Today*, 1 April 1984).

To sum up, the working of the bureaucracy, the judiciary, the Parliament and the president became increasingly influenced by political considerations that, over time, made them lose their institutional aura. While the judiciary strenuously fought for its independence and eventually resisted to a large extent to the attacks of the executive, the Parliament and the president surrendered without fighting. As a consequence, their subjugation to the executive became an accepted norm of India's institutional life. The bureaucracy split into three groups: "the 'wives' (those officers who are attached to one party), the 'nuns' (officers who remain unattached to any party), and the 'prostitutes' (who attach themselves to whichever party is in power and switch when there is a change of government)"—the share of the "prostitutes" being "quite high" (Krishnan and Somanathan 2005, 306).

Overall, the politicisation of institutions caused them to function in distorted ways and at the service of partisan political calculations. Also it reinforced the idea—widespread in Indian society—that politics is omnipotent and that no restraint to the power of politicians exists. This is indeed one of the most harmful legacies of Mr Gandhi's rule.

Erosion of Institutions: The Rule of Law and the Constitution

A set of institutions that were seriously undermined during Mrs Gandhi's rule were those forming India's democratic framework and, more specifically, the constitution. I have already mentioned how Mrs Gandhi's attempts to subject the institutions of the state to the executive culminated into the proclamation of the emergency and in the draconian amendments of the constitution, which were then enacted. We will now see in greater detail how these tendencies continued in the early 1980s.

From this point of view, Mrs Gandhi's final term in office stands in complete continuity with her earlier terms. Along with a series of disturbing trends which we have already dealt with—above all, the spread of corruption, the virtual annihilation of the Congress party, and the appointment of people whose democratic credentials were far from being solid to important positions—the declining quality of India's democracy was the result of the enactment of a set of quasi-authoritarian laws. These concerned three main areas: preventive detention, labour, and freedom of expression.

Let's start with preventive detention. Three pieces of legislation are particularly important. One of the few achievements of the Janata government had been the restoration of the democratic character of the Constitution and the repealing of the Maintenance of Internal Security Act (MISA), which had given the government sweeping powers for the management of political disorder. However, a similar piece of legislation (the Preventive Detention Ordinance (PD)) was passed by Charan Singh's caretaker government in late 1979. A well-known lawyer and intellectual, A. G. Noorani, indeed compared the two laws (*Indian Express*, 15 October 1979). Shortly after Mrs Gandhi's return to power, the Lok Sabha converted the Ordinance into law (*Indian Express*, 3 February 1980). Apparently, the desire for dealing with growing social unrest with severe limitations of citizens' rights was something that cut across party barriers.

A few months later, the president promulgated yet another ordinance, which was converted into law in December 1980 (*Indian Express*, 17 December 1980). The National Security Act (NSA) gave the government the right to arrest and detain without trial those suspected of undermining national security and essential economic services. The NSA was subsequently amended in Summer 1984 by an ordinance, which established that a detention order made under the act would not be deemed to be invalid because one or more of the grounds were held to be unsustainable (*Indian Express*, 22 June 1984). The fact that these provisions could be used to curb political dissension was clearly demonstrated the very day the ordinance was promulgated: the government released two of the Akali Dal leaders—Operation Bluestar had just taken place—and immediately re-arrested them under the amended NSA.

In July 1984, supposedly in response to the civil war-like situation in Punjab, the government made the president promulgate an ordinance (the Terrorist Affected Areas (Special Courts) Ordinance), which was converted into law in August the same year. The Act, which extended to the whole of India (barring Jammu and Kashmir), gave the central government the power to declare any area of the country as a terrorist-affected area. In such cases, it was possible to establish special courts for trial of some specified offences. These included, among others, "waging war against the state, abetting mutiny, promoting enmity between classes, assertions or imputations prejudicial to national integrity and certain serious offences relating to human body and property like murder and dacoity" (*Indian Express*, 15 July 1984). In other words, the Act gave the government the power to establish special courts for prosecuting an extremely broad (and vaguely defined) array of crimes. Moreover, the definition of the word "terrorist" was so broad that even workers raising their demands through strikes fell within its purview. The act ensured that a "terrorist" remained in detention for at least six months, before an Advisory Board was summoned to evaluate the grounds on which that person had been arrested. In any case, even if the Advisory Board held the detention order to be invalid, the government was allowed to re-arrest the same person on the very same grounds. Furthermore, the act, by modifying Section 111A of the Evidence Act, put the burden of the proof on the accused, thus reverting one of the basic principles of most democratic penal codes in the world—namely, that one is to be presumed innocent until guilt is proven. Rajiv Nayar compared the Terrorist Affected Areas Act to the colonial Rowlatt Act (*Seminar*, No. 302, October 1984).

A second area in which Mrs Gandhi's government actively intervened was labour relations. We have already seen in chapter 3 that Mrs Gandhi sought some sort of corporatist solution to labour unrest. However, along with the setting up of tripartite talks between the business community, the central government, and the unions, Mrs Gandhi's government enacted a set of laws designed to suppress labour unrest. The most notorious provision—along with the Terrorist Affected Areas Act mentioned above—which sought to curb workers' rights was the Essential Services Maintenance Act 1981. The Act enabled the government to ban strikes in certain "essential" services and gave the police the power to arrest without warrant any person "reasonably" suspected of having committed an offence under the ordinance. Not only was the list of "essential" services very long and vaguely defined, but it was open to further extension:

> any other service connected with matters with respect to which Parliament ha[d] power to make laws and which the Central Government being of opinion that strikes therein would prejudicially affect the maintenance of any public utility service, the public safety or the maintenance of supplies and services necessary for the life of the community or would result in the infliction of grave hardship of the community, may, by notification in the Official Gazette, declare to be an essential service for the purposes of [the] act (ESMA 1981, art. 2.17).

Furthermore, the definition of "strike" included the refusal to work "overtime". In short, the government conferred on itself the right to suppress strikes altogether. However, as we have already seen in chapter 3, results were disappointing; even excluding the Bombay textile strike from the count (which lasted almost two years), the man-days lost for strikes steadily increased during the early 1980s (*Economic Survey*, various issues).

The third area in which the Congress (I) government curbed citizens' rights was freedom of expression. Four provisions are worth noting. First, in the 1981 Budget, a 15 per cent levy on imported newsprint was introduced (*Budget Speech*, 1981). The move was unprecedented, as newsprint had been exempted from custom duties since 1947. Small and medium newspapers would have been put in serious difficulty by the provision, which was however ultimately cancelled for small newspapers and reduced to 5 per cent for medium-sized ones (*Indian Express*, 23 April 1983).

Second, the central government backed a piece of legislation introduced in the Bihar Legislative Assembly (controlled by the Congress (I)) which threatened to jeopardise the freedom of expression in the state. The legislation, known as the Bihar Press Bill, introduced a new kind of offence, namely scurrilous writing. According to the bill, judicial and executive magistrates—the latter being petty functionaries of the state government—had the power to issue a warrant against a journalist for scurrilous writing. The offence was not an ordinary criminal offence, but a non-bailable one (*Times of India*, 18 September 1982). Mrs Gandhi defended the bill on the grounds that the press in India was in the hands of the opposition and it indulged in "character assassination" (*Times of India*, 8 September 1982). The bill was eventually withdrawn after it aroused nation-wide protests, a national press strike, innumerable *bandhs*, and a march to the Parliament.[19]

Third, in August 1982, the government attempted to amend the Post Office Act 1898. The provision aimed at conferring on the government the right to intercept private mail on the "occurrence of any public emergency or in the interest of public safety or tranquillity" (*Indian Express*, 14 August 1982). Once again, the very general and broad scope of the bill left ample space for abuses. However, the legislation was eventually withdrawn.

Fourth, the government-controlled media became (in continuity with the previous decade) an instrument for the ruling family's propaganda. However, the skyrocketing spread of the radio and TV even in very remote corners of the country—a result of well-targeted government policies (*India Today*, 16 June 1983), including a Rs 68 crore hardware expansion plan (*India Today*, 16 August 1983)—made the effects of this kind of limitation of the public media's independence qualitatively and quantitatively different from the past. Not only was the number of people reachable through these means considerably higher than in the previous decades, but this "new" media was acquiring a growing influence on the urban middle class, which, as we have seen, had been chosen as one of the major constituent parts of Mrs Gandhi's national social base.

In this respect it is worth pointing out that all provisions aiming at limiting the citizens' freedom of expression were finally withdrawn. It is likely that Mrs Gandhi, although apparently willing to subject the press to her will, did not want to push things too far, as this was an issue that was particularly important for the middle class. Indeed, during the emergency, press censorship had been one of the major sources of concern for the middle class. Mrs Gandhi knew that in order to "conquer" the middle class's heart she had to restore her democratic credentials, or, at least, she had to respect those freedoms which the middle class was not ready to renounce.

The general decline of the quality of democracy in India was parallel to a somewhat latent threat to the Constitution. Throughout Mrs Gandhi's final term, some of her closest associates repeatedly referred to the possibility of transforming the parliamentary system into a presidential form of government. The debate was not new. Indeed, the constituent assembly itself had taken into consideration the presidential system before opting for the more familiar Westminster model. Since then, the debate has resurfaced regularly.[20] In 1966, R. Venkataraman—one of the closest associates of the prime minister in the early 1980s—made a powerful plea for switching to a presidential system at the Chandigarh session of the AICC. The following year, in the wake of the "confusion" sparked off by the results of the 1967 elections, the India International Centre hosted an important seminar on the topic, during which several exponents of India's intellectual, political, and economic life backed the switch to a presidential form of government, in order to provide stability to the political system. In 1970, the distinguished civil servant, diplomat and relative of Mrs Gandhi, B. K. Nehru, proposed the establishment of a presidential system in order to ward off the "sunset of democracy" (quoted in Noorani 1989, 14). In a private letter to the prime minister written during the emergency (dated 9 September 1975, B. K. Nehru Private Papers, NMML), B. K. Nehru suggested a detailed scheme for switching to a presidential system inspired by the French model. Again during the emergency, an anonymous[21] paper titled "A Fresh Look at Our Constitution: Some Suggestions" (reproduced in Noorani 1989, appendix I) circulated among Congress members suggesting the imposition of a presidential system (see also Austin 1999, ch. 16). However, unlike earlier proposals, the latter did not aim at switching from one democratic form of government to another, but at the suppression of democracy through the imposition of a quasi-dictatorial regime. In 1979, during the process of disintegration of the Janata government, N. A. Palkhivala, a well-known lawyer, returned to the theme, advocating a presidential system as a remedy to instability and political confusion.

Therefore, on the eve of the 1980s, the debate on the presidential system was far from being unfamiliar to Indian public opinion. For some (including J. R. D. Tata and several important businessmen (*Indian Express*, 19 October 1979)) switching to a presidential system was a remedy to political instability; for some others, especially after the emergency, it evoked the spectre of authoritarian rule (*Indian Express*, 11 February 1981).

The debate resurfaced shortly after Mrs Gandhi came back to power. What were new were the forms in which the debate took shape. In previous decades, mainly intellectuals and bureaucrats, rather than politicians, had raised the issue. In those rare cases in which politicians had taken part in the debate, this had happened at party forums, as when R. Venkataraman proposed to reform the Constitution during the AICC session in Chandigarh in the mid-1960s. In the 1970s also, the anonymous paper describing a new constitutional order was circulated among party members and eventually leaked to the press.

In the early 1980s, the issue was raised most times by politicians universally considered to be the most loyal among the loyalists to the prime minister and debated in public. Moreover, in the late 1970s, all neighbouring countries had adopted a strong presidential system. In Bangladesh, the forth amendment (1975) of the Constitution introduced a presidential form of government. In Sri Lanka, a French-style presidential system came into being, with the enactment of the third constitution since independence. In Pakistan, Zulfikar Ali Bhutto's constitution, although formally establishing a parliamentary system, envisaged a strong role for the prime minister, which configured Pakistan's setting as a de facto presidential form of government. In Burma, the promulgation of the 1974 Constitution had made General Ne Win the president of the republic. In other words, presidentialism was "in the air".

The first proposal to switch over to a presidential system came from Chenna Reddy, the then chief minister of Andhra Pradesh. In Summer 1980, he called for the summoning of a Constituent Assembly to frame a new Constitution establishing a presidential form of government (*Indian Express*, 4 June 1980; 8 June 1980). The opposition and virtually the entire national English press reacted vehemently, foreseeing the end of democratic rule in India. The Law Minister, P. Shiv Shankar, felt obliged to say before the Rajya Sabha that Chenna Reddy's statement had been made "in his individual capacity" (*Indian Express*, 10 June 1980). However, few were reassured by the Law Minister's declarations (*Indian Express*, 3 July 1980). This became a familiar pattern. One of Mrs Gandhi's men—including the former President of the Republic, V. V. Giri (*Indian Express*, 22 June 1980), the Maharashtra Chief Minister A. R. Antulay (*Indian Express*, 8 December 1980; 29 January 1981), the Congress (I) MPs Vithal Gadgil (*The Hindu*, 2 March 1981) and Kamalapathi Tripathi (*Indian Express*, 15 December 1980), and Union Minister Vasant Sathe (*Indian Express*, 29 April 1984; *Times of India*, 27 August 1984; *India Today*, 30 September 1984)—would call for the establishment of a presidential form of government; the opposition would express its concerns in the strongest possible terms; a member of the government or the prime minister herself would deny in rather ambiguous terms the existence of any plan to change the Constitution "in the near future" (Mrs Gandhi cited in *Indian Express*, 28 January 1981), which provoked those opposing the change even more.

We will now look at three of these episodes in further detail. The first one occurred in October 1980, when Mrs Gandhi inaugurated the All-

India Conference of Lawyers. In her speech, the Prime Minister welcomed the initiative, as it was an opportunity to debate the question of whether "there was any form of government better suited to India than the present system" (quoted in *Indian Express*, 26 October 1980). The lawyers' conference, which had been organised by the legal cell of the Congress (I) (*Indian Express*, 24 October 1980) and sponsored by a "well-known businessman, who [had] no single lawyer in the family" (*Indian Express*, 25 October 1980), at first recommended the switching over to a presidential form of government (*Indian Express*, 27 October 1980), but later specified that that was the view of only part of the participants (*Indian Express*, 28 October 1980). Mrs Gandhi "reassured" those who feared the establishment of a presidential system saying that she was not interested in changing the constitution, but that she welcomed debates on these topics because she thought it was good for the "people" to know "how different systems worked" (*Indian Express*, 24 January 1981).

The second episode had among its protagonists the Chief Minister of Maharashtra, A. R. Antulay, who had authored the anonymous paper proposing a presidential system circulated during the emergency (Noorani 1989). He proposed to switch to a presidential form of government several times. The first one was through a long interview in the *Times of India* shortly after the 1980 lawyers conference (16 November 1980). The second one was during the AICC(I) session in December 1980 when, along with many other Congress (I) members, he advocated the immediate approval of a constitutional amendment and, if necessary, the re-imposition of the emergency (*Indian Express*, 7 December 1980). Shiv Shankar did not reassure many when, in the wake of the opposition's protests, he said before the Lok Sabha that no plan for changing the Constitution existed, and that, in any case, the presidential form of government was "a democratic one" (*Indian Express*, 15 December 1980). The third time, Antulay called for a referendum on the presidential form of government in a long interview published in the *Indian Express* (26–28 January 1981). Referring to the issue a few months later, the prime minister, sitting next to Antulay himself, reiterated that she was not in favour of a presidential form of government, but that she believed that "if the people's expectations are consistently belied, it goes without saying that the people will opt for new institutions in the hope that they might serve better" (*Indian Express*, 20 April 1981). Answering a question on why one of her closest associates kept calling for switching over to a system of which she was not in favour, Mrs Gandhi replied, "you know in which direction he [Antulay] is going. Who can restrain him?" (*Indian Express*, 20 April 1981). A year later, when the prime minister was asked once again whether there were efforts to switch over to a presidential system she replied that the government was trying to find "ways and means to remove obstacles in the functioning of the system" (*Hindustan Times*, 14 February 1982). Similar answers were given every time the issue was raised (e.g. *The Hindu*, 4 March 1982; *Indian Express*, 28 August 1984).

The third episode occurred shortly before the general election, which was due, at the latest, in January 1985. In April 1984, Union Minister Vasant Sathe, relaunched the debate on presidentialism, first by writing a letter to Rajiv Gandhi (then a Congress (I) General Secretary) (reproduced in Noorani 1989, appendix III), and later through a series of press statements (*Times of India*, 29 April 1984). In the meantime, the convenor of the legal cell of the Congress (I), Lalit Bhasin, issued a statement demanding a constitutional amendment, which could make the opposition "more responsible" (*Indian Express*, 4 May 1984). Mrs Gandhi released the umpteenth ambiguous declaration in a press interview, in which she said that both the parliamentary and presidential systems had advantages and disadvantages (*Blitz*, 2 June 1984). In the same weeks, according to *India Today* (16 May 1984), the government appointed a cell comprising former Supreme Court judges A. N. Mulla and Baharul Islam,[22] that was given the task of reviewing all the articles of the Constitution and suggesting appropriate changes.

Vasant Sathe continued his campaign for constitutional reform for several months. In August 1984, a Congress (I) MP, Sat Paul Mittal, hosted a dinner for 50 Congress (I) MPs (including Sathe, Darbara Singh, and A. P. Sharma). A press note was released, in which the minister argued that given the serious threats the national unity and integrity "arising out of regional, parochial, linguistic and communal urges", strong actions were needed in order to ensure stability (*Indian Express*, 27 August 1984). The problem was, Sathe argued, that it was extremely unlikely that any party would secure an absolute majority in the forthcoming elections. The same prediction had been made by district-level chiefs of the Congress (I) and members of the party's frontal organisations, who had gathered in Delhi in June 1984 (*India Today*, 16 June 1984). A presidential system, the minister's note continued, would provide the system with the necessary stability and with a national figure democratically elected, who could protect national integrity. The following day, Pranab Mukherjee tried to reassure the opposition parties by saying before the Lok Sabha that they should not worry before actual measures were taken (*Indian Express*, 28 August 1984). At the same time, Mrs Gandhi, speaking in front of Assam's MPs and MLAs, stressed the need for the people to be educated about suitable changes to the Constitution, while Kamal Nath—one of the few among Sanjay's loyalists who had remained in a position of power after his death—drafted a resolution to be adopted by the Madhya Pradesh Congress (I) asking for the switching over to a presidential system (*Indian Express*, 31 August 1984). Finally, in September 1984, Vasant Sathe—after Mrs Gandhi had invited people "to study the different systems of government prevailing in other parts of the world" (*India Today*, 16 September 1984)—spelled out in greater detail his proposition. He suggested[23] amending only two articles, namely articles 54 and 55, to make the election of the president by direct universal franchise. All other constitutional provisions would not be changed. This would have given the president both democratic legitimation and virtually absolute powers—to name just one, that of declaring President's Rule (*Economic and Political Weekly*, 20 October 1984).

It is very possible that the whole debate was just political chitchat.[24] It is also plausible that a debate on the forms of government was intentionally aroused in order to leave "less time for a debate about sugar" (Shourie 1983, 224). However, in August–September 1984, for the first time since the emergency, the constitutional requirements that were needed for amending those articles of the constitution were met. First, Mrs Gandhi enjoyed a two-thirds majority in the Lok Sabha. In the Rajya Sabha, after Zail Singh had nominated two more members because of their "special knowledge" of "literature, science, art and social service"[25] (Constitution, Art. 80) the Congress (I) was just nine MPs short of a two-thirds majority. However, it was likely that the AIADMK (which had 11 members in the Upper House) would vote with the Congress (I), as it had done on several other occasions—including for the election of Zail Singh to the presidency. Moreover, the AIADMK's leader, M. G. Ramachandran (popularly known as MGR), had earlier suggested turning the Lok Sabha into a Constituent Assembly to give "a fresh look" at the Constitution (*Indian Express*, 14 June 1980). Also, Tamil Nadu's chief minister was probably thankful to Mrs Gandhi for her covert support to Tamil insurgents in Sri Lanka.

Second, according to the Constitution (Art. 368), in order to modify the articles 54 and 55, in addition to a two-thirds majority in both Houses of Parliament, at least half of the Legislative Assemblies had to ratify the amendments. In September 1984, the Congress (I) enjoyed an absolute majority in eight (out of twenty-two) states,[26] including Assam, where the Congress (I) had won 91 out of 126 seats the previous year, when most opposition parties boycotted the elections that the central government had decided to impose. In three more states, namely Jammu and Kashmir, Sikkim, and Andhra Pradesh, the respective non-Congress (I) chief ministers had been dismissed (in what were constitutionally dubious and politically unwise moves) and new coalitions (that included Mrs Gandhi's party) had been formed.[27] In other states, the Congress (I) was either part of a coalition government or enjoyed a wafer-thin majority.

In any case, nothing came out of the debate. Since then the issue resurfaced regularly, but technical and/or political difficulties have blocked any attempt to abandon the Westminster model (Wallack 2008; Rudolph and Rudolph 2001; Verney 2003).

Informalisation of Institutions: The Federal Setting

Arguably the most severe and potentially dangerous institutional breakdown in the early 1980s occurred in federal relations. In fact, if there is one problem of the early 1980s to which scholars have dedicated a great deal of attention, this is the deterioration of centre-state relations (Frankel 2005; Guha 2007; Hardgrave and Kochanek 2008). Indeed, the crises that exploded in several states—above all, Punjab, Jammu and Kashmir, and Assam—dominated both the political and the academic debates. As a result, many extremely detailed accounts—more than this study could possibly be—for each of these crises exist. For this reason, rather than re-proposing a detailed narration of the events which upset India's federal structure in the early 1980s, in the rest of this chapter we will first put the crisis of federal relations into a broader framework, and later see how this framework contributed to shape the federal relations in the early 1980s.

In doing so, we will see how, since independence, the functioning of the federal structures had heavily relied upon the Congress's dominance over the party system. Or, to put it in other words, federal relations were managed (by Nehru and Mrs Gandhi alike) in an informal way, i.e.

through the Congress party organisation. By informal federalism we mean two things: first, the management of centre-state relations which does not occur within an institutional framework; second, the emptying of any institutional significance to institutions supposedly designed for the management of centre-state relations. As we will see, on the one hand, the Constitution envisaged federal institutions, but these were for the most part not designed to *manage* centre-state relations; on the other hand, those institutions that were supposed to regulate federal relations were "swallowed up" by the one-party-dominant party system.

In the last part of the chapter we will see how Mrs Gandhi attempted to re-impose an informal federal framework even though this was not sustained by a one-party-dominant system anymore, thus paving the way for the breakdown of federal relations in the early 1980s. Finally, we will note that the early 1980s witnessed the emergence of an institutionalisation of federal relations.

India's Federal Institutions

Paradoxically, the informalisation of federal institutions had an institutional root. The constitution provided the centre with large and very flexible powers but, at the same time, it did not envisage strong institutional mechanisms for the management of centre-state relations. If a certain degree of flexibility was intentionally envisaged in order to let federal institutions adapt to changing circumstances (Arora 1995), the lack of institutional constraints to the exercise of such flexibility paved the way for the informal management of centre-state relations, and, at the same time, all sort of abuses. In other words, the federal system came to rely heavily on the party system and on the personality of the political leaders, each factor mattering more or less according to the actual political context.

It is worth spelling out briefly what were the main features of India's federal system at the time of the promulgation of the Constitution. It must be considered that the construction of federal institutions was difficult from the very beginning, not only because of the violent context in which the constitution was framed, which made the disintegration of the country appear like a very concrete possibility, but also because the Constitution was based upon the colonial Government of India Act (1935), which grouped together hundreds of different administrative systems. Furthermore, examples of other democratic federations accommodating ethnic diversity were scarce—Canada being the most proximate case (Dasgupta 2001, 55).

What came out, rather than a federal polity, was a "centralized federation"[28] (e.g. Singh and Verney 2003), which left a high degree of flexibility to central authorities. Five institutional provisions are worth noting.[29] First, the constitution divides the legislative power between the centre and the states. Certain subjects are left to the states, some others to the centre, and still others to concurrent legislation. All residual subjects are considered in the Union's domain. In case of a conflict between central and a state's legislation on subjects included in the concurrent list, the former would prevail. Further, the Parliament has the right (Constitution, art. 249) to legislate on state and concurrent subjects, if the Rajya Sabha, "in the national interest", allows it to do so. Therefore, legislative power is unbalanced in favour of the central government, which in addition can legitimately invade the states' legislative domain. However, this does not mean that the states do not have significant powers. Indeed, the powers reserved by the constitution to the states offered enough incentives to political parties to develop along regional lines and to make the conquering of power at the state level extremely attractive (Sridharan 2003).

Second, India's fundamental law envisages a set of emergency provisions. The most important (and controversial) one as far as federal relations are concerned is the so-called "President's Rule", established by article 356. If the president—that, in actual terms, means the prime minister—is satisfied, on the basis of the report of the governor—another central organ—that the "government of the State cannot be carried on in accordance with the provisions of [the] Constitution", he/she may assume direct executive powers and transfer the state's legislative power to the central Parliament. Until 1994 (Mozoomdar 1995), no justification had to be provided, which left an immense amount of flexibility to the central government. Moreover, the imposition of President's Rule is translated into a government of bureaucrats, who are accountable only to the central government, thus creating space for multiple and discretionary centres of power to emerge.

Third, the constitution confers on the central government the right to deploy the army and/or paramilitary forces in the states, if it is satisfied that the state government cannot handle law and order—a state subject—on its own. "To decide when that happens has been left by the constitution to the judgement and good sense of the Union government" (Marwah 1995). Central forces were deployed in the states 475 times between 1951 and 1979 and 375 times between 1981 and 1984 (Austin 1999, 600 n11).

Fourth, the Constitution created the figure of the governor, who is thought to be the equivalent of the president of the republic, at the state level. However, his powers, although very significant, are not clearly defined and this leaves the governors—who are appointed by and remain in office at the discretion of the centre—an ample margin of autonomy. As we shall see, the governors became New Delhi's long arm in the early 1980s, when they were repeatedly asked to dismiss non-Congress (I) governments.[30]

Fifth, the constitution partly regulates financial relations between the centre and the states. In particular, article 280 rules that the president must appoint a Finance Commission every five years. The latter recommends the share of personal income tax and union excise duties (both collected by the central government) that must be devolved to the states. The commission also recommends the amount of non-plan grants to the states—in the 1980s about 30 per cent of the total central grants—the remaining 70 per cent being allocated on a completely discretionary basis by the Planning Commission (another central organ) (*India Today*, 16 August 1983). Given that income tax and excise duties were by large the most important sources of revenues (and given the unwillingness of virtually all states to tax agricultural income, which would be collected by the states), constitutional provisions in fact made the states financially dependent upon the centre, especially because the former are responsible for a sizeable share of governmental spending. In fact, the proportion of revenue expenditure that the states were able to finance out of their own resources fell from about 80 per cent in the early 1950s to about 60 per cent in the 1970s (Bagchi 2003).

To sum up, the constitution not only conferred on the central government large powers which in fact established the supremacy of the centre over the states, but left such an ample margin of flexibility and discretion in dealing with local polities, that the institutional functioning of centre-state relations was almost completely left to the goodwill and self-restraint of those ruling at the centre.

Informal Federalism: Nehru's Years

Nehru's government did little to build up a strong institutional framework for the management of centre-state relations. On the contrary, on the one hand, it worked for further strengthening the centre vis-à-vis the states; on the other hand, he inaugurated the informal way of managing federal relations.

A fundamental push towards a more centralised political system came from the establishment of a planned economy and of the Planning Commission. Not only were the states called to formulate plans that had to be consistent with the national plan, but they were highly dependent on the Planning Commission for the resources necessary to implement their plans (Bhargava 1984). In other words, the Planning Commission, especially during Nehru's years, became the "economic Cabinet, not merely for the Union but also for the States" (Asok Chanda quoted in Austin 1999, 620). Moreover, till 1969[31] plan transfers to the states were allocated on a complete discretionary basis by the commission. Finally, the establishment of a centrally planned economy was accompanied by the coming into being of the centrally controlled license-Raj, which placed the authority to regulate all major industries under central control (Bagchi 2003). In short, even before the government came to control the "commanding heights" of the economy, fiscal federalism and the planned economy were firmly in the hands of the Union.

The high degree of flexibility left to the central government by the framers of the constitution allowed the ruling party at the centre to manage centre-state relations in an informal way, i.e. through its own internal organisation. This was not only the most natural choice, given the configuration of the national party system as a "Congress system" (Kothari 1964), but also a somewhat obligated one, since the constitution had not designed strong institutional mechanisms for the management of centre-state relations, with the partial exception of the Finance Commission (which, beside being a centrally-appointed organ, was to be overshadowed by the over-centralised Planning Commission (Sarkaria 1988, ch. 10)), and of the inter-state council (which was not even established until the early 1990s).

Other institutions theoretically designed to manage centre-state relations were inevitably swallowed up by the Congress system and lost much of their institutional significance. The National Development Council (NDC), for example, rather than working as an "apex institution for arriving at a consensus among the Union and the States on various matters relating to planning and socio-economic development", in fact became a "forum for the ventilation of individual grievances" (Sarkaria 1988, ch. 11). In other terms, given the dominance of the Congress party at the centre and in a great majority of the states, it became some sort of internal party forum. Indeed, not only did the NDC only meet at the initiative of the Planning Commission (which is chaired by the prime minister), but, according to the Sarkaria Commission (1988, ch. 11), the contribution to the formulation of the plans was limited to the approval of the approach papers and of the draft plans—and this was not even always the case. For instance, some chief ministers claimed that the Third Plan was presented to them *after* the Parliament had approved it (Austin 1999, 619 n20). The NDC was not even meeting as often as it was supposed to.[32] In short, states did not participate in any significant manner to the planning process and when they did, it was through informal consultations within the party high command, rather than through the institutional channels officially envisaged. Other institutions such as the multi-state councils or various sub-state institutions did not play any significant role in most parts of India (Arora 1995).

It is also worth noting that one of most utilised institutional mechanisms designed to manage centre-state relations—article 356 of the constitution—was seldom used according to the meaning it was supposed to have—i.e. as a potentially very useful device to avoid the breakdown of the country in (real) emergency situations (Manor 2001). Of course, most of the abuses of article 365 occurred after Nehru's death (Dua 1979); however, the institute of the President's Rule was misused even earlier. The very first instance (in Punjab in 1951) occurred not to handle an emergency situation in the state, but to solve—through an informal usage of federal institutions—an internal squabble within the state Congress party (Marwah 1995, 142). Few years later, at the explicit initiative of the Congress President, Indira Gandhi, the government of Kerala was dismissed with no other apparent reason than being led by an opposition party (Malhotra 1989, 70). Once again, not only did the move reveal how informally centre-state relations were managed—the president of the ruling party should not have a voice in such cases—but it showed that when federal issues arose outside the "Congress system", the likelihood of abuse on the part of the central government increased.

To sum up, during the Nehru period, centre-state relations worked because the federal "bargaining" (Morris-Jones 1971, 152) took place prevalently within the Congress. In other words, the configuration of the party system as a "Congress system", on the one hand, let the ruling party manage federal relations informally; and, on the other hand, gave India's democracy a consociational element that was extremely important for managing potentially explosive conflicts (Adeney 2007). For example, the states' re-organisation in 1956 was managed mostly within the Congress party. It is therefore not very surprising that it was the Congress itself that collected the political dividends of the operation.

However successful this way of managing federal relations, with hindsight, it was a short-sighted game on the part of the Congress: instead of building up institutional—and therefore long-lasting—mechanisms which could survive the demise of the Congress system, it preferred to postpone the problem under the illusion that Congress rule would last forever.

Informal Federalism: Indira Gandhi's Years

This long introduction has helped us to put the rise to power of Indira Gandhi into a broader historical perspective. Our contention is twofold. On the one hand, Mrs Gandhi's centralising policies constituted, rather than a radical reversal of the trend, a continuation and then a very steep acceleration and degeneration of previous tendencies. On the other hand, Mrs Gandhi, rather than weakening (barely) existent federal institutions, refused to build them up when the need arose, in the wake of the changes that occurred in the party system.

The electoral dominance of Mrs Gandhi's party till 1977—and the increasing personification of power within the party—reduced centre-state relations "to a state of near non-existence as a problematic of federal politics in India" (Sathyamurthy 1997, 245), thus compensating the lack of institutional mechanisms for their management. In fact, the only significant development was the severe centralisation process that paralleled Mrs Gandhi's growing authoritarianism throughout the 1970s. This involved, as we have seen in chapter 2, the Congress party as well as the government apparatus, the two overlapping to a significant extent. To give just one example of this well-known story, during the Nehru period (1950–64) article 356 was invoked nine times; from 1966 to 1977, the government resorted to President's Rule as many as thirty-six times (Ray and Kincaid 1988, 152), not to speak of the endless replacement of Congress chief ministers by the party high command. However, the persistence of a (somewhat artificial) Congress system, rendered over-centralisation feasible and the annihilation of centre-state relations tolerable.

All this changed in the early 1980s. The Janata phase had irremediably changed the party system (Manor 1997). The regional units of the parties ruling at the centre started influencing political dynamics in Delhi more than ever before (Jaffrelot 2003), exercising an influence arguably bigger than that exercised by the centre on the states. Not only were regional units capable of influencing political dynamics within the ruling coalition in Delhi, but their influence was also translated into larger resources allocated to the states. The outlay of the states' and union territories' annual plans taken together for 1978–79 was in fact bigger than that of the central government (Dasgupta 2002, 363).

Further, as we have already seen, the rise of a demand for political representation among large strata of the electorate, the breakup of the Congress party in 1978 and of the Janata Party in 1979, and the emergence of new forms of political mobilisation in the early 1980s combined to produce immense changes in the political system which, in turn, were inevitably reflected in the working of federal relations.

Indira Gandhi was not willing either to take cognizance of the changes that had occurred, or to suffer the consequences. She chose instead to continue managing centre-state relations the way she had done in the previous decade. On the one hand, as we have seen in chapter 2, she kept treating her party as a personal fiefdom,—the "I" added to the party's name in 1978 was there to remind anyone in doubt—substituting chief ministers at will (Dua 1985), imposing drastic changes in the list of candidates for state elections (e.g. *India Today*, 1 March 1980), and holding a firm control on states' administrative apparatuses (*The Hindu*, 3 November 1981). On the other hand, when it became clear, after the state elections in 1982 and, even more so, those in early 1983, that the one-party-dominant party system was gradually but steadily coming to an end, Mrs Gandhi tried to reverse the process of change through a series of subterfuges that eventually resulted in the outbreak of four major crises in as many states. In what follows, we will first see how Mrs Gandhi managed federal relations in Congress-led states and during "ordinary" times. We will then turn our attention to the ways in which Mrs Gandhi's inability to deal with political actors that did not share her own goals led to the outbreak of severe crises in Assam, Jammu and Kashmir, Andhra Pradesh and Punjab.

Centre-state Relations in Congress (I) States

A few weeks after Mrs Gandhi's return to power, nine legislative assemblies—all opposition-led—were dissolved and President's Rule was imposed. Law Minister P. Shiv Shankar adduced three reasons for the move. First, he said that these assemblies were responsible for the delays in the ratification of the constitutional amendment extending reservations for the Scheduled Castes and Tribes. For some mysterious reason, the same was apparently not true for those Congress-controlled states that had not ratified the provision yet. Second, the law minister feared that states controlled by opposition parties would block the implementation of "other progressive measures". Finally, the result of the general elections showed that the people had lost faith in the Janata Party which was therefore not, in Shiv Shankar's eyes, legitimised to govern anywhere in India[33] (*Indian Express*, 19 February 1980). The Congress (I) managed to win the elections in eight of the states (the exception was Tamil Nadu, where the AIADMK obtained an absolute majority). The one-party-dominant party system was restored.

States controlled by the Congress (I) were considered a personal property of the Gandhis, not only by the family, but also by most chief ministers themselves. Babasaheb Bhosale, who was chosen as chief minister of Maharashtra because his was the first name on the list that Mrs Gandhi recognised as familiar (James Manor, in a conversation with the author), candidly stated that he perfectly knew that he and all his colleagues could retain their posts only as long as Mrs Gandhi wished so (*India Today*, 16 July 1981). In some cases, the chief ministers were chosen for no apparent reason: T. Anjaiah, for example, chief minister of Andhra Pradesh, did not even know why he had been chosen to substitute Chenna Reddy (*India Today*, 01 March 1982); Jagannath Pahadia explicitly admitted that he was not the right man to lead a state like Rajasthan (*India Today*, 16 July 1981). In many cases, chief ministers were chosen in order to hinder other faction leaders' emergence as important political figures, who could threaten Mrs Gandhi's power position (Dua 1985). Further, in order to limit the power of the new chief ministers, Mrs Gandhi usually imposed the inclusion of their rivals either in the local Pradesh Congress (I) Committee or in the Cabinet. In any case, Congress (I) chief ministers had very little autonomy, not only regarding the composition of their own cabinets, but also with respect to policy-making. To give just one example, in the first hundred days of government, the chief minister of Rajasthan spent 48 days in Delhi. In general, Congress (I) chief ministers spent about 30 per cent of their time in the capital (Jeffrey 1986, 195).

The subordination of Congress (I) chief ministers—and, to a significant extent, also of non-Congress ones—to the central executive was nearly absolute. Mrs Gandhi's visits were followed by "inspections" in the states' secretariats by Mrs Gandhi herself and by central government officials (*The Hindu*, 16 September 1981). In some cases, a "teleguided administration" (Arora 1983, 80) came into being. The state bureaucracy, despite officially being accountable to the chief minister, in fact acted at the orders of the central government. In some cases, Mrs Gandhi was even able to force a chief minister to substitute the chief secretary with a man of her choice (e.g. in Punjab)[34] (*India Today*, 16 June 1982).

The subordination of the states was evident also from rhetorical and symbolic points of view. For example, when Mrs Gandhi visited the state capitals she usually sat in the chief minister's chair (Dua 1985). Moreover, the prime minister used to stress the need for "committed states" (e.g. *Indian Express*, 19 May 1980), in order to harmonise development strategies (*Hindustan Times*, 5 May 1982) and ensure effective implementation of plan programmes (*Hindustan Times*, 12 May 1982). In some instances she even made it clear that, from the central government's point of view, "pro-centre" states had priority when it came to the allocation of resources or the identification of suitable locations for public investments (*Times of India*, 24 October 1982).

Centre-state Relations in non-Congress (I) States: Assam and Punjab

The apparent restoration of a one-party-dominant party system and the extreme degree of centralisation of the Congress (I) made centre-state relations in most parts of the country smooth—i.e. virtually non-existent—as they mostly were in the 1970s. There were at least two important exceptions. The first was Assam; the second one, the Punjab. The two crises had several elements in common: both began before Mrs Gandhi came back to power; both originated from local issues, which had little to do with centre-states relations; both degenerated into major crises thanks to the excessive intrusion of the central government in the states' affairs and to the sordid manipulation of ethnic identities on the part of the Congress (I); and finally, in both cases a solution could not be found because Mrs Gandhi could not accept that her interlocutors did not share her own political goals.

We have already dealt with the crisis in Assam in chapter 3, with reference to Mrs Gandhi's "defence" of the Muslims' interests. Here we will see how the lack of an institutional framework for the management of the crisis gave the central government a complete degree of flexibility in dealing with the Assam agitation. It is my contention that the complete breakdown of governance which followed the centre's decision to impose state elections in early 1983 and the subsequent few thousand deaths were completely avoidable and that the crisis degenerated because there were no institutional mechanisms which could "guide" both parties towards an acceptable solution.

This is not to say that the relations of the north-east region with the rest of the country were not a very delicate issue. Indeed, the extreme socio-economic complexity of the area and the very delicate demographic equilibrium within the region, combined with the sensitive geopolitical location, has constituted a continuous challenge for New Delhi. It is certainly not a coincidence that most of the special provisions included in article 371 of the constitution—which allows the central government to grant special concessions to certain states or regions—concerned this area; and it is certainly not a coincidence either that the area from where the highest number of states was carved out after the states' reorganisation in the 1950s was the north-east. Therefore, I am not suggesting that the underpinning issues were easily solvable; indeed, I am not even sure if they were solvable at all (Manor 2001). Instead, we are pointing out that the actual crisis which broke out in the early 1980s could have been avoided had a mechanism for an institutional bargaining process existed or had Mrs Gandhi been able to negotiate with someone who did not have among their goals the electoral prospects of the Congress (I).

As I mentioned in chapter 3, the bone of contention in Assam was the revision of the state electoral rolls, which contained many non-Indian citizens who had thus no right to vote. Indeed, Mrs Gandhi herself, shortly before the 1980 general elections, said that free elections were not possible in Assam, unless the electoral rolls were revised (*Indian Express*, 4 December 1979). However, after she came back to power, Mrs Gandhi apparently changed her mind. The talks were conducted in an extremely informal fashion. Sometimes it was the home minister who bargained with the leader of the AASU (*Indian Express*, 26 February 1980). Other times it was the external affairs minister (*Indian Express*, 22 October 1980). Still other times, it was the finance minister (*Times of India*, 9 March 1982), or the prime minister herself, or the chief minister of Manipur, or the Gandhi Peace Foundation who led the negotiations (*Indian Express*, 28 January 1980). A great deal of confusion resulted from the several rounds of talks and no solution could be found. In the meanwhile, several Congress (I) governments—which had a majority thanks to major defections from the Janata Party—were appointed, only to be rapidly followed by long periods of President's Rule.[35] Further, the leaders of the agitation were repeatedly arrested (e.g. *Indian Express*, 30 January 1981; 22 February 1981; 5 February 1982), which brought about even more confusion around the negotiating table. In any case, the framework of informal federalism could not work if the parties involved in the negotiation had diverging political goals. To put it in very simple terms, the AASU was asking the government two things: first, to delete several thousand Congress (I) voters from the electoral roll; second, to guarantee them an "honourable" way out of the agitation that they had promoted and led. Neither of these two things was acceptable to Mrs Gandhi.

The prime minister then sought a way out of the impasse. A democratically elected Congress (I) government, in her eyes, would have been a more suitable interlocutor in the framework of informal federalism: hence the decision to call for fresh elections on the basis of the unrevised electoral rolls.

The government justified this decision—which ultimately led to the most violent elections since independence (*India Today*, 1 May 1983)—on two grounds. First, there was a constitutional obligation to hold elections before March 1983, since five years had passed since the Legislative Assembly had been elected. In order for the postponement of the elections to be constitutionally permissible, an amendment allowing the government to prolong President's Rule beyond one year was needed. Indeed, a bill was introduced in the Parliament (*Times of India*, 3 November 1982) and the opposition parties agreed to give their consent in the Rajya Sabha, where the Congress (I) did not have a two-third majority yet (*Economic and Political Weekly*, 29 November 1983). However, the Congress (I) decided instead to withdraw the bill and go ahead with the elections, despite the fact that the army had estimated that no less than 120 battalions would be needed to ensure acceptable law and order conditions during the elections—to put things into perspective, the whole Central Reserve Police Force amounted to 76 battalions (*India Today*, 1 May 1983). Moreover, according to intelligence reports, the RSS on the one side, and Mrs Gandhi on the other, were using an explicitly communitarian idiom, which contributed to inflaming feelings and radicalising the situation (*India Today*, 1 March 1983).

Second, the government justified the decision to hold elections on the basis of the unrevised electoral rolls saying that there was no time to do otherwise, since the decision had only been taken on 7 January 1983, about five weeks before the elections. Revising the electoral rolls could take from six weeks to six months, according to the methodology utilised (*India Today*, 16 May 1983). However, it is absolutely not credible that the electoral commission was taken by surprise by the government communication on 7 January. First, that the limit for holding an election was March 1983 had been known since the election of the Legislative Assembly five years before. Second, the imposition of President's Rule (which could last no more than a year) and the dissolution of the Legislative Assembly in March 1982 should have sounded as a reminder to the electoral commission; apparently, it did not. In addition, in the preceding year, several public declarations by a series of institutional actors did not leave any doubt about the constitutional obligation to hold elections. Bishma Narain Singh, a cabinet minister at the time, recalled that "everyone" knew that elections would be held in March 1983 (interview, Delhi, 16 January 2011). Third, preparations for the elections had begun in May 1982 and detailed reports had been sent to the prime minister regarding the number of officials and polling booths needed, and similar technical matters (*India Today*, 16 May 1983). Despite all this, the chief of the Election Commission, R. K. Trivedi, did not realise that elections were about to be held. It sounds more credible that the electoral rolls were not revised intentionally.[36]

After the imposition of President's Rule in March 1982, the central government had resorted to growing repression in Assam. Shortly before the elections, Rajesh Pilot, at that time a Congress (I) official in charge of the party's electoral campaign in neighbouring Tripura, spelled out the Congress (I)'s strategy towards Assam to the journalist Shekhar Gupta. Pilot said that people wanted elections and a "political government". Therefore, the central government was planning to arrest some five thousand agitators for the elections period. In this way, the agitators would be "finished politically" and normalcy could be restored in Assam (reported in Baruah 1999, 131). The plan was actually implemented and the entire leadership of the AASU was arrested the very day the elections were announced (*Indian Express*, 8 January 1983). A probably unintended consequence of the crackdown on AASU's militants was to hand in the leadership of the movement to the most extremist elements. Further, the entire operation was accompanied by an "invasion" by central personnel of Assam. Given the reluctance—out of fears and/or political beliefs—of state officials to work at the organisation of the elections, several thousand officials had to be "imported" from outside the state. The same happened for the security apparatus. The local police were definitely not happy to repress the Assam movement (another similarity with the agitation in Punjab). In some cases, clashes erupted between the police and the Central Reserve Police Force, which even caused some casualties (*India Today*, 16 May 1983). On top of this, the central government imposed censorship in the state, thus creating the rather paradoxical situation by which in order to promote the democratic process, the government suppressed the most fundamental civil liberties (*India Today*, 16 January 1983).

Most parties boycotted the elections—the only exception, beside the Congress (I), were the parties of the Left. The Congress (I) eventually won 91 out of 126 seats. In several constituencies the turnout was lower than 1 per cent. About 3,000 people died in the days preceding the elections (Baruah 1999, 133).

The new chief minister, Hiteswar Saikia, an ethnic Assamese belonging to the Ahom (upper) caste (like most of the leadership of the agitation), promoted a set of policies aiming to accommodate this or that tribal group and, according to what the press reported, actively tried to split the AASU on communal lines (*India Today*, 1 May 1983), a strategy which was successful to a certain extent. Eventually, a weaker AASU and, more importantly, another government at the centre—not so keen on maintaining its political hold on the state and able to conceive centre-state relations outside the informal federalism framework—led to the signing of the Assam accord in 1985 and to the subsequent state elections, which were handsomely won by the Assam Gana Parishad. However, problems in Assam were not solved as the rise of the United Liberation Front of Assam (ULFA) and the following decades of guerrilla activities clearly demonstrate.

Let us turn our attention to the second crisis that haunted Mrs Gandhi's government from the very beginning to the very end of her final term. Indeed, if asked what they remember the early 1980s for, virtually all observers this author spoke to would respond "the Punjab". Understandably, the Punjab story has called the attention of several journalists who produced a set of extremely detailed analyses, from which this study will heavily draw (in particular: Tully and Jacob 1985; Nayar and Singh 1984). Indeed, it is unlikely that new facts will emerge before the opening of the archival records and of Mrs Gandhi's papers (if they are ever opened).

It is my contention that the Punjab problem was, on the one hand, completely avoidable and, on the other hand, easily manageable had Mrs Gandhi been able to negotiate with actors who did not share her own political objectives. To put it in other words, although deeper socio-economic factors did play a role—especially in terms of providing Sikh militancy with a growing following among the educated unemployed (Wallace 1990; Telford 1992)—the crisis emerged, degenerated and could not be solved for eminently political reasons.

The Punjab-India relations were not easy since their inception. This area was the only one left out of the state reorganisation process along linguistic lines. Nehru believed that the request for a state for the Punjabi-speakers ill-concealed a demand for a state for the Sikhs. In fact, when Mrs Gandhi agreed to the creation of the state of Punjab in 1966, Sikhs constituted about roughly 60 per cent of the population. However, the net separation within the Sikh community along caste and class lines—the most important one being between Jats and non-Jats, the former forming the great majority of land proprietors in the state,[37] the latter (along with many rural Hindus) constituting the bulk of the agricultural labour force—prevented the coming into being of a regional party system dominated by the party of the Sikhs, the Akali Dal. Indeed, since 1966, the Akali Dal headed, in alliance with the Jana Sangh, a set of rather unstable governments, which were frequently interrupted by periods of President's Rule. In 1972, the "*garībi hatao*" wave hit Punjab too. Zail Singh became the chief minister. The new Punjab government represented one of the best instances of the political environment that was essential for the working of informal federalism. No problem arose and Zail Singh's government lasted till the end of the legislature in 1977. However, in 1973 the Akali Dal, in an attempt to reverse the political trend and in response to Zail Singh's attempt to compete with the Akalis for the leadership of the (Jat) Sikhs, issued a document—the so-called

Anandpur Resolution[38]—in which they spelled out a set of religious and political demands to the central government.

The end of the emergency—during which many thousands of Akalis were jailed—brought about the end of the Congress's rule in Punjab. The Akali Dal formed a government in alliance with the Janata Party. In the altered national party system that the anti-emergency wave brought about, regional polities became more important. In this context, the Akali Dal's demands on the central government were renewed and slightly modified (*Indian Express*, 30 October 1978). The Sikh's demands contained both general and specific requests. On the one hand, they asked for the respect of the letter of the constitution as far as federal relations were concerned (Anandpur 1982, pt. II), thus asking for less intervention in the states' affairs on the part of the centre. On the other hand, the Akalis listed a series of administrative demands. The most significant ones were the handing over of the city of Chandigarh to Punjab[39] and the annexation of some areas dominated by Punjabi-speakers in neighbouring states; the demand for a better share of the water of the rivers crossing Punjab; and the right of the Shiromani Gurdwara Parbandakh Committee (SGPC) to administer Sikh temples—and their finances—outside the Punjab. Some religious and symbolic demands (e.g. the resolution asked for Amritsar to be granted the status of "Holy city") provided the "ideological" framework of the resolution (Anandpur 1982, pt. I).

The Prime Minister, Morarji Desai, to put it mildly, was not sympathetic towards these demands (Jeffrey 1986, ch. 8). However, the Akalis, although not accommodated, were left the autonomy they had so eagerly been looking for in the previous decade, so they did not press too hard for the implementation of the Anandpur resolution.

However, the demise of the Congress party in north India was not without consequences in Punjab. It is now widely accepted that, shortly after the establishment of an Akali Dal-Janata government, Sanjay Gandhi and Zail Singh began to look for a Sikh who could steal the Akalis' thunder in Punjab. Their choice fell on a hitherto unknown Sikh preacher, Sant Jarnail Singh Bhindranwale. Apparently, Sanjay Gandhi and Zail Singh thought they could manipulate the Sant into breaking the tenuous unity of the Akali Dal. With this purpose in mind, they financed and promoted him. During the 1980 general elections, Bhindranwale even campaigned for the Congress (I) party in at least three constituencies (Frankel 2005, 671).

Punjab was among the states that were brought under President's Rule in February 1980. Once again a non-Congress government in the state was not allowed to come to its natural end. In the following elections, the Akali Dal, badly divided into a number of warring factions (*Indian Express*, 4 September 1979), suffered a resounding defeat. The Congress (I) came back to power and Mrs Gandhi installed Darbara Singh as chief minister. Zail Singh, who had by then been appointed as Union Minister of Home Affairs, was definitely not pleased to see his arch rival at the head of the state government. However, Zail Singh still had an ace in the hole with which he could make his rival's life tough. Bhindranwale was therefore not left to his own destiny. On the contrary, the central government's backing guaranteed him almost complete impunity.

This became clear when the Sant was arrested, at Darbara Singh's insistence, for the murder of Lala Jagat Narain, the editor of the Hindi newspaper, *Punjab Kesari*, which had sharply criticised Bhindranwale. Narain had also been a witness against the Sant in a trial on the attack by 200 of Bhindranwale followers against the heterodox Sikh sect of the Nirankaris.

The arrest of the Sant was a tragicomic event. He was first helped to escape from Haryana to Punjab by the police (under orders issued by Zail Singh) (Tully and Jacob 1985, 67). He was then allowed to choose the date and place of his own arrest and, before being taken into custody, he was permitted to preach a sermon against the Punjab government. As soon as the police took him into custody, his followers opened fire against the police and 12 people lost their lives (*India Today*, 1 October 1981).

In the following days the law and order situation degenerated: government properties were attacked, a train was derailed and a plane was hijacked. Despite all this, the home minister—not the High Court—decided that there was no evidence against Bhindranwale and that he was to be released (*Times of India*, 15 October 1981). Mark Tully, on the base of an interview to the President of the Delhi Gurudwara Management Committee (DGMC), Santokh Singh, claims that it was Mrs Gandhi herself who ordered the release of the Sant, because she had been told that the DGMC would have stopped supporting the Congress (I) in the capital unless Bhindranwale was set free (Tully and Jacob 1985, 71). In any case, Bhindranwale was released and allowed to "celebrate" in Delhi with 80 of his followers who rallied in the streets of New Delhi shouting slogans and embracing illegal weapons.

At this point Bhindranwale was a hero. Even the so-called moderate Akali leaders—the president of the party, Harcharan Singh Longowal, former chief minister, Prakash Singh Badal, and the president of the SGPC, Gurcharan Singh Tohra—started (although reluctantly) begging for Bhindranwale's support, in order to maintain a hold over Punjab politics. In the meanwhile, the Sant's followers began to systematically eliminate those on Bhindranwale's black list—policemen, journalists, civil servants et cetera—and, a few months later, to kill Hindus at random. President's Rule was imposed in October 1983.

In the meantime, the Akali Dal leaders had launched an agitation, parallel and partially overlapping with the Sant's campaign, for the implementation of the Anandpur resolution. The negotiating process with the government was an extremely complicated one, and was influenced by an extremely high number of factors. The actual issues at stake—in particular, the share of the rivers' waters, the fate of Chandigarh and the control over the gurudwaras—were the least important. First, the talks were influenced by a series of state elections. The April 1982 talks failed because Mrs Gandhi was not willing to concede anything to the Akalis on the eve of the elections in neighbouring Haryana and Himachal Pradesh. The breakdown of the talks was usually followed by various initiatives on the part of the Akalis, which in turn forced Mrs Gandhi to reopen the negotiations; but then the Delhi and the Jammu and Kashmir elections came, and Mrs Gandhi's political priorities changed; and so on and so forth.

Second, the talks were also influenced by a set of initiatives undertaken by both the Akalis and the government, which had the net effect of raising tension to barely manageable levels. For example, the Akalis publicly threatened to disrupt the Asian Games in Delhi, which, as we have seen, were a top political priority for the central government (and, perhaps more importantly, Rajiv Gandhi's first important task after his entry into politics). The central government reacted by ordering the Haryana government (headed by the loyal Bhajan Lal) not to let any Sikh pass the border with Delhi. All sorts of abuses—including forced shavings (*India Today*, 1 December 1982; 16 December 1982)—occurred.

Third, the talks were also not facilitated by the anarchic situation within the Congress (I) and by petty intraparty political games. On several occasions the local unit of the party actively boycotted the talks, by spreading false information about the nature of the agreements reached or by misleading both Mrs Gandhi and the Akalis about the other's intentions (Prem Shankar Jha, interview, Delhi 2 December 2010). In another case, Zail Singh secretly called Longowal to tell him to reject Mrs Gandhi's proposal to include Swaran Singh in a high-level meeting, which obviously did not contribute to building a positive climate for the upcoming round of talks (Nayar and Singh 1984, 45). In still another case, Mrs Gandhi decided that the details of the accord reached with the Akalis regarding the river waters had to be approved by Parliament; however, what she presented in the Lok Sabha differed significantly from the agreement that she had reached with the Akalis, who then decided to abandon the negotiating table (Jeffrey 1985, 154). All this humiliation of the moderate Akalis, on the one hand, served Mrs Gandhi's goal to reduce their influence over Punjab politics; on the other hand, they served the leadership of the Sikhs to Bhindranwale on a golden plate.

In the meanwhile, on the one hand, Bhindranwale—from his safe shelter inside the Golden Temple—was spreading terror across Punjab and, at the same time, taking the agitation away from the moderate Akalis. Paradoxically, he remained in contact with Mrs Gandhi at least until May 1984, barely a month before Operation Bluestar (Tully and Jacob 1985, 121). On the other hand, the institutional set up of Punjab completely broke down. Not only had the administration been virtually paralysed by the Darbara Singh–Zail Singh dispute, but the imposition of President's Rule had created even more confusion, alternative centres of power, and mutual vetoes (Nayar and Singh 1984, 56). More dramatically, the police in the state were more and more reluctant to make use of their powers as more and more policemen either became admirers of the Sant, or were too afraid to take the necessary actions, thus making the enactment of draconian provisions like the Terrorist Affected Areas Act quite useless. Similarly to what happened in Assam, the Central Reserve Police Force clashed with the Punjabi police on several occasions.

The talks failed because Mrs Gandhi acted as if the Akali Dal shared her same political goals, or, to use the terminology I have adopted, she acted as if she was in a context of informal federalism. In political terms, all that the Akalis were asking for was "a victory" (Akbar 1985, 196), which would enable them to restore their credibility as the party of the Sikhs and eventually isolate the Sant. However, as we have seen, too many actors were competing for the same role, all with their own agenda and with their own means. Moreover, the agendas of all these actors dangerously overlapped in one way or another. Crucially, Mrs Gandhi was not willing to concede a political victory to a non-Congress (I) party at any cost. As in Assam, in Punjab too her adversaries had to be "politically finished". The defeat of the Congress (I) in a series of by-elections in May 1984—only a few months away from the general elections—convinced Mrs Gandhi that a growing section of Indian society—most and foremost the middle class—expected her to undertake strong action. Operation Bluestar (the storming of the holiest Sikh shrine, the Golden Temple, by the army) followed. Bhindranwale was eventually killed, along many hundreds of his followers. The Indian army lost a very high number of men. Hundreds of pilgrims who were in the temple were killed and many more injured. The Sikh community was outraged.

Centre-state Relations in non-Congress States: the "Constitutional revolt" and the Crises in Andhra Pradesh and Jammu and Kashmir

Two other instances show how the breakdown of federal relations that occurred in the early 1980s stemmed from Mrs Gandhi's inability to rule a federal polity outside a one-party-dominant party system. The crises that developed in Jammu and Kashmir and Andhra Pradesh in 1984 also show how the prime minister did not hesitate either to violate the constitution, or to endanger her own party's electoral prospects in the states, in order to re-impose a Congress (I)-dominated national party system.

We mentioned in chapter 3 that N. T. Rama Rao (NTR), Ramakrishna Hegde and Farooq Abdullah won elections in Andhra Pradesh, Karnataka and Jammu and Kashmir, respectively, in the course of 1983. The fragmentation of the party system along regional lines received a decisive boost. Indeed, five of the major states were ruled by non-Congress parties (the remaining two were West Bengal and Tamil Nadu). Feeling stronger than ever before, they joined hands to confront the centre in a concerted way. We saw that, in a series of meetings, regional parties sought to build a confederal national alternative to the Congress (I) party. Here we will see how non-Congress chief ministers set up a "Constitutional revolt" (Austin 1999, 541) whose main objective was demanding an institutionalisation of federal relations, which could overtake the informal federalism model of the previous decades.

Perhaps NTR's very first public declaration addressed to the centre demanded the setting up of a commission to study centre-state relations (*The Hindu*, 24 January 1983). Indeed, the demand for a complete decentralisation of powers—on the lines suggested by the Anandpur resolution—was included in the TDP's election manifesto (*India Today*, 16 January 1983).

Bolder initiatives were undertaken in the following months. In late March 1983, Hegde hosted in Bangalore a meeting of the chief ministers of the south—Congress (I) Kerala chief minister, K. Karunakaran, declined the invitation labelling the initiative as "seditious" (*Economic and Political Weekly*, 26 March 1983). Alongside many rhetorical declarations, the meeting issued a set of recommendations to the central government. The chief ministers asked for the setting up of a commission on federal relations, suggested the amendment of articles 256 and 257 of the constitution in order to give more powers to the states, and demanded the repeal of the provision which obliged the states to seek the president's (i.e. the prime minister's) assent to enact laws on certain state-reserved subjects—the Tamil Nadu Land Reform (Fixation of Ceiling on Land) Second Amendment of 1980 had been denied the presidential assent, therefore impeding Tamil Nadu to acquire about 1 lakh acres of land (*India Today*, 1 April 1983). The chief ministers also asked for a fairer and less discretional distribution of central resources. For example, they claimed that Andhra Pradesh's first steel project had been starved of funds since the January 1983 elections, or that Kerala was receiving bigger allocations of rice than Tamil Nadu, despite the latter's bigger population (*India Today*, 1 April 1983). Shortly after the meeting, NTR explained that he saw the initiative as a "nucleus for a bigger body" (*The Hindu*, 6 April 1983). What he had in mind was the setting up of a council of all chief ministers that could function as a forum for discussing centre-state relations in an institutional setting.

The Congress (I) reacted vehemently to the meeting of the southern chief ministers, claiming that the initiative was "extra-constitutional" and "highly dangerous" (*Indian Express*, 1 April 1983). However, it did accept one of the recommendations, namely the setting up of a commission for the study of centre-state relations—although Mrs Gandhi denied that the establishment of the Sarkaria[40] Commission had anything to do with the chief ministers' meeting or with the agitation in Punjab[41] (*The Hindu*, 25 March 1983). Granville Austin (1999, 542–43) underlines the scant enthusiasm with which the prime minister instituted the Commission. According to Austin, Mrs Gandhi tried to limit Sarkaria's range of action by asking him to conduct his study "within the constitution", by not allowing him to choose the number and the composition of the commission,[42] and by delaying the beginning of the enquiry by about ten months.

The setting up of the commission did not satisfy the opposition parties' demand for an institutionalisation of centre-state relations. As we saw in chapter 3, another meeting was held in late May in Vijayawada in Andhra Pradesh, and still another one in Srinagar shortly after Farooq Abdullah's victory in Jammu and Kashmir. In addition, Hegde hosted a seminar about federal relations in Bangalore in August 1983, which was attended by some of the most prominent academics, civil servants and commentators. The papers of the conference formed the base for the discussion held in Srinagar in October 1983. Here the opposition leaders issued quite a detailed statement in which some ten articles of the constitution were indicated as the means through which the Union government exercised wide discretionary powers and imposed its dominance upon the states (Srinagar 1984).[43] In particular, they questioned the legitimacy of President's Rule—according to the Sarkaria Commission only 26 out of 75 impositions of article 356 were "inevitable" (Sarkaria 1988, ch. 6)—and other emergency provisions; they asked for a revision of the constitutional distribution of powers and for the setting up of institutional mechanisms which could ensure the states' exclusive right to legislate in states-reserved subjects; they strongly argued for the formation of an Interstate Council (as envisaged by article 263 of the constitution, which had hitherto not been implemented); they asked for a provision which would make it mandatory for the central government to obtain a state's assent before deploying the army within its boundaries; and they put into question the overall structure of financial relations.

The Srinagar meeting, as pointed out by Jyoti Basu in his statement, claimed to speak not only for opposition state-governments, but for Congress (I)-ruled states too (Srinagar 1984). Indeed, that most chief ministers were not at ease with the framework of informal federalism would be confirmed by Justice Sarkaria himself, who claimed that some Congress (I) chief ministers, although scared of stating this in public, actually backed many of the opposition-sponsored reforms (Austin 1999, 627).

Opposition leaders mounting such an unprecedented challenge to the centre were not forgiven by Mrs Gandhi. Within months, most of the protagonists of the "constitutional revolt" had been somehow punished. The first victim was Farooq Abdullah.

The state of Jammu and Kashmir, for well-known historical reasons (Schofield 2003; Bose 2003), has always been particularly sensitive to the issue of its autonomy from Delhi. Nevertheless, despite the special provisions envisaged by article 370 of the constitution, the centre's intrusion in the state's affairs had been considerable. In fact, it was during Nehru's rule that the most apparent abuses occurred. The arrest of Sheikh Abdullah in 1953, the irregularity of virtually all state elections till 1977, and the severe erosion of the letter of article 370,[44] all contributed, on the one hand, to making the issue of the state's autonomy even more sensitive, and, on the other hand, to the coming into being of a state Congress-dominated party system, thus creating the conditions for a framework of informal federalism to work. In an ironic reversal of roles, it was Indira Gandhi who reached an agreement with the sheikh—the "Kashmir Accord" in 1975—which eventually led to the first authentically democratic elections in the state in 1977, which the sheikh's National Conference handsomely won. Delhi's presence was still very much intrusive, but the democratic process was at least put into operation. However, Abdullah made a huge mistake, from Mrs Gandhi's point of view. He chose to support the Janata government after the end of the emergency. Mrs Gandhi never forgave him (*India Today*, 16 April 1980).

After January 1980, life became harder for the Lion of Kashmir. The local unit of the Congress (I) constantly tried to destabilise his government. The state Congress (I)—supposedly the state unit of a national party—even attacked the sheikh when he said that article 370 was not sacrosanct, a statement which, from a national point of view, should have been welcomed (Letter to the prime minister dated 21 May 1981, B. K. Nehru Private Papers, NMML). In April 1981, all major financial backers of the National Conference were the target of a tax raid which, not very surprisingly, found many irregularities (*India Today*, 16 May 1981), while many other "prominent black marketers" were left out (B. K. Nehru's report to the prime minister dated 21 May 1981, B. K. Nehru Papers, NMML). Abdullah was aware of these attempts and repeatedly complained to the Governor of Jammu and Kashmir, B. K. Nehru. However, as the latter made clear to the prime minister on the just cited report, "till he [was] alive there [was] no chance to remove him from power or to constitutionally come to power, let alone winning elections".

This changed when the sheikh's son inherited the chief ministership in September 1982. Farooq Abdullah's position was extremely precarious from the very beginning. First, the National Conference was far from being a unitary formation. In fact, two of the sheikh's closest advisors, namely Mirza Afzal Beg and Farooq's brother-in-law, Ghulam Mohammed Shah, deeply resented Farooq's appointment as chief minister, a post they thought they deserved more. The fact that, in order to "clean" the image of the National Conference, Farooq sidelined most of his father's collaborators certainly did not help him in securing his position within the party. Second, Indira Gandhi was not willing to tolerate an unfriendly chief minister, especially at the top of India's most strategically important state. She first looked for an electoral alliance with the National Conference, but Farooq's unwillingness to leave any seat to the Congress (I) in the Kashmir valley, and more importantly, to be Delhi's pawn in Srinagar for the forthcoming five years, set the stage for Mrs Gandhi's attempts to remove him from power "at any cost" (Arun Nehru, quoted in Malhotra 1989, 297).

In fact, the Congress (I)'s attempts to topple Farooq's government began a few weeks after the National Conference won the July 1983 state elections. A few months later, in a letter to the prime minister, B. K. Nehru explained that he would not swear in Ghul Shah, as asked by many Congress (I) members including the party chief Mufti Mohammed Sayeed, simply on the grounds of their claim that the chief minister had lost his majority. Instead, he stated his constitutional obligation to ask the chief minister to summon a meeting of the Assembly so that the dissidents could vote him out of power. He added that the congressmen's argument that the dissidents' group would not hold together for a week was not a good reason to unconstitutionally dismiss a democratically elected government (Letter to the prime minister dated 1 September 1983, B. K. Nehru Papers, NMML).

P. C. Alexander, Mrs Gandhi's personal secretary, was not convinced by Nehru's arguments. Instead, he said that the centre was of the view that a no confidence vote was not necessary and that the chief minister should be dismissed straightaway (Letter to B. K. Nehru dated 19 September 1983, B. K. Nehru Papers, Subject File 80, NMML). The correspondence continued on these terms until Nehru was finally moved to Gujarat (March 1984) and replaced by Jagmohan who, in four months' time, dismissed Farooq Abdullah and swore in Shah on the basis of a letter signed by thirteen defectors (*Indian Express*, 3 July 1984). The very day Farooq's dismissal was announced, protests erupted throughout

Kashmir. The Central Police Reserve Force, which had been sent from Delhi the day before (Schofield 2003, 149), was ordered to maintain law and order. In the first ninety days of G. M. Shah's chief ministership, curfew was imposed on seventy-two days (Bose 2003, 92).

Three techniques were used to destabilise the National Conference government. First, the Congress (I) state unit deliberately tried to "create a law and order situation" to convince the governor to impose Governor's Rule[45] ('Notes on the present situation in J&K discussed with the PM on 5th Jan 1984', B. K. Nehru Papers, Subject File 80, NMML). The strategy included preventing the movements of the chief minister by *dharnas*[46] on the road, disturbing National Conference meetings, creating disturbances in Courts and Offices of Deputy Commissioners, Assistant Commissioners, Tahsildhars, and the like. Virtually all observers denounced the Congress (I)'s deliberate attempt to create chaos (e.g. Tavleen Singh, quoted in Schofield 2003, 146; Arun Shourie in *India Today*, 16 July 1983 and 1 September 1983).

Second, Mrs Gandhi repeatedly accused Farooq of being a secessionist and in a secret alliance with Muslim fundamentalists inside and outside India. The central government linked Farooq Abdullah with virtually any law and order situation in the country, especially in the Punjab (*Economic and Political Weekly*, 11 February 1984) and insistently portrayed him as a CIA agent.

Third, the Congress (I) contacted potential defectors from the National Conference trying to "convince" them to join Ghul Shah's newly formed party, the Awami National Conference. The standard offer was "Rs. 2 lakhs in cash plus a Ministership" ('Notes on the present situation in J&K discussed with the PM on 5th Jan 1984', B. K. Nehru Papers, Subject File 80, NMML). The fact that all thirteen defectors did obtain a ministership in Ghul Shah's Cabinet would confirm the governor's claim. However, until Mrs Gandhi decided to send Jagmohan to Srinagar, the only results that the Congress (I) obtained were, on the one hand, to escalate tensions in the Kashmir Valley and, on the other hand, to increase the hitherto marginal consensus of Islamist organisations such as the Jamat-e-Islami (Widmalm 1997, 150). The insurrection that exploded in the Valley in the late 1980s drew heavily on both these outcomes.

At the following National Development Council in Summer 1984, the non-Congress (I) chief ministers of Tripura, West Bengal, Karnataka and Andhra Pradesh designated the latter to read a joint statement, protesting against Farooq Abdullah's dismissal. Afterwards, they would walk out, thus trying, perhaps for the first time, to give political significance to a meeting of the National Development Council. However, Mrs Gandhi would not allow them to raise the issue. As Rama Rao tried to read his statement, "there were interruptions by the Buta Singhs and the Bhajan Lals". The chief ministers finally walked out, instructing their officials to remain seated. However, Mrs Gandhi ordered them to leave along with their chief ministers, "as if these states had ceased to belong to the Union" (Ashok Mitra, *Illustrated Weekly of India*, 5 January 1986). Within two weeks, a grant of Rs. 325 crore that West Bengal was supposed to receive in line with the Finance Commission's recommendations was cancelled (*Economic and Political Weekly*, 8 September 1984). Two weeks later, NTR was dismissed in yet another unconstitutional move (*Indian Express*, 17 August 1984; see also Tummala 1986).

We have already mentioned NTR's dismissal earlier in this chapter. The Congress (I)'s plot to get rid of NTR was very similar to that for Farooq's removal. First, the local party unit compiled a list of potential defectors. Then congressmen tried to convince them to defect, offering money and ministerships. Newspapers reported that about Rs 20–30 million were sent from New Delhi to Andhra to tempt legislators (Tummala 1986, 391). Attempts intensified during NTR's stay in the United States for medical treatments in July 1984. In this period Mrs Gandhi even paid a surprise visit to her constituency (Medak) in Andhra Pradesh (*Indian Express*, 19 July 1984). However, despite the large sums invested, the Congress (I)'s search for defectors was unsuccessful. Nevertheless, the party convinced the Governor, Ram Lal, to dismiss NTR's government anyway (*India Today*, 15 November 1983) and swear in Bhaskara Rao (*The Hindu*, 16 August 1984). The Congress (I) thought that many more TDP legislators would defect once NTR was out of power. However, they had not taken into account the strong popular reaction to NTR's dismissal. The TDP's leader was still very popular and the Congress (I)'s move only reinforced NTR's electoral message that the Telugu pride was being trampled on by Delhi. Most of the TDP legislators were smart enough not to fall into the Congress (I)'s trap, also thanks to NTR's decision to bring them all to neighbouring Karnataka, where they were less exposed to the Congress (I)'s offers (Raghavan and Manor 2009, ch. 7). Eventually, NTR was sworn back in mid-September.

A very similar plot was planned in Karnataka. E. Raghavan and James Manor (2009, ch. 7) provide a very detailed and first hand account of these attempts, which, however, failed. A few months earlier, in May

1984, the Sikkim Janata Parishad chief minister, Nar Bahadur Bhandari had been dismissed, after the state Congress (I) unit had "encouraged" defections[47] (*Indian Express*, 12 May 1984). As a result (perhaps not wholly unintended) of these attempts to re-impose a one-party-dominant party system that could sustain a framework of informal federalism, the Congress (I) had an absolute majority in more than half of the Legislative Assemblies, which was a requisite for amending the articles of the Constitution concerning the elections of the president of the republic.

A certainly unintended result was the collapse of the Congress (I)'s support in those states where Mrs Gandhi had tried to re-impose a one-party-dominant system by resorting to unconstitutional means. Paradoxically, she accelerated the emergence of a multi-party system in which the states played a key role. The erosion of the Congress (I)'s popularity in these states was very evident. In the December 1984 general elections, just after Mrs Gandhi's assassination and in the midst of Rajiv's wave that gave the Congress the largest victory of its history, Andhra Pradesh elected only six Congress (I) legislators (in 1980 there had been 41 of them) vis-à-vis 30 belonging to the TDP, which became the single largest party in the Lok Sabha (after the Congress (I)). In Karnataka, where the plot was well known—a Congress (I) member's attempts to bribe a potential defector were even recorded on tape (Raghavan and Manor 2009, 171)—but was not put into operation, Rajiv Gandhi's party swept the polls. However, in the state elections in the following years, the trend was confirmed. Punjab, Andhra Pradesh, Sikkim, Assam and Karnataka all chose non-Congress (I) governments. The Congress system was over.

In the following years, parallel to the process of regionalisation and fragmentation of the national party system, the demand for institutionalisation of federal institutions was partially responded to: the anti-defection law[48] enacted in 1985 made the toppling of state governments a much more difficult endeavour; the establishment of the inter-state council in the early 1990s provided a forum for expressing state grievances; and the 1994 ruling of the Supreme Court made the imposition of President's Rule much more difficult.

Conclusion

This chapter has sought to put into a broader perspective the severe institutional crisis of the early 1980s. In doing so, it has tried to qualify the process of deinstitutionalisation which took place in the previous decades by distinguishing between the three sub-processes of politicisation, erosion, and informalisation of the state institutions. We highlighted both severe discontinuities, but also some important continuities in the relation between the executive and the other institutions of the state throughout India's independent history.

Mrs Gandhi managed to subjugate state institutions to a significant extent. Particularly significant was her attempt to force the maintaining of a one-party-dominant party system despite the fact that regional players were assuming an increasingly important role in India's political system. Federalism has worked throughout India's independent history as a rather effective mechanism for conflict regulation (Adeney 2007). Also, what I called "informal federalism"—i.e. the management of centre-states relations within the Congress's fold—added a consociational element to India's democracy that was crucial for the maintenance of the democratic order in a highly diverse society. However, such a consociational element was crucially depending on the configuration of the party system. When new players started claiming their place in the national party system, informal federalism cracked. The consequences for India's governability were enormous, especially in Punjab, Assam and Jammu and Kashmir.

The relation between Mrs Gandhi and the other institutions of the state is important in two other senses. First, as suggested by Ashis Nandy (cited in *India Today*, 16 September 1984), Mrs Gandhi herself became an institution. This was a reflection of the incredible personalisation of power that resulted from almost two decades of her rule. After her assassination, it became clear that dynastic succession too had become somehow institutionalised, as today's proliferation of political dynasties shows.

Second, Mrs Gandhi contributed to the spreading of a political culture that had no respect for the institutional set up of the country. What almost two decades of her ruling left behind—among politicians and common people alike—was the idea that politicians are omnipotent. Hence a somewhat paradoxical process developed. On the one hand, as argued by Rajni Kothari, quite large sections of the electorate were losing faith in the state as an agent of social change (*Illustrated Weekly of India*, 8 June 1984); on the other hand, more and more people believed that access to political power remained the best way to pursue their private interests, thus further strengthening their demand for political representation. In other words, while the legitimacy of the state as a public institution faded, its recognition as a tool for private benefits thrived. This indeed must be seen as one of the most important—and most detrimental—of Mrs Gandhi's legacies.

CONCLUSION

Indira Gandhi was assassinated on the morning of 31 October 1984 by two of her bodyguards. Both were Sikhs. One of the assassins, senior officer Beant Singh, reportedly said, "I have done my duty. It is now for you to do yours". Shortly after Operation Bluestar, officials in the prime minister's office had advised the prime minister not to post any Sikh bodyguards. But Mrs Gandhi, whose personality was a somewhat paradoxical combination of cynicism and naivety, rejected the advice simply saying "aren't we secular?" (Jayakar 2007, 486).

The assassination of Indira Gandhi opened one of the darkest pages of India's independent history. Violence against Sikhs started on 31 October in the area surrounding the All India Institute of Medical Sciences in New Delhi, where the prime minister was declared dead in the early afternoon. The following day, violence spread across the capital and North India. According to the Ahuja Commission, between 31 October and 7 November,[1] 2,733 Sikhs were killed in Delhi alone (Nanavati Commission 2005, 3).

That the state apparatus was not able to maintain law and order in its capital city was bad enough. But the ways in which the events unfolded revealed a much deeper malady of India's institutions than simple administrative incapacity. Indeed, the anti-Sikh riots of 1984 can be seen as an example of what kind of institutional set-up Indira Gandhi left behind.

A number of civil society organisations and government commissions[2] established that the riots were far from being a spontaneous reaction to the prime minister's assassination. Rather, the state apparatus was used by Congress (I), including its MPs and ministers, to promote, facilitate and direct the vengeance against the Sikhs.

According to the testimony of eye-witnesses collected during the last 30 years, the Congress (I) workers, including MPs Jagdish Tytler, Sajjan Kumar and Lalit Maken, and Minister H. K. L. Bhagat, incited the mobs to kill as many Sikhs as possible (BBC News, 23 December 2012). They distributed cash, liquor, iron rods, and kerosene; they ensured that the buses of the Delhi Transport Corporation were made available for bringing the mobs to Sikh neighbourhoods; they distributed voter lists, school registration forms and ration card lists to identify Sikhs' houses and properties; the police marked Sikhs' houses with huge white "Xs" (*Time*, 28 October 2009). Sajjan Kumar was even seen by a local Congress (I) worker promising Rs 1,000 for each Sikh that was killed (Ensaaf 2006, 28). According to some witnesses, Jagdish Tytler complained that the small number of Sikhs killed in his area would undermine his position inside the party (*The Tribune*, 19 December 2007). The police not only refused to file First Information Reports against arsonists, rapists and killers, but in many cases actively participated in the looting.

In short, what clearly emerges is that the members of the ruling party could make free use of the state apparatus to take vengeance for their assassinated leader. The fact that Congress (I) workers saw the promotion of killings and arsons as a way to prove their loyalty to the new prime minister—Rajiv Gandhi had been sworn in the very day his mother died—tells a lot about the state of the ruling party and about the degree of subjugation of the state's institutions to the rulers' wishes. Only when the army was deployed on 3 November was law and order restored.

What happened after the riots is perhaps even more revealing of the way Indian institutions have been working since the 1980s. The Indian state has been incapable of ensuring justice. Ten commissions of inquiry and numerous trials led to only a handful of convictions. The recommendations of the commissioners' reports have been largely ignored and no or little follow-up action was taken (e.g. *Tehelka* 18 April 2009; BBC News, 1 November 2009). Not a single senior politician has been convicted. There have been widespread allegations that key witnesses have been threatened or bribed (*Tehelka*, 25 September 2009). Serious efforts were made to destroy or lose track of files and evidence, in what has been called "the Mother of all cover-ups" (*The Asian Age*, 9 August 2005).

The first Sikh (Congress) Prime Minister, Dr Manmohan Singh, in the wake of the publication of the Nanavati Commission Report in 2005—which established in very clear terms that "Congress (I) leaders and workers ... either incited or helped the mobs in attacking the Sikhs" (Nanavati Commission 2005, 182)—apologised to the Sikh community and to the entire nation for what happened in 1984. This was indeed a rare and commendable gesture.[3] He even forced Jagdish Tytler to resign from the Cabinet on the base of the serious accusations against him contained in the report. Both Tytler and Sajjan Kumar were later forced to withdraw their candidature to the 2009 Lok Sabha elections. Yet, this could hardly be considered enough.

The anti-Sikh riots best represent the short-term legacy of Indira Gandhi. In short, she left behind a "divided nation" (Guha 2007, 572). This does not mean that she left a country on the brink of disintegration. In fact, fears about India's balkanisation have always been greatly exaggerated. However, it is hardly deniable that the Indian social fabric was badly cracked in the mid-1980s. The northeast, Punjab and Kashmir were on the edge of civil war. Caste conflicts were as acute as never before, communal clashes were on the increase, and the stage for the destruction of the Babri Masjid in Ayodhya had been set, while Maoist groups spread to new areas. The anti-Sikh pogroms left an indelible mark not only on the Sikh community, but also among large strata of Indian society, which understood that the state was something to be wary of. In fact, some authors' contention (Chandra et al. 2008; Malhotra 1989) that Mrs Gandhi's major contribution was her strenuous defence of India's unity and integrity is hardly sustainable. Similarly, the argument that Mrs Gandhi helped preserving democratic stability and secularism (Frankel 2005, 633) is hardly convincing too, given her direct and indirect contributions to the rise of Hindu politics. In at least two cases (Assam and Jammu and Kashmir) the consequences of Mrs Gandhi's inability to deal with social and political unrest are still visible today.

Indira Gandhi's Legacy

As it should be evident from this study, Indira Gandhi's prime ministerships had a number of long-term consequences on India's political system. We can divide Mrs Gandhi's legacy into what she destroyed and what she contributed to create.

On the destructive side, we can identify three major long-term consequences of Indira Gandhi's rule. First, she contributed to the institutionalisation of corruption as a key feature of India's political system. One of the key reasons why corruption is so widespread is that India lacks a legitimate system for financing political activity (Jha 1993; Gowda and Sridharan 2012). Since Mrs Gandhi banned corporate donations to political parties in the 1970s a parallel economy of gigantic proportions came into being, which eventually resulted in the crystallisation of corruption as a systemic feature of the Indian political system. The uninterrupted emergence of scams in recent years confirms how deeply rooted the phenomenon is. The economic reforms of the early 1990s were supposed to curb corruption through the retreat of the state from the economic sphere. However, the only visible effect has been the increased magnitude of corruption. The Bofors scam in 1989 cost the public exchequer Rs 65 crores. The 2010 2G scam is estimated to have led to a loss of almost Rs 60,000 crores. And this is by no means a problem limited to the central government or to the Congress party. The illegal mining scam in BJP-led Karnataka could have cost a mind-boggling Rs 1 lakh crore (*The Hindu*, 18 June 2013), i.e. the equivalent of running the Mahatma Gandhi National Rural Employment Guarantee Scheme—the largest anti-poverty programme in the world—in the whole country for almost three years.

Corruption is something that can be found in every society. However, what is worrying in India is that corruption is now a systemic feature of the Indian polity. There is a widespread consensus across party lines that black money is an acceptable way of financing political activities. One observer recalls that, in late 2010 at a Congress Working Committee meeting, Prime Minister Manmohan Singh proposed to pass a piece of legislation that, on the one hand, would tighten the controls on parties' funding mechanisms, and, on the other hand, would institute public funding. According to this observer, not a single member of the CWC voted in favour of this proposal (interview, New Delhi, January 2011). But this is something that is by no means limited to the Congress party. In mid-2013 the Central Information Commission issued an order that the six national parties had to be taken under the purview of the Right to Information Act (RTI). This would have forced them to handle their finances in a much more transparent way. However, a broad consensus emerged in the Parliament and a specific legislation was passed that excluded political parties from the purview of the Act. These are just two among many examples that show how corruption is inextricably intertwined with politics.

Strictly related to what I just said, Indira Gandhi contributed to the development of an even more disturbing trend. This is the entry into politics of a number of politicians who are hardly distinguishable from criminals. This process of criminalisation of the political arena was started and somewhat legitimised by Sanjay Gandhi. Today, most political parties include in their ranks well-known criminals. Among sitting MPs, 34 per cent have criminal records, up from 30 per cent in 2009 and 24 per cent in 2004. Those who are accused of serious crimes like murder or rape constitute 20 per cent of the MPs, up from 15 per cent in the previous legislature (*New York Times*, 23 May 2014). Although in many cases these criminal MPs are seen as some sort of "Robin Hoods" in their constituencies, it is undeniable that the high concentration of legislators with criminal records does not help to make the system more accountable and more transparent.

The second major long-term consequence of Indira Gandhi's rule is that the state institutions became a vehicle for pursuing personal and partisan ends. In other words, Mrs Gandhi's age left behind an idea of power which is "highly personalized and weakly institutionalized" (Saxena 2010, 447). We saw how Indira Gandhi used the state apparatus for pursuing a project of personal domination and to "finish politically" the enemies of the Congress (I). Institutions were so badly eroded that, after Mrs Gandhi's death, the personalisation of institutions became a systemic feature of the political system. This is true especially at the state level. Chief ministers are in many cases able to centralise powers in their hands and to use the state apparatus for their own, personal ends.

This is a process strictly intertwined with the institutionalisation of corruption. Chief ministers in most states are able to squeeze ministries at will, and to amass enormous wealth for themselves and for their parties. Chandrababu Naidu and Y. S. Rajasekhara Reddy from Andhra Pradesh, B. S. Yeddyurappa from Karnataka, O. P. Chautala from Haryana, Karunanidhi and Jayalalitha from Tamil Nadu, Mulayam Singh Yadav and Mayawati from Uttar Pradesh, Lalu Prasad Yadav from Bihar, Madu Khoda from Jharkand, and Sharad Pawar from Maharashtra are just the most prominent examples of chief ministers that were accused of (and, in certain cases, convicted for) serious corruption-related crimes. In all cases, they managed to amass huge wealth that is completely disproportionate to their "legal" economic status.

At the central level the situation is similar. According to the Association for Democratic Reform, the average assets of 396 MPs from the

2009 Lok Sabha increased by 145 per cent by 2014, from 5.82 crore to 14.29 crore.[4] This widespread tendency to use one's power position to amass wealth is a reflection of the absence of a public mechanism to finance political activity. "Investments" made during the electoral campaign must have a return.

The use of the state institutions for partisan ends is not limited to raising illegal funds. For example, the central government is able to keep political allies on a leash through its control of the Central Bureau of Investigation. There have been numberless allegations of the politicised role that this institution plays. In some cases, it became fairly evident that the support of a party to the central government crucially depended on the latter's ability to stop or allow the prosecution of senior political leaders. Another example can be drawn from the aftermath of the anti-Sikh riots. The Indian state has been substantially unable to prosecute and convict the (powerful) culprits.

A very evident instance of the private use of institutions is the politicisation of the bureaucratic apparatus. We have seen in chapter 4 how this process unfolded during the 1970s and the early 1980s. Political loyalty became the key organising principle of the bureaucratic apparatus (both at the centre and in the states). However, since 1989, things have changed to a certain extent. The main reason is the profound transformation that affected the party system. Alternations in power and coalition governments have become the norm. This by itself has led to a change in the incentive structure of the bureaucrats. Whereas during the heyday of the "Indira System" political commitment to the Congress party was highly incentivised, today the key mechanism seems to be what two senior civil servants call "passive political neutrality", i.e. "total submission to *whoever is in power*" (Krishnan and Somanathan 2005, 306). "Total submission" often includes engaging in illicit activities, especially for those officers appointed to "wet ministries".[5]

The politicisation of the bureaucratic apparatus is particularly important in the Indian context because the state has significant discretionary powers, especially concerning the regulation of economic activity. This is a legacy of the "licence-Raj system" that was built by Nehru and reinforced by Indira Gandhi to the extent that India became "one of the most comprehensive systems of control and regulation of the private sector of the non-communist world" (Kochanek 1987, 1283). The economic liberalisation of the early 1990s did little to change the situation. The bureaucratic apparatus still retains a great deal of discretion, which obviously facilitates the usage of institutions for personal ends by senior politicians.

Both these consequences of Indira Gandhi's rule (the institutionalisation of corruption and the personalisation of the institutions) contributed to make India's political system not transparent and largely unaccountable; and they provided very strong incentives to keep the system so. A ray of hope came in 2005, when the Indian government enacted the RTI. This is a potentially revolutionary piece of legislation that has already had a very positive impact on India's polity. It remains to be seen to what extent the RTI and a growing concern about corruption among India's society[6] will succeed in creating a culture of transparency and in curbing the massive black economy that gravitates around politics.

The third long-term destructive consequence of Mrs Gandhi's prime ministership is the institutionalisation of dynastic politics. Indira Gandhi first became an institution herself. Her will became synonymous with the Congress (I)'s will. After her assassination in October 1984 and the smooth succession of Rajiv Gandhi, dynastic leadership became the accepted norm within the party. But the consequences went far beyond the Congress. In the mid-1980s, hardly any observer thought that the institutionalisation of political dynasties would become an enduring feature of India's democracy (Romesh Thapar in *Seminar*, No. 30, December 1984). Today, 30 years after Mrs Gandhi's death, virtually every party—barring the Left—has its own political dynasties (*Hindustan Times*, 30 October 2009). The institutionalisation of dynastic politics contributed to making political parties less representative (Chhibber 2013) and their workers less inserted into the social fabric. Moreover, among the key tasks that political parties undertake is the selection and training of new leaders (Randall and Svåsand 2002). Dynastic politics impedes political parties in playing such a role. In other words, the institutionalisation of dynastic politics contributed—along with the erosion of institutions—to make the system less responsive to the demands coming from below. Both the very high anti-incumbency factor and the growing number of parties that contest national and state elections is a sign that the demand for political representation coming from a sizable part of the Indian electorate goes largely unanswered and that voters keep looking for alternatives.

Indira Gandhi's legacy can be seen from a creative point of view too. In short, what Mrs Gandhi left behind was a new political system, very different from the one which she had found, and quite similar to today's one. There are three main features of the system that Mrs Gandhi contributed—sometimes intentionally, sometimes not—to build. First, the establishment of a "tripartite pact" between the state, the middle class and big business became an enduring feature of India's politics. Since 1980 India's development path changed remarkably. Emphasis was shifted from the rural to the urban sectors of the economy, or, as argued in chapter 3, Mrs Gandhi sought to make the Congress (I) the representative of the (rising) new middle class and of the corporate sector, while the poor and the agricultural world were relegated into a secondary position. Since then, all Indian governments adopted a similar approach, especially after the liberalisation of the economy in 1991 (Maiorano 2014a). It was only in 2004, with the election of the United Progressive Alliance government, that a greater effort to enlarge the social coalition benefiting from the central government's economic policies was made, especially through a marked increase in spending in the social sector and through massive investments in the rural economy. However, the "tripartite pact" between the state, the middle class and the corporate sector was not put into question, as shown by the continuation of a set of policies favouring the better offs.

Second, Indira Gandhi contributed (directly and indirectly) to the rise of Hindu politics. In the early 1980s, this form of political mobilisation remained in an embryonic form. But by the end of the decade it had become extremely important. The rise of the BJP as one of the two national poles of the multi-party system that emerged in the 1990s owes much to the campaign for the "liberation" of Ram's birthplace in Ayodhya that began in 1983. Mrs Gandhi in part contributed directly to make this form of mobilisation politically acceptable. We saw in chapter 3 how, as part of her political strategy, she adopted a form of soft (or subtle) majoritarianism. On the one hand, during her final term in office, Mrs Gandhi started expressing her religiosity publicly. On the other hand, she started using in her speeches a lexicon borrowed from political Hinduism and on several occasions she even accepted the support of the RSS during the electoral campaigns.

A more indirect contribution to the rise of political Hinduism was the refusal to act firmly when the RSS and the VHP started organising a set of religious-cum-political processions. Admittedly, this was something difficult to do. Not allowing a religious procession to take place would have been politically very harmful. However, a more clear defence of the secular values that she claimed to be standing for would certainly have been possible. Another indirect contribution to Hindu politics was the emphasis that she put on the dangers that the country was facing. In fact, the RSS's idea that Hindus were under siege in their own homeland and Mrs Gandhi's message that the nation was under constant threat did not differ much and actually reinforced each other.

Third, Indira Gandhi overlooked (and unwittingly contributed to) the regionalisation of India's politics. This is a process that started before Mrs Gandhi came to power and, no doubt, would have unfolded anyway. It is the result of a combination of many complex factors, among which Mrs Gandhi's actions were certainly not the most important one. However, she gave a decisive (and unintentional) contribution to accelerate the process.

The deinstitutionalisation of her own party made it virtually impossible for the Congress (I) to include new groups in its fold. This weakened the consociational elements of India's democracy. This meant that the growing demand for political representation coming from below could not be accommodated within the Congress (I). Consequently, Indian voters started looking for political alternatives at the state level. We have seen in chapter 3 how regional parties emerged as serious contestant for power in a number of states, including Andhra Pradesh, Assam, Jammu and Kashmir, Punjab, Karnataka, West Bengal, Kerala[7] and Tamil Nadu. In addition, Kanshi Ram founded the Bahujan Samaj Party in 1984, which would become an enormously important political player in Uttar Pradesh. Moreover, the entire Hindi belt was about to be stormed by regional parties too (see below).

The regionalisation of Indian politics was intertwined with other three important political processes. The first one is the centralisation of power that occurred during Mrs Gandhi's prime ministership. We saw in chapter 3 that this process, on the one hand, resulted in the Congress (I)'s inability to respond to regional demands; on the other hand, as seen in chapters 3 and 4, it provoked a reaction from the regional parties that started mobilising the electorate by appealing to regional sentiments. In particular, Mrs Gandhi's unwillingness to deal politically with regional demands and to allow the emergence of a multi-party system—adversaries had to be "finished politically"—accelerated the process of regionalisation of Indian politics.

Second, the regionalisation of Indian politics, especially in the Hindi belt, was greatly accelerated by the implementation of the recommendations of the Mandal Commission report by V. P. Singh in 1989. Indira Gandhi had chosen to bury the report, fearing that her party was not able to manage the political energy that its implementation would have unleashed. Also, Mrs Gandhi did not want to compromise her strategy aimed at winning the heart of the (upper-caste) middle class.

When V. P. Singh eventually implemented the report, the soil was fertile for regional and caste-based political formations to storm north India. V. P. Singh's Janata Dal soon disintegrated into its regional constituent units, giving birth to the Samajwadi Party in Uttar Pradesh, the Rashtriya Janata Dal and the Janata Dal (United) in Bihar, the Biju Janata Dal in Orissa and the Janata Dal (Secular) in Karnataka. All these parties came to power in their respective states and exercised an enormous influence on national politics. Between 1996 and 2014, no single party was able to secure an absolute majority in the Lok Sabha and therefore the two major parties (the Congress and the BJP) had to form coalition governments that necessarily included regional parties.

Finally, regionalisation was reinforced by the liberalisation of the economy in 1991, a process that, as we saw, Mrs Gandhi started in the early 1980s. It is certainly true that the states had become the most important units for economic decision-making even before liberalisation; however, the dominance of the Congress and the degree of centralisation of power made the centre extremely influential. The liberalisation of the economy gave the states much more freedom, especially in terms of attracting private investment. This also resulted in much greater scope for chief ministers to amass (illegal) wealth that could be used to strengthen their position.

The new political system that emerged is, in sum, more elitist, less secular, and more federal, but also deeply corrupt, scarcely accountable and institutionally weak. It is also a system that is less prone to authoritarianism though. Since 1989, the collapse of the one-party-dominant party system resulted in a radical redistribution of power, from the prime minister's office to other institutions of the central government, and from the central government to the states.

This new system proved to be relatively stable. Federalism, in particular, facilitated the inclusion of new groups into the political system and proved to be an effective power-sharing mechanism.

The elitist nature of India's developmental path since 1980, however, brought about an increase of inequalities (Dreze and Sen 2013) and, at least till the election of the UPA government in 2004, a very slow poverty reduction rate. This has contributed to the spread of armed Maoist groups in about one third of the country. According to former Prime Minister Manmohan Singh, this is today the "biggest threat to internal security" (*The Hindu*, 24 October 2010).

The rise of Hindu politics resulted in a number of extremely serious incidents, foremost among them the destruction of the Babri Masjid in Ayodhya in 1992 and the Gujarat riots in 2002. In both cases, thousand of people died, mainly belonging to the Muslim minority. However, generally speaking, the system that Mrs Gandhi contributed to build is more stable and more governable than the one that she presided over. The key factor in determining this stability is the emergence of a multiparty, federal system that does not permit the concentration of power at the centre. However, the massive electoral victory of the BJP in 2014, which obtained an absolute majority on its own, has altered (perhaps only temporarily) the configuration of the party system. The appointment of Narendra Modi as prime minister in 2014, whose centralizing and even authoritarian tendencies strongly remind one of Indira Gandhi, may constitute a source of danger for India's democratic institutions.

It is finally worth mentioning two other legacies of Mrs Gandhi's rule, much more positive for India's democracy than those that I outlined so far. The first one is that, rather paradoxically, Indira Gandhi contributed to the democratisation of the political system. Her direct appeal to the country's poor since the 1971 general elections had no small role in accelerating the awakening of the Indian masses. In a way, Indira Gandhi was a victim of her own success, since governing an increasingly assertive electorate became more and more challenging; but the awakening of the subalterns contributed to the weakening of patron-client relations that subjugated the poor and made them passive actors in India's democracy.

Secondly, and strictly connected to this point, Indira Gandhi brought poverty to the centre of the political discourse. Her promise to "abolish poverty" in the early 1970s, although not followed by any concrete attempt to reduce poverty, shifted the attention of politicians on to the poor. Since then, every single party has had to address the question of poverty. Most of the time, this translated into merely rhetorical commitment. But, in recent years, the UPA's government did try to give some substance to the Congress's social democratic tradition. There is still a lot to do. But the emergence of an embryonic welfare state in India is also due to her former Empress.

NOTES

INTRODUCTION

1. i.e. the lower house of the Indian Parliament.
2. *The Times* (London) referred to Indira Gandhi as "the Empress of India" in 1971.
3. For simplicity's sake I will refer to the Indian National Congress simply as the Congress.
4. Yogendra Yadav in a conversation with the author, New Delhi, 23 January 2011.
5. The reshaping of the Congress (I)'s social base as a consequence of the impact of national economic policies on national social groups has been the subject of Maiorano (2012).
6. West Bengal was ruled by the Communist Party of India (Marxist) (hereafter CPI(M)). This is registered as a national party, but, in practice, it functions as a regional party.
7. We will call "informal federalism" the way in which centre-state relations were managed during the Nehru's years, in a framework of one-party-dominant system in which the Congress party was in power at the centre and in most states.
8. None of these studies is exclusively dedicated to the early 1980s.

1. INDIAN POLITICS AND SOCIETY IN THE 1970s

1. The Congress obtained 40.72 per cent of the votes.
2. These were Bihar, Kerala, Orissa, Punjab, Tamil Nadu and West Bengal.
3. In fact defections began before the elections, at the time of the distribution of the party tickets (Kashyap 1970).
4. That young people were "rewriting" their loyalty to the Congress would be confirmed by the analysis prepared by the Indian Institute of Public Opinion cited in Frankel 2005, 353–4.
5. The "syndicate" was the collective leadership of the Congress party, consisting mainly of strong regional leaders. Particularly important were the defeats of Atulya

Ghosh, S. K. Patil and, above all, Kumarasami Kamaraj, who was defeated by an unknown 28-year old student.

6. Morris-Jones (1978a) notes that Congress dissidents could not be held in the party because severe intra-party competition played a fundamental role in determining the election outcomes in all the states where the Congress was defeated, except Tamil Nadu.
7. I use the term "class" not in the classic Marxist sense. Rather, the term is simply to indicate a social group that shares a set of economic interests but whose boundaries are blurred rather than rigidly defined.
8. Similarly, when the term "class" is referred to the other dominant groups, it does not imply that these are homogeneous social formations that act in a coordinated way.
9. This includes tenants enjoying proprietorship rights.
10. Not much land was redistributed to the landless. The literature on these topics is monumental. See for example (Frankel 2005).
11. Of course, Scheduled Castes and Scheduled Tribes were duly represented in the assemblies because of the policy of positive discrimination envisaged by the Constitution.
12. The Gram Panchayats are elected local councils.
13. Francine Frankel (1988) argues that in the south, accommodating middle status groups was easier because the sharing of power at the state level did not compromise the overall socio-economic structure of dominance of elite groups.
14. This does not mean that this section of the business elite did not finance the Congress. It simply means that they were less generous and, more importantly, they did not finance the ruling party exclusively.
15. One crore is equivalent to 10 million. One lakh is equivalent to 100,000.
16. Given that the Congress was the ruling party, "donations" from industrialists would have come anyway.
17. Indeed, industrialists were often threatened by government officials. For example, if a businessman refused to donate the requested amount of money to the party, it was extremely likely that a tax-raid would have been ordered against that industrialist (see Kochanek 1987).
18. See next section.
19. From this point of view, it is significant that virtually every biography of Mrs Gandhi published before 1975 is written in rather hagiographic terms (see Vasudev 1974). Even Zareer Masani, who was to become one of the sharpest critics of Mrs Gandhi, used a rather sympathetic tone in his excellent biography published shortly before the proclamation of the emergency (Masani 1975).
20. This does not mean that vote-banks and factional networks ceased to be important for building up electoral support. Indeed, they remained one of the most important political tools throughout the 1970s, especially when patron and cli-

ent were bound by a creditor-debtor relationship. Anyway, the importance of vote-banks gradually, but steadily, declined.

21. In addition to the references cited above see Hart 1976; Kohli 1990b; Kochanek 2002.
22. The word "warlords" would probably need some qualifications.
23. This does not mean that Mrs Gandhi's branch did not include factional leaders. In fact she had to compromise with many of them in the selection of Congress (R)'s candidates for the 1971 general elections. See Kochanek 2002, 84.
24. Two good accounts of these developments are Masani 1975, ch. 7–8, and Malhotra 1989, ch. 7. I will deal with the relation between the prime minister and other formal institutions in chapter 4.
25. Her popularity was eroded after the emergency, as shown by the electoral data of the 1977 election. However, this was only temporary, as the rapidity with which Mrs Gandhi came back to power shows. Tavleen Singh collected a few interviews just before the 1980 general elections that show how many voters did not blame Indira Gandhi directly for the excesses of the emergency (Singh 2012, 116).
26. As far as internal politics was concerned.
27. What follows is just a very brief account of the process of submission of state institutions by the prime minister immediately before the proclamation of the emergency. Further details will be provided in chapter 4.
28. In the Kesevananda Bharati case in 1973.
29. Indira Gandhi was found guilty of minor technical offences.
30. Apparently the prime minister received some reports from the Intelligence Bureau concerning a "conspiracy" against her by Hemvati Nandan Bahuguna and Jagjivan Ram (Austin 1999, 302 n18).
31. Patrick Clibbens (2013) argues that urban clearance programs were not limited to Delhi and North India.
32. These figures probably over-estimate the actual redistribution of land. Certain states submitted bogus reports. It should also be noted that the redistribution of land was by no means limited to the Hindi belt. In Karnataka, for example, a good amount of land was actually redistributed (Raghavan and Manor 2009).

2. THE PARTY THAT DIDN'T WORK: THE CONGRESS (I) IN THE EARLY 1980s

1. The argument according to which Mrs Gandhi called for fresh election because she was a democrat (Malhotra 1989; Frank 2001) is not very convincing.
2. The constituent parties of the Janata Party were the Jana Sangh, the BLD, and the Congress (O). The Congress for Democracy (a newly formed party headed by Jagjivan Ram) did not merge with the Janata Party, but contested the elections

under the same symbol. Also rebels from the Congress (R) like Chandra Shekhar and Mohan Dharia joined the Janata Party.

3. We will see below how the argument that the 1977 (and 1980) elections were marked by "national" waves (Rudolph and Rudolph 1987) is not entirely convincing.
4. For the detailed electoral data see Election Commission of India—Statistical Report 1977, available online at http://eci.nic.in/eci_main1/ElectionStatistics.aspx. Two electoral analyses are Weiner 1978a and Manor 1978.
5. Sanjay Ruparelia (2014) revisited the Janata Party government in a recent book on coalition politics.
6. Even though it was substituted by a similar provision (the National Security Ordinance), enacted during Charan Singh's brief prime ministership and subsequently converted into law by Mrs Gandhi in 1980.
7. The Janata Party argued that the Congress had been massively rejected at the general elections, it was necessary to hold fresh elections in those states where the Congress was in power. Out of these, seven were conquered by the Janata Party (Uttar Pradesh, Bihar, Haryana, Orissa, Madhya Pradesh, Rajasthan and Himachal Pradesh), one by a coalition Akali Dal-Janata (Punjab) and one by the National Conference of Sheik Abdullah (Jammu and Kashmir).
8. He was substituted by Banarsi Das.
9. The 5-point programme was Sanjay Gandhi's political programme. The points were education; eradicating the dowry system; tree plantation; family planning; eradication of the caste system.
10. Most of the following factual information is taken from Mirchandani 1980, ch. 4 and Malhotra 1989, ch. 12.
11. Arunchal Pradesh, Meghalaya, Maharashtra, Andhra Pradesh, and Karnataka.
12. For details about the dubious legitimacy of this move see Austin 1999, ch. 22.
13. See chapter 3 for further details.
14. For example, in Punjab tension between orthodox Sikhs and Nirankaris was very high.
15. Bahuguna had been part of Charan Singh's caretaker government till late October, 1979.
16. Formally, the Jana Sangh had ceased to exist with the formation of the Janata Party in 1977.
17. Formally, the Janata coalition broke up because most of the Jana Sangh members were also members of the RSS.
18. Gopal Singh was at that time the Chairman of the High Power Panel for Minorities, Scheduled Castes, Scheduled Tribes and the Weaker Section.
19. Gopal Singh Private Papers, Letter D.O.No. Ch/19/80 dated 19 November 1980, Nehru Memorial Museum and Library, hereafter NMML
20. The following information is taken from *Indian Express*, *The Hindu*, and *Times of India*, various issues, September–December 1979].

21. Wallace refers to Punjab and Haryana only, but the same situation applied throughout the country.
22. Most of the electoral data is taken from two sources: Weiner 1983a and Election Commission of India—Statistical Report 1980.
23. In 1971 the Congress polled 63.18 per cent; in 1977 47.02 per cent; in 1980 53.3 per cent. The Congress (U) in 1980 polled 11.81 per cent.
24. In 1971 the Congress polled 46.6 per cent; in 1977, 32.47 per cent; in 1980, 47.2 per cent.
25. In 1971 the Congress polled 45.96 per cent; in 1977, 34.85 per cent; in 1980, 52.45 per cent.
26. In 1971 the Congress polled 55.73 per cent; in 1977, 57,36 per cent; in 1980, 56,24 per cent.
27. In 1971 the Congress polled 38.46 per cent; in 1977, 38.18 per cent.
28. The reasons behind this sharp increase deserve closer attention.
29. In 1971 the Congress got 28.2 per cent; in 1977 29.37 per cent; in 1980, 36.51 per cent.
30. Elections could not be held in 12 out of 14 constituencies in Assam, due to the agitations against "foreigners".
31. This argument probably needs some qualification, as we cannot know how the voters would have behaved if the opposition had been united. However, it is certainly true that many seats conquered by the Congress (I) were due to the divisions of the opposition in an FPTP electoral system.
32. From the initials of the social groups to whom the Congress (I) appealed in Gujarat, namely Kshatriya (a low-status caste cluster in Gujarat), Harijans, Adivasis, and Muslims.
33. These were Punjab, Rajasthan, Uttar Pradesh, Bihar, Orissa, Madhya Pradesh, Gujarat, Maharashtra, and Tamil Nadu.
34. There were three reasons given for justifying this doubtfully legitimate move: a) the central government feared that opposition-led legislative assemblies could slow down the ratification of the extension of reservation for the Scheduled Classes and Tribes; b) similarly, the central government feared that other "progressive measures" could be blocked; c) it was evident, from the government's point of view, that people had lost faith in the Janata Party and other opposition parties, as shown by the results of the general elections (*Indian Express*, 19 February February 1980).
35. Bahuguna contested the elections from Garhwal. However, given the high number of violent incidents which occurred in the constituency, the Election Commission ordered a repoll, which was later postponed for more than two years. In 1982 Bahuguna finally won his seat.
36. i.e. the State Legislative Assembly.
37. A history sheet is a police record. It does not necessarily mean that one has been

in jail or that he/she has been convicted. It means that one has been involved in some criminal activity which required the intervention of the police.

38. Of course, the political context was favourable to Sanjay Gandhi. Only three years before most of the Congressmen had (rightly) reputed him to be mainly responsible for the demise of the Congress.
39. Another important source of money for the ruling party was the kickbacks on foreign contracts. However, given the limited effects of the phenomenon on the internal political situation, we will not deal with the topic.
40. Manor (1984) describes this process with reference to Karnataka.
41. 18.34 per cent of the votes.
42. 25.33 per cent of the votes.
43. 27.99 per cent of the votes.
44. The Congress (I) won 186 seats and 44.5 per cent of the votes.
45. i.e. the elective body at the district level.
46. This occurred only after Rajiv Gandhi obtained a massive mandate in the December 1984 general elections.
47. In February 1982 Mrs Gandhi launched the "new 20-point programme" as the "new" ideological platform of the party. Further details will be given in chapter 3.
48. Further details about these programmes will be provided in chapter 3.
49. Further details will be given in chapter 4.
50. Linguistic conflicts did not occur on a large scale during the first half of the 1980s.
51. i.e. the Akali Dal's leadership.
52. The turnout was as low as 20 per cent. In some constituencies a few hundred people voted (*India Today*, 1 March 1983).
53. Further details will be provided in chapter 3.

3. POLITICAL MOBILISATION IN THE EARLY 1980s

1. The construction of a national social base through a set of economic policies has been the subject of Maiorano 2012.
2. *India Today* (01 January 1980) called that of 1980 "the sugar and kerosene election".
3. All data are taken from *Ministry of Finance: Economic Survey 1981*.
4. For further details see Charan Singh's Budget Speech before the Lok Sabha in 1979.
5. The Plan was not approved due to the changed political situation. When the Congress (I) came back to power, a new Planning Commission was established.
6. The huge number of atrocities against low-caste members, or Charan Singh's anti-urban rhetoric, or the deteriorating communal situation are all examples of other important factors which contributed to the defeat of the Janata Party in 1980.

7. This was the best-known slogan of the Congress (I) electoral campaign.
8. Since 1980 India's economic growth has been steady and sustained (if one excludes 1991—the year of the fiscal crisis). However, in the wake of the global recession that started in 2008, India's growth rate slowed down significantly, particularly since 2011/12.
9. Baldev Raj Narain (2006) argues that the "Hindu" rate of growth ended in 1974–75, when, according to the author, the first liberalizing measurers were implemented.
10. Indeed Indira Gandhi's anti-capitalist stance had always been more rhetorical than practical (Bardhan 1998, 41).
11. Imports were relatively liberalised in 1981, probably under the pressure of the International Monetary Fund, with which India had signed an agreement. However, import controls were soon reimposed following the strong protests of the business community (*Economic and Political Weekly*, 10 July 1982).
12. The factual information provided below is taken from the newspapers and periodicals indicated in the bibliographical references and from various official publications.
13. That the Indian business community was not ready to accept complete liberalisation became apparent when Rajiv Gandhi initiated a policy of external liberalisation. Opposition to such a policy by the business community resulted in a reversal of the process of liberalisation.
14. The figure refers to the total allocation for Energy, Industry and Minerals, and Transport.
15. Figures in 1982–83 and 1983–84 would be even higher if man-days lost due to the two-year long textile strike in Bombay had been taken into account.
16. It is likely that Indira Gandhi used the Budget as an instrument to appease or penalize supporters and adversaries within the business community. This was the feeling of many observers at that time. However, no definite proof exists.
17. Figures refer to the 1980–81 to 1990–91 period.
18. Even though, as already noted, all-India generalisations are not usually accurate, it is likely that urban middle class opposition to the Congress (I) was a nationwide phenomenon.
19. A majority of the Indian middle class belong to upper-caste groups (see Frankel 1988, 225–6).
20. Hansen's and Jaffrelot's argument is that this feeling of alienation was largely responsible for the middle class's support for the Bharatiya Janata Party (BJP) in the late 1980s and early 1990s.
21. Similar arguments can be found in Khilnani 1998, 48.
22. The following factual information is taken from Budget Speeches, Economic Surveys, and major national newspapers.
23. Examples are the scheme providing incentives to those investing in a life insur-

ance (1980), the National Savings Certificate (1981), the Social Security Certificate and the Capital investment Bond (1982) and the National Deposit Scheme (1984).

24. Thus the latter group constitutes what we have called "rich farmers".
25. State governments had the power to pay higher procurement prices to farmers. However, it was politically difficult, especially for Congress (I)-led governments.
26. Bihar and UP were probably the most striking examples see Frankel 1989; Jaffrelot 2003.
27. This was evident with respect to the Maratha lobby.
28. The first one was that organised by Rammanohar Lohia on Charan Singh's birthday in 1978. Two other impressive farmers' demonstrations were the Congress (I)-led in February 1980 and the opposition's in March 1980.
29. Factual information is taken from the already mentioned newspapers and from official publications specified in the text.
30. Agriculture and allied services plus Irrigation and flood controls.
31. For details see *Ministry of Finance: Economic Survey* 1980–85.
32. Prices of agricultural inputs started rising from the 1970s (*Seminar*, No. 267, Nov. 1981, tab. II, 29).
33. See *Ministry of Finance: Economic Survey*, various issues. Prices were slightly lowered in following years.
34. Defined as an income of Rs 49 a month at October 1973–June 1974 rural prices.
35. The national figure is 43 per cent.
36. According to some scholars (e.g. Rudolph and Rudolph 1987, 377) small farmers tend to identify more with independent farmers than with rural poor. However, for reasons spelled out below, small farmers will be included in our definition of poor.
37. In January, 1982 Mrs Gandhi presented the "recast and redefined" 20-point programme (*Indian Express*, 15 January 1982).
38. Many other smaller programmes were financed by the central or the state governments e.g. the Small Farmers Development Agency, the Drought Prone Areas Programme and numerous programmes for the betterment of the Scheduled Castes and Scheduled Tribes.
39. For the exact amount of resources allocated to anti-poverty programmes see *Seventh Five-Year Plan*: for IRDP tab. 2.1; for NREP tab. 2.2; for Basic Needs Programme tab. 19.1; for special programmes for Scheduled Castes and Tribes tab. 15.5.
40. Figure calculated on the basis of the 1981 census.
41. Of course, this does not mean that Indian Muslims form a monolithic bloc. Muslims living in Srinagar, coastal Kerala and rural UP for example, live in extremely different socio-economic conditions, not to mention the linguistic and caste differences.

42. However, the imam's backing of Mrs Gandhi was apparently more linked to the number of tickets allocated to Bahuguna's followers than to the promotion of the interests of Muslims, as it became clear after the resignation of Bahuguna from the Congress (I) a few months after the elections (*Indian Express*, 2 May 1980).
43. These figures were probably inflated, as suggested by Sanjoy Hazarika (2000, 30).
44. Even though Bangladesh's official position was that there were no Bangladeshi illegal immigrants in India. Thus deportation of Bengali speakers to Bangladesh would have had serious consequences on the international level.
45. The agitation in Assam as an aspect of the deteriorating centre-state relations in the first half of the 1980s will be dealt with in chapter 4.
46. This perception was also due to the fact that Bengali speakers outnumbered Assamese speakers in the urban world.
47. This distinction was officially envisaged by the Government of India until the 1960s.
48. i.e. the RSS centres.
49. Most parties boycotted the elections and consequently the turnout was extremely low. In some constituencies it was lower than 1 per cent.
50. Bengali Hindus in most cases preferred the CPI(M) (Weiner 1983b).
51. Mrs Gandhi even felt the need to send a Muslim envoy to the Persian Gulf to explain the Assam situation to the governments in the area (*India Today*, 1 May 1983).
52. This was probably due to the extensive coverage by the press of one particularly bloody episode in the village of Nellie, where during the elections some 1,500 people—mostly Muslims—were massacred.
53. This was the actual reason why they were nationalised (*Indian Express*, 28 April 1980).
54. In May 1982 the Congress (I) party released a document, known as Manifesto-82, which served as the common base for the electoral campaigns of the party in four states, namely Haryana, Himachal Pradesh, West Bengal and Kerala. The national manifesto was supplemented by state-level election manifestos (*Hindustan Times*, 1 May 1982).
55. Farooq Abdullah was the leader of the ruling party, the National Conference. Farooq had replaced his father, Sheikh Abdullah, after his death in September 1982.
56. This is certainly not to say that Mrs Gandhi's decision to modernise India's military equipment was exclusively or even mainly due to the need to appease the middle class. But this is something that the middle class appreciated.
57. This is not to say that the Soviet Union ceased to be an important partner in the field of military cooperation. Indeed, it remained India's most important arms supplier.

58. Virtually every person who has been interviewed pointed this out. See also Prem Shankar Jha's article in Tehelka, 10 September 2011.
59. Further details will be given in chapter 4.
60. Needless to say, this does not apply to the strongest of India's neighbours, namely China.
61. As envisaged by the National Security Act.
62. This does not mean that the modernisation of India's military equipment was undertaken just because Mrs Gandhi wished to please the middle class. There were crucial strategic reasons behind the move, which, however, cannot be covered within the scope of this study.
63. The citation refers to the atomic test in Pokharan in 1974. However, the argument is extendable to the development of the early 1980s just described.
64. This became one of the central themes in the electoral campaign for the Municipality of Delhi. Oddly enough, the construction of new infrastructures in Delhi was used as a campaign theme also in other parts of the country, even in places as far as Karnataka and Andhra Pradesh (*India Today*, 16 January 1983).
65. Again, this does not imply that Mrs Gandhi's foreign policy was dictated by her attempts to appease the middle class. However, the path undertaken was congenial to a middle class view of the world.
66. These did not include the Scheduled Classes and the Scheduled Tribes.
67. In addition to reservations for SC and ST, thus bringing the total amount of places reserved close to 50 per cent. Many states had passed similar legislations in the previous decades.
68. The most famous one was Swamy Dhirendra Brahmachari, a sordid individual involved in all kind of odd manoeuvres, who was granted a virtual immunity because of his long-standing friendship with the Gandhi family. See the report in *India Today* (16 November 1980).
69. In fact, sporadic references to themes that were usually associated with Hindu communal politics occurred even before mid-1982. However, it is after that date that it became a persistent feature of Mrs Gandhi's political strategy.
70. One notable exception, which shows how contradictory Mrs Gandhi's political behaviour was in the early 1980s, was the defence of the Bengali immigrants in Assam.
71. The government of Jammu and Kashmir introduced a bill in the Assembly according to which persons who had left the state and fled to Pakistan in 1947 were allowed to resettle in Jammu and Kashmir (which, in most of the cases meant in the Jammu region).
72. Apparently Mrs Gandhi had discovered Farooq's alleged links with Pakistan and the Jamaat-e-Islami only after the breakdown of the talks with Abdullah's party regarding an electoral alliance in the state (*Economic and Political Weekly*, 28 May 1983).

73. This was at least partially true and quite natural indeed, being that it was in the Kashmir Valley that the National Conference had its stronghold (*India Today*, 1 June 1983).
74. Even though, as explained in private to the Governor of the State, B. K. Nehru, these were purely pre-electoral strategies (B. K. Nehru's Private Papers, letter to Mrs Gandhi dated 27 July 1983, NMML).
75. More details will be provided below.
76. Stephen was one of the AICC(I) general secretaries.
77. This is how the *London Times* once described her.
78. It is quite difficult to compare the results of the state elections in West Bengal, Himachal Pradesh and Haryana with the state elections in the states in 1977. Not only were these elections held in a particular political context, but the Congress was still undivided. In Kerala, where the state elections took place together with the general elections in 1980, results are perhaps more comparable, even though this is a state where regional considerations are even more important than in other states. In 1980 the Congress (I) polled 17.03 per cent in Kerala, whereas in 1982 the percentage fell to 11.9 per cent.
79. We have made sporadic citations to the importance of identity (mainly in terms of caste) politics at the state level. However, at the national level, its importance had always been marginal.
80. The construction of a national Hindu vote has been the subject of extensive research, e.g. Jaffrelot 1996; Hansen 1999; Van Der Veer 1994; Andersen and Damle 1987. All these works have looked at "the saffron wave" (Hansen 1999) of the 1980s, and have described the set of strategies adopted by the RSS network in great detail. What follows relies heavily on these works.
81. See chapter 4 for further details.
82. See Suri (2003, 55) for some qualifications on this argument, mainly due to the lack of reliable empirical evidence.
83. A somewhat similar argument was made by D. L. Sheth in *Seminar*, January 1982.

4. INSTITUTIONS: POLITICISATION, EROSION, AND INFORMALISATION

1. A shorter version of this chapter appeared in *Modern Asian Studies* (Maiorano 2014b).
2. Members of all-India services serve both at the centre and in the states. There are two other all-India services, namely the Indian Police Service (IPS) and the Indian Forest Service (IFoS).
3. In part, this applies to the Supreme Court too. However, the profound difference between the colonial and the democratic state radically changed the nature and the task of the highest court.
4. David Potter (1994, 77) identifies this trend, but, in my opinion, he underestimates the extent to which it transformed the bureaucratic apparatus.

5. Jagmohan would hold several cabinet positions in the 1990s.
6. Further details about this sordid operation can be found in Raghavan and Manor 2009, ch. 7.
7. One of the best accounts of the relationship between Mrs Gandhi and the judiciary is that of Granville Austin (1999).
8. Formally, the clash was between the legislature and the judiciary. However, as we shall see below, the Parliament has never had a high degree of autonomy from the executive.
9. The Directive Principles, contained in Part IV of the Constitution, are guidelines to the central and state governments which should be kept in mind while framing policies.
10. The Fundamental Rights, contained in Part III of the Constitution, is a charter of rights similar to that of most liberal democracies.
11. Of course, this was only part of the problem. Indeed, the fact that the Congress party had the most significant part of its social base in most states among the landowning castes explains to a great extent why the land reform was implemented the way it was.
12. Namely, Justice A. N. Grover, Justice K. S. Hegde and Justice J. M. Shelat.
13. Law Minister H. R. Gokhale even threatened the Supreme Court in Parliament, see Noorani 1994, 106.
14. The note is reproduced in Noorani 1994, 108.
15. From the Bar Council of India's reply to the government press note, reproduced in Noorani 1994, 109.
16. The word "relatively" needs to be stressed here. Especially in times of political crisis, the President of the Republic can and indeed must play a decisive role, as it happened in India during the period of political instability post-1989, or as it happened in this author's country (Italy) during the severe political and economic crisis in late 2011.
17. MPs' fear of being arrested surely played a role.
18. Reddy had been chosen by the Congress to be the party's candidate for the presidency in 1969, but Mrs Gandhi decided instead to back V. V. Giri in the course of the dramatic struggle for power between her and the "Syndicate", which eventually led to the split of the party. Zareer Masani (1975) and Inder Malhotra (1989) have provided two richly detailed accounts of this episode.
19. The central government backed another piece of legislation introduced in the Orissa Legislative Assembly—controlled by the Congress (I)—which threatened to subject newspapers to the will of the state government, see (Alva 1982).
20. The following brief summary of the debate is largely drawn from Noorani 1989 and Austin 1999.
21. It later turned out that the author was A. R. Antulay.
22. We have seen above how Baharul Islam was appointed to the Supreme Court.

23. He made the same proposition at the Press Club of Calcutta few days before Mrs Gandhi's assassination. The full text of his address is reproduced in Noorani 1989, Appendix IV.
24. Indeed, this is the view of most of the observers this author has spoken with in Delhi in late 2010–early 2011. Interviewees included Sir Mark Tully, Prem Shankar Jha, Inder Malhotra, George Verghese, and Subhash Agrawal. Politicians who were close to Mrs Gandhi also denied there was any plan to change the constitution on the eve of the elections (interviews with Vasant Sathe, Bishma Narain Singh, and Natwar Singh).
25. These were K. Ramamurthi, a Congress (I) member from Tamil Nadu, and Gulam Rasool Kar, a Congress (I) member in Jammu and Kashmir.
26. Namely, Assam, Bihar, Gujarat, Madhya Pradesh, Maharashtra, Orissa, Rajasthan and Uttar Pradesh.
27. In Sikkim, President's Rule was imposed.
28. Some analysts call India a "quasi-federal" polity, while others even deny its federal character: for some references see Bagchi 2003 or Verney 1995.
29. What follows is by no means a comprehensive list of the constitutional provisions which shaped Indian federalism. Our attention will be limited to those provisions that made the federal structure flexible and unbalanced in favour of the Union government.
30. The Tamil Nadu and Andhra Pradesh governments proposed the abolition of the governors in the late 1980s (Sarkaria 1988, ch. 4).
31. In 1969, following the states' protests, the Planning Commission adopted the Gadgil formula as the basis for the distribution of plan resources to the states [This is obviously a significant change, but it tells the reader very little—who was Gadgil, what was his formula, how did it change plan allocations, and where should we look for details?].
32. The NDC was supposed to meet twice a year. However, between 1952 and 1989, it met only 39 times.
33. The Janata Party had set the precedent in 1977 when it dismissed nine Congress-led state assemblies, on the ground that, having the people badly rejected Mrs Gandhi at the centre, her party was not legitimised to govern in the states. The Supreme Court had endorsed this view. On the Janata Party's defence, one could argue that the post-emergency context was completely different from that of early 1980.
34. The Punjab case reached the national press. However, as many former bureaucrats told this writer, many other instances occurred.
35. President's Rule was imposed from December 1979 to December 1980; from June 1981 to January 1982; and from March 1982 to February 1983.
36. I am not suggesting that revising the electoral rolls would have solved all problems in Assam or that detecting foreigners would have been easy or even feasi-

ble. Rather, I am arguing that revising the electoral rolls or at least trying to do so would have eased the tension and perhaps the 1983 bloodbath would have been avoided.

37. Jats constituted nearly 20 per cent of the population, but they owned about 60 per cent of the arable land in the state (Puri 1983).
38. Several versions of the resolution exist. In 1982, Sant Longowal endorsed one of these, which is reproduced in Nayar and Singh (1984, annexure A).
39. This had been promised by Mrs Gandhi as early as 1969, when Sant Fateh Singh, an Akali Dal faction leader, threatened to burn himself to death if Chandigarh was not handed over to Punjab (Tully and Jacob 1985, 51).
40. From the name of its chairman, former Justice Rajinder Singh Sarkaria.
41. The appointment of a Sikh as the chairman of the commission was probably not accidental.
42. The other members of the commission were former Cabinet secretary and IAS member B. Sivaraman and former member of the Planning Commission S. R. Sen.
43. The statements presented at the Srinagar meeting were published in 1984 [Srinagar 1984].
44. See Bose 2003, ch. 2 for further details.
45. As the Jammu and Kashmir version of President's Rule is called. In practical terms, little changes.
46. A *dharna* is a non-violent sit-in protest.
47. The Congress (I) government in Sikkim lasted about two weeks, after which President's Rule was imposed.
48. i.e. the 52th Amendment to the Constitution.

CONCLUSION

1. Law and order was by and large restored on 3rd November, when the army was deployed and curfew enforced.
2. These include ten government commissions (for details see the introduction to the Nanavati Commission 2005 Report). Civil Society reports include Ensaaf 2006; PUCL 1984; CFD 1985.
3. In what is the other major pogrom in India's independent history, the anti-Muslim riots in Gujarat in 2002, Narendra Modi, Chief Minister of Gujarat at that time, has so far refused to offer an apology.
4. http://loksabha.adrindia.org/lok-sabha/analysis-assets-comparison-re-contesting-MPs-in-the-2014-lok-sabha-elections accessed on 28 May 2014.
5. i.e. those ministries (like Mining or Telecommunications, for example) where it is easier to extract bribes from businessmen in exchange for permits.
6. The attention that the anti-corruption movement led by Anna Hazare in 2011

and the Aam Admi Party led by Arvind Kejriwal managed to get is a clear sign of the growing pressure from below on this issue.

7. The Communist parties that were in power in West Bengal and Kerala, although officially recognised as national parties, function as regional formations for all practical pursposes.

BIBLIOGRAPHICAL REFERENCES

Official Documents and Reports

2FYP Planning Commission: Second Five-Year Plan, 1956–1961.

3FYP Planning Commission: Third Five-Year Plan, 1961–1966.

4FYP Planning Commission: Fourth Five-Year Plan, 1969–1974.

5FYP Planning Commission: Fifth Five-Year Plan, 1974–1979.

D6FYP Planning Commission: Draft Sixth Five-Year Plan, 1978–1983.

6FYP Planning Commission: Sixth Five-Year Plan, 1980–1985.

7FYP Planning Commission: Seventh Five-Year Plan, 1985–1990.

Budget Speech, 1977–1986: Ministry of Finance.

Census 1981: Government of India.

Constitution of India.

Election Commission of India—Statistical Report, all-India and States reports 1971–1987: http://eci.nic.in/eci_main1/ElectionStatistics.aspx (ECI), last accessed 4 September 2014.

Economic Survey 1979–1986: Ministry of Finance.

ESMA 1981: Essential Services Maintenance Act, 1981.

LS: Parliament of India 1985: The Seventh Lok Sabha, 1980–84. New Delhi: Lok Sabha Secretariat.

MOA 1987: Ministry of Agriculture, *Concurrent Evaluation of IRDP: The Main Findings of the Survey for October 1985-September 1986*, New Delhi.

MHA: Ministry of Home Affairs Annual Report 1979–1984.

Nanavati Commission 2005: *Justice Nanavati Commission of Inquiry Report—The anti-sikh riots 1984*, Submitted to the Ministry of Home Affairs in August 2005, New Delhi.

RBI: Reserve Bank of India 2009: *Handbook of Statistics on the Indian Economy*, Mumbai.

Sarkaria 1988: Report of the Sarkaria Commission on Centre-State Relations. 1988.

World Bank 1999: *India—Reducing Poverty, Accelerating Development*. New Delhi: Oxford University Press.

Party and Civil Society Organisation Documents

AICC 1983a: All India Congress (I) Committee, Resolutions—20–21 October 1983, Bombay.

AICC 1983b: All India Congress (I) Committee, Political resolution Calcutta 1983 (77th plenary session).

Anandpur 1982: Akali Dal, Anandpur Resolution as endorsed by Sant Longowal, 1982.

CFD 1985: Citizens for Democracy, *The truth about Delhi violence: Report to the Nation*, New Delhi, 1985.

CIM 1980: Congress (I) Election Manifesto 1980.

CIM 1982: Congress (I) National Electoral Manifesto for the Haryana, Himachal Pradesh, West Bengal and Kerala state elections, 1982.

ENSAAF 2006: Jaskaran Kaur, *Twenty Years of Impunity*, October 2006.

JPM 1980: Janata Party Election Manifesto 1980.

LDM 1980: Lok Dal Election Manifesto 1980.

PUCL 1984: People's Union for Democratic Rights and People's Union for Civic Liberties, Delhi—*Who are the Guilty?*, Delhi.

Srinagar 1984: Collection of Statements presented at the Srinagar Meeting 5–6–7th Oct. 1983.

Private Papers held at Nehru Memorial Museum and Library (NMML)

B. K. Nehru

Gopal Singh

Interviews cited in the text

Bishma Narain Singh, New Delhi, 16 January 2011.

George Verghese, New Delhi, 17 January 2011.

Inder Malhotra, New Delhi, 16 December 2010.

Mark Tully, New Delhi, 10 December 2010.

Col. Mohan Kaktikar, New Delhi, 27 January 2011.

Naresh Chandra, New Delhi, 14 December 2010.

Natwar Singh, New Delhi, 20 January 2011.

Prem Shankar Jha, New Delhi, 2 December 2010.

Salman Haider, New Delhi, 24 January 2011.

S. K. Mishra, New Delhi, 21 December 2010.

Subash Agrawal, New Delhi, 17 November 2010.

Vasant Sathe, New Delhi, 11 December 2010.

Yogendra Yadav, New Delhi, 4 February 2011.

BIBLIOGRAPHICAL REFERENCES

Newspapers and Periodicals

Blitz, Bombay.
BBC News (www.bbc.com/news).
The Economist, London.
Economic and Political Weekly, Bombay.
Hindustan Times, New Delhi.
Indian Express, New Delhi.
India Today, New Delhi and Bombay.
Illustrated Weekly of India, Bombay.
New York Times, New York.
Outlook, Chennai.
Seminar, New Delhi.
Tehelka, New Delhi.
The Asian Age, New Delhi.
The Hindu, Chennai.
The Tribune, Chandigarh
Time, New York
Times of India, New Delhi and Bombay.

Books and Articles

Adeney, Katharine. 2007. *Federalism and Conflict Regulation in India and Pakistan*. New York: Palgrave.

Ahluwalia, M. S. 2002. 'Economic Reforms in India Since 1991: Has Gradualism Worked'. *Journal of Economic Perspectives* 16 (3).

Akbar, M. J. 1985. *India: The Siege Within*. Harmondsworth: Penguin.

Ali, Ifzal, B. M. Desai, R. Ramakrishna, and V. S. Vyas. 1981. 'Indian Agriculture at 2000—Strategies for Equity'. *Economic and Political Weekly* 16 (10/12), Annual Number.

Alva, Chittaranjan. 1982. 'What the Bihar Press Bill Means'. *Social Scientist* 10 (12).

Andersen, Walter K. 1982. 'India in 1981: Stronger Political Authority and Social Tension'. *Asian Survey* 22 (2).

Andersen, Walter K. and Shridhar D. Damle. 1987. *The Brotherhood in Saffron—The Rashtriya Swayamsevak Sangh and Hindu Revivalism*. New Delhi: Vistaar Publications.

Appadurai, A. 1996. *Modernity at Large: Cultural Dimension of Globalization*. Minneapolis: University of Minnesota Press.

Arora, Balveer. 1983. 'Political Control Over Administration in a Federal Context'. In R. B. Jain (ed.), *Public Services in a Democratic Context*. New Delhi: Indian Institute of Public Administration.

———. 1995. 'Adapting Federalism to India: Multilevel and Asymmetrical

Innovations'. In Balveer Arora and Douglas V. Verney (eds), *Multiple Identities in a Single State: Indian Federalism in Comparative Perspective*. New Delhi: Konark Publishers.

Austin, Granville. 1996. *The Indian Constitution: Cornerstone of a Nation*. New Delhi: Oxford University Press.

———. 1999. *Working a democratic constitution: A history of the Indian experience*. New Delhi: Oxford University Press.

Bagchi, Amaresh. 2003. 'Rethinking Federalism: Changing Power Relations between the Center and the States'. *Publius* 33 (4).

Banaji, Jairus. 1995. 'The Farmers' Movements: A Critique of Conservative Rural Coalitions'. In Tom Brass (ed.), *New Farmers' Movement in India*. Ilford: Frank Cass.

Bardhan, Pranab. 1998. *The Political Economy of Development in India*. New Delhi: Oxford University Press.

Baru, Sanjaya. 1995. 'Continuity and Change in Indian Industrial Policy'. In T. V. Sathyamurthy (ed.), *Industry and Agriculture in India since Independence*. Oxford: Oxford University Press.

Baruah, Sanjib. 1986. 'Immigration, Ethnic Conflict, and Political Turmoil: Assam, 1979–1985'. *Asian Survey* 26 (11).

———. 1999. *India Against Itself: Assam and the Politics of Nationality*. Philadelphia: University of Pennsylvania Press.

Bayly, C. A. 1985. 'The Pre-History of "Communalism"?—Religious Conflict in India, 1700–1860'. *Modern Asian Studies* 19 (2).

Bhargava, P. K. 1984. 'Transfers from the center to the states in India'. *Asian Survey* (24) 6.

Bhatia, B. M. 1994. *India's Middle Class: Role in Nation Building*. New Delhi: Konark Publishers.

Bhattacharya B. B. 1979. 'Union Budget, 1979–80'. *Economic and Political Weekly* 14 (14).

Blair, Harry W. 1980. 'Rising Kulaks and Backward Classes in Bihar—Social Change in the Late 1970s'. *Economic and Political Weekly* 15 (2).

Bose, Sumantra. 1997. *The Challenge in Kashmir: Democracy, Self-determination, and a Just Peace*. New Delhi: Sage.

———. 2003. *Kashmir: Roots of Conflict, Paths to Peace*. Cambridge (Massachusetts): Harvard University Press.

Brass, Paul R. 1981. 'Congress, the Lok Dal, and the Middle-Peasant Castes: An Analysis of the 1977 and 1980 Parliamentary Elections in Uttar Pradesh'. *Pacific Affairs* 54 (1).

———. 1984a. 'National Power and Local Politics in India: A Twenty-Year Perspective'. *Modern Asian Studies* 18 (1).

———. 1984b. *Caste, Faction and Party in Indian Politics—Vol. 1*. New Delhi: Chanakya Publications.

———. 1985. *Caste, Faction and Party in Indian Politics—Vol. 2*. New Delhi: Chanakya Publications.

Brass, Paul 1997: *The Politics of India since Independence*. Cambridge: Cambridge University Press.

Brass, Tom (ed.). 1995. *New Farmers' Movement in India*. Ilford: Frank Cass.

Byres, Terence J. 1981. 'The new technology, class formation and class action in the Indian countryside'. *Journal of Peasant Studies* 8 (4).

———. 1988. 'Charan Singh, 1902–87: An assessment'. *Journal of Peasant Studies* 15 (2).

Calman, Leslie J. 1989. 'Women and Movement Politics in India'. *Asian Survey* 29 (10).

Chandra, Bipan, Mridula Mukherjee, and Aditya Mukherjee. 2008. *India Since Independence*. New Delhi: Penguin Books.

Chandrashekar, C. P. and Jayati Ghosh. 2002. *The Market that Failed: A Decade of Neoliberal Economic Reforms in India*. New Delhi: Leftword.

Chhibber, Pradeep K. 2013. 'Dynastic Parties: Organization, Finance, Impact'. In *Party Politics* 19 (2).

Chhibber, Pradeep K. and John R. Petrocik. 1990. 'Social Cleavages, Elections, and the Indian Party System'. In Richard Sisson and Ramashray Roy (eds), *Diversity and Dominance in Indian Politics. Volume 1: Changing Bases of Congress Support*. New Delhi: Sage.

Chaudhry, Praveen K., Vihay L. Kelkar, and Vikash Yadav. 2004. 'The Evolution of "Homegrown Conditionality" in India–IMF Relations'. *The Journal of Development Studies* 40 (6).

Clibbens, Patrick. 2013. '"The Destiny of this city is to be the spiritual workshop of the nation": clearing cities and making citizens during the Indian Emergency, 1975–77'. *Contemporary South Asia* 22 (1).

Corbridge, Stuart and John Harris. 2000. *Reinventing India: Liberalization, Hindu Nationalism and Popular Democracy*. Cambridge: Blackwell.

Damodaran, Harish. 2008. *India's new Capitalists: Caste, Business and Industry in a Modern Nation*. Basingstoke: Palgrave MacMillan.

Dasgupta, Jotirindra Das. 1979. 'The Janata Phase: Reorganization and Redirection in Indian Politics'. *Asian Survey* 19 (4).

———. 1980. 'India in 1979—The Prize Chair and the People's Share—Electoral Diversion and Economic Reversal'. *Asian Survey* 20 (2).

———. 1981. 'India in 1980—Strong Centre, Weak Authority'. *Asian Survey* 21 (2).

———. 2002. 'The Janata Phase: Reorganization and Redirection in Indian Politics'. In Zoya Hasan (ed.), *Parties and Party Politics in India*. New Delhi: Oxford University Press.

De Janvry, Alain and K. Subbarao. 1986. *Agricultural Price Policy and Income Distribution in India*. Delhi: Oxford University Press.

Dhanagare, D. N. 1995. 'The Class Character and Politics of the Farmers' Movement In Maharashtra during the 1980s'. In Tom Brass (ed.), *New Farmers' Movement in India*. Ilford: Frank Cass.

Dreze, Jean. 1990. 'Poverty in India and the IRDP Delusion'. *Economic and Political Weekly* 25 (39).

Dreze, Jean and Amartya Sen. 2013. *An Uncertain Glory: India and Its Contradictions*. New Delhi: Allen Lane

Dua, Bhagwan D. 1979. 'Presidential Rule in India: A Study in Crisis Politics'. In *Asian Survey* 19 (6).

———. 1985. 'Federalism or Patrimonialism: The Making and Unmaking of Chief Ministers in India'. *Asian Survey* 25 (8)

Dubey, Suman. 1992. 'The Middle Class'. In Leonard Gordon and Philip Oldenburg (eds), *India Briefing, 1992*. Oxford: Westview.

Engineer, Ashgar Ali. 1981. 'Biharsharif Carnage: a Field Report'. *Economic and Political Weekly* 16 (20).

Fernandes, Leela. 2006. *India's New Middle Class: Democratic Politics in an Era of Economic Reform*. Minneapolis: University of Minnesota Press.

Frank, Katherine. 2001. *Indira: The Life of Indira Nehru Gandhi*. London: Harper Collins Publishers.

Frankel, Francine R. 1971. *India's Green Revolution: Economic Gains and Political Costs*. Princeton: Princeton University Press.

———. 1988. 'Middle Classes and Castes in India's Politics: Prospects for Political Accommodation'. In Atul Kohli (ed.), *India's Democracy: An Analysis of Changing State-Society Relations*. Princeton: Princeton University Press.

———. 1989. 'Dominance in Bihar: Breakdown of the Brahmanical Social Order'. In Francine R. Frankel and M. S. A. Rao (eds), *Dominance and State Power in Modern India, Vol. 1*. New Delhi: Oxford University Press.

———. 2005. *India's Political Economy 1947–2004: The Gradual Revolution*. New Delhi: Oxford University Press.

Frankel, Francine R. and M. S. A. Rao (eds.) 1989. *Dominance and State Power in Modern India, Vol. 1*. New Delhi: Oxford University Press.

———. 1990. *Dominance and State Power in Modern India, Vol. 2*. New Delhi: Oxford University Press.

Gaiha, Raghav. 2000. 'Do Anti-poverty Programmes Reach the Rural Poor in India?' *Oxford Development Studies* 28 (1).

Gill, S. S. 1997. *The Dynasty: A Political Biography of the Premier Ruling Family of Modern India*. New Delhi: Harper Collins.

Gowda, M. V. Rajeev and E. Sridharan. 2010. 'Reforming India's Party Financing and Election Expenditure Laws'. *Election Law Journal* 11 (2).

Graff, Violette. 1990. 'Aligarh's Long Quest for 'Minority' Status: AMU (Amendment) Act'. *Economic and Political Weekly* 25 (32).

Guha, Ramachandra. 2007. *India after Gandhi*. London: Macmillan.

Guhan, S. 1980. 'Rural Poverty: Policy and Play Acting'. *Economic and Political Weekly* 15 (47).

Hansen, Thomas Blom. 1999. *The Saffron Wave: Democracy and Hindu Nationalism in Modern India*. Princeton: Princeton University Press.

Hara Gopal, G. and C. H. Bala Rumulu. 1989. 'Poverty Alleviation Programmes: IRDP in an Andhra Pradesh District'. *Economic and Political Weekly* 24 (35–36).

Hardgrave, Robert L. Jr. 1985. 'India in 1984: Confrontation, Assassination and Succession'. *Asian Survey* 25 (2).

Hardgrave, Robert L. Jr., and Stanley A. Kochanek. 2008 [1980]. *India: Government and Politics in a Developing Nation*. Boston: Thomson Wadsworth Publishing.

Hart, Henry C. (ed.) 1976. *Indira Gandhi's India: A Political System Reappraised*. Boulder: Westview Press.

Hasan, Zoya. 1989. 'Power and Mobilization: Patterns of Resilience and Change in Uttar Pradesh Politics'. In Francine R. Frankel and M. S. A. Rao (eds), *Dominance and State Power in Modern India, Vol. 1*. Delhi: Oxford University Press.

———. 1995. 'Shifting Ground: Hindutva Politics and the Farmers' Movement in Uttar Pradesh'. In Tom Brass (ed.), *New Farmers' Movement in India*. Ilford: Frank Cass.

Hazarika, Sanjoy. 2000. *Rites of Passage: Border Crossings, Imagined Homelands, India's East and Bangladesh*. New Delhi: Penguin Books.

Jaffrelot, Christophe. 1996. *The Hindu Nationalist Movement and Indian Politics: 1925 to the 1990s*. London: Hurst & Co.

———. 2003. *India's Silent Revolution: The Rise of the Lower Castes in North India*. London: Hurst & Co.

Jayakar, Pupul. 1995. *Indira Gandhi: A Biography*. New Delhi: Penguin Books

Jeffrey, Robin. 1986. *What's Happening to India?: Punjab, Ethnic Conflict, Mrs Gandhi's Death and the Test for Federalism*. London: MacMillan.

Jha, Prem Shankar. 1993. *In the Eye of the Cyclone: The Crisis in Indian Democracy*. New Delhi: Viking.

Joshi, Vijay and I. M. D. Little. 1994. *India: Macroeconomics and Political Economy, 1964–9*. Washington: World Bank.

Katju, Manjari. 2003. *Vishwa Hindu Parishad and Indian Politics*. New Delhi: Orient Longman Limited.

Kashyap, Subhash C. 1970. 'The Politics of Defection: The Changing Contours of Political Power Structure in State Politics in India'. *Asian Survey* 10 (3).

Kaviraj, Sudipta. 1984. 'On the Crisis of Political Institutions in India'. *Contributions to Indian Sociology* 18 (2).

———. 1988. 'A Critique of the Passive Revolution'. In Partha Chatterjee (ed.), *State and Politics in India*. New Delhi: Oxford University Press.

Khilnani, Sunil. 1997. *The Idea of India*. London: Hamish Hamilton.

Kochanek, Stanley A. 1987. 'Briefcase Politics in India: The Congress Party and the Business Elite'. *Asian Survey* 27 (12).

———. 2002. 'Mrs Gandhi's Pyramid: The New Congress'. In Zoya Hasan (ed.), *Parties and Party Politics in India*. New Delhi: Oxford University Press.

Kohli, Atul. 1988. 'The NTR Phenomenon in Andhra Pradesh: Political Change in a South Indian State'. *Asian Survey* 28 (10).

———. 1990a. 'From Elite Activism to Democratic Consolidation: The Rise of Reform Communism in West Bengal'. In Francine Frankel and M. S. A. Rao (eds), *Dominance and State Power in Modern India: Decline of a Social Order, Vol. 2*. Delhi: Oxford University Press.

———. 1990b. *Democracy and Discontent: India's Growing Crisis of Governability*. Cambridge: Cambridge University Press.

———. 2004. *State-Directed Development: Political Power and Industrialization in the Global Periphery*. Cambridge: Cambridge University Press.

———. 2006. 'Politics of Economic Growth in India, 1980–2005—Part I: The 1980s'. *Economic and Political Weekly* 41 (13).

Kothari, Rajni. 1964. 'The Congress 'System' in India'. *Asian Survey* 4 (12).

———. 1970a. 'Continuity and Change in India's Party System'. *Asian Survey* 10 (11).

———. 1970b. *Politics in India*. Boston: Little Brown.

———. 1988. 'Integration and Exclusion in Indian Politics'. *Economic and Political Weekly* 23 (43).

———. 1997. 'Rise of the *Dalits* and the Renewed Debate on Caste'. In P. Chatterjee (ed.), *State and Politics in India*. Delhi: Oxford University Press.

Krishnan, K. P. and T. V. Somanathan. 2005. 'Civil Service: An Institutional Perspective'. In Devesh Kapur and Pratab Bhanu Mehta, (eds), *Public Institutions in India: Performance and Design*. New Delhi: Oxford University Press.

Kurian, N. G. 1989. 'Anti-Poverty Programme: A Reappraisal'. *Economic and Political Weekly* 24 (12).

Lele, Jayant. 1990. 'Caste, CLass and Dominance: Political Mobilization in Maharashtra'. In Francine Frankel and M. S. A. Rao (eds), *Dominance and State Power in Modern India, Vol. 2*. New Delhi: Oxford University Press.

Lijphart, A. 1996. 'The Puzzle of India's Democracy: A Consociational Interpretation'. *American Political Science Review* 90 (2).

Mahendra Dev, S. and N. Chandrasekhara Rao. 2009. *Agricultural Price Policy, Farm Profitability and Food Security: An Analysis of Rice and Wheat*. Delhi: Commission for Agricultural Costs and Prices.

Maiorano, Diego. 2012. 'Mrs. Gandhi's Final Term and the Remaking of the Congress (I)'s Social Base'. *India Review* 11 (1).

———. 2014a. 'Continuity amid Change in India's Political Economy from 1980 to 2004'. *Economic and Political Weekly* 49 (9).

———. 2014b. 'Indian Institutions in the early 1980s: the pre-history of the Great Transformation'. *Modern Asian Studies* 48 (5): pp. 1389–1434.

Malhotra, Inder. 1989. *Indira Gandhi: A Personal and Political Biography*. London: Hodder and Stoughton.

Malik, Yogendra. 1988. 'Indira Gandhi: Personality, Political Power and Party Politics'. In Yogendra K. Malik and Dhirendhra K. Vajpeyi (eds), *India: The Years of Indira Gandhi*. Leiden: E. J. Brill.

Manor, James. 1978. 'Where the Congress Survived. Five States in the Indian General Election of 1977'. *Asian Survey* 18 (8).

———. 1981. 'Party Decay and Political Crisis in India'. *The Washington Quarterly* 4 (3).

———. 1983a. 'The Electoral Process amid Awakening and Decay: Reflections on the Indian General Election of 1980'. In P. Lyon and J. Manor (eds), *Transfer and Transformation: Political Institutions in the New Commonwealth*. Leicester and New York: Leicester University Press.

———. 1983b. 'Anomie in Indian Politics—Origins and Potential Wider Impact'. *Economic and Political Weekly* 18 (19/21) Annual Number: pp. 725–34.

———. 1984. 'Blurring the Lines between Parties and Social Bases—Gundu Rao and Emergence of a Janata Government in Karnataka'. *Economic and Political Weekly* 19 (37): pp. 1623–1632.

———. 1989. 'Karnataka: Caste, Class, Dominance and Politics in a Cohesive Society'. In Francine Frankel and M. S. A. Rao (eds), *Dominance and State Power in Modern India, Vol. 1*. New Delhi: Oxford University Press.

———. 1994. 'The Prime Minister and The President'. In James Manor (ed.) *Nehru to the Nineties: The Changing Office of Prime Minister in India*. London: Hurst & Co.

———. 1997. 'Parties and the Party System'. In Partha Chatterjee (ed.), *State and Politics in India*. New Delhi: Oxford University Press.

———. 2001. 'Centre-State Relations'. In Atul Kohli (ed.), *The Success of India's Demcoracy*. Cambridge: Cambridge University Press.

———. 2005. 'The Presidency'. In Devesh Kapur and Pratab Bhanu Mehta (eds), *Public Institutions in India: Performance and Design*. New Delhi: Oxford University Press.

———. 2010. 'What Do They Know of India Who Only India Know? The Uses of Comparative Politics'. *Commonwealth and Comparative Politics* 48 (4).

Marwah, Ved. 1995. Use and Abuse of Emergency Powers: The Indian Experience'. In Balveer Arora and Douglas V. Verney (eds), *Multiple Identities in a Single State: Indian Federalism in Comparative Perspective*. New Delhi: Konark Publishers.

Masani, Zareer. 1975. *Indira Gandhi: A Biography*. New Delhi: Oxford University Press.

Mehta, Pratap Bhanu. 2005. 'India's Judiciary: The Promise of Uncertainty'. In Devesh Kapur and Pratab Bhanu Mehta (eds), *Public Institutions in India: Performance and Design*. New Delhi: Oxford University Press.

Minhas, B. S., L. R. Jain, and S.D. Tendulkar. 1991. 'Declining Incidence of Poverty in the 1980s—Evidence versus Artefacts'. *Economic and Political Weekly* 26 (27–28).

Mirchandani, G. C. 1980. *The People's Verdict*. New Delhi: Vikas Publishing House.

Misra, V. N. and Peter B. R. Hazell. 1996. 'Terms of Trade, Rural Poverty, Technology and Investment—The Indian Experience, 1952–53 to 1990–91'. *Economic and Political Weekly* 31 (13).

Mohanty, Manoranjan. 1990. 'Class, Caste and Dominance in a Backward State: Orissa'. In Francine Frankel and M. S. A. Rao (eds), *Dominance and State Power in Modern India: Decline of a Social Order, Vol. 2*. New Delhi: Oxford University Press.

Morris-Jones, W. H. 1957. *The Parliament in India*. London: Longmans Green.

———. 1971. *The Government and Politics of India*. London: Hutchinson & Co.

———. 1978a. 'From Monopoly to Competition in India's Politics'. In W. H. Morris-Jones, *Politics Mainly Indian*. Bombay: Orient Longman.

———. 1978b. 'Dominance and Dissent: Their Interrelations in the Indian Party System'. In W. H. Morris-Jones, *Politics Mainly Indian*. Bombay: Orient Longman.

———. 1985. 'India after Indira: A Tale of Two Legacies'. *Third World Quarterly* 7 (2).

Mozoomdar, Ajit. 1995. 'The Supreme Court and President's Rule'. In Balveer Arora and Douglas V. Verney (eds), *Multiple Identities in a Single State*. Delhi: Konark.

Nadkarni, Mangesh Venktesh. 1987. *Farmers' Movements in India*. Ahmedabad: Allied Publishers.

Nagaraj, R. 2000. 'Indian Economy since 1980—Virtuous Growth or Polarisation?'. *Economic and Politcal Weekly* 35 (32).

Nandy, Ashis. 1988. 'The Political Culture of the Indian State'. *Daedalus* 118 (4).

Nayar, Kuldip and Khushwant Singh. 1984. *Tragedy of Punjab: Operation Bluestar and After*. New Delhi: Vision Books.

Noorani, A. G. 1989. *The Presidential System: The Indian Debate*. New Delhi: Sage Publications.

———. 1994. 'The Prime Minister and the Judiciary'. In James Manor (ed.) *Nehru to the Nineties: The Changing Office of Prime Minister in India*. London: Hurst & Co.

Pai, Sudha. 2011. 'The Congress Party and Six National Elections 1964–1984'. In Pranab Mukherjee and Aditya Mukherjee (eds), *A Centenary History of the Indian National Congress—Vol. V: 1964–1984*. New Delhi: Academic Foundation.

Palshikar, Suhas. 2004. 'Revisiting State Level Parties'. *Economic and Political Weekly* 39 (14/15).

Panagariya, Arvind. 2008. *India: The Emerging Giant*. New York: Oxford University Press.

Potter, David. 1994. 'The Prime Minister and the Bureaucracy'. In James Manor (ed.), *Nehru to the Nineties: The Changing Office of Prime Minister in India*. London: Hurst & Co.

Puri, Harish K. 1983. 'The Akali Agitation, an Analysis of Socio-Economic Bases of Protest'. *Economic and Political Weekly* 18 (4).

Raghavan, E. and James Manor. 2009. *Broadening and Deepening Democracy: Political Innovation in Karnataka*. New Delhi: Routledge.

Rajagopal, Arvind. 2011. 'The Emergency as Prehistory of the New Indian Middle Class'. *Modern Asian Studies* 45 (5).

Raj Narain, Baldev. 1975. *Violence and Crime in India: A Quantitative Study*. New Delhi: Macmillan.

———. 2006. 'When Did the "Hindu" Growth End?' *Economic and Political Weekly* 41 (19).

Randall, Vicky and Lars Svåsand. 2002. 'Party Institutionalization in New Democracies'. *Party Politics* 8 (2).

Rath, Nilakantha. 1985. '"Garibi Hatao": Can IRDP Do It?'. *Economic and Political Weekly* 20 (6).

Ray, Amal and John Kincaid. 1988. 'Politics, Economic Development, and Second-Generation Strain in India's Federal System'. *Publius* 18 (2).

Reddy, G. Ram. 1989. 'The Politics of Accomodation: Caste, Class and Dominance in Andhra Pradesh'. In Francine Frankel and M. S. A. Rao (eds), *Dominance and State Power in Modern India, Vol. 1*. New Delhi: Oxford University Press.

Rodrik, Dani and Arvind Subramanian. 2004. 'From "Hindu Growth" to Productivity Surge: The Mistery of the Indian Growth Transition'. IMF Working Paper.

Rudolph, Lloyd I. and Susanne Hoeber Rudolph. 1987. *In Pursuit of Lakshmi: the Political Economy of the Indian State*. Chicago: University of Chicago Press.

———. 2001. 'Redoing the constitutional design: from an interventionist to a regulatory state'. In Atul Kohli (ed.), *The Success of India's Democracy*. New York: Cambridge University Press.

Sahgal, Nayantara. 1978. *Indira Gandhi's Emergence and Style*. New Delhi: Vikas Publishing House.

Sathyamurthy, T. V. 1997. 'Impact of Centre-State Relations on Indian politics: An Interpretative Reckoning 1947–87'. In Partha Chatterjee (ed.), *State and Politics in India*. New Delhi: Oxford University Press.

Saxena, N. C. 2010. 'The IAS Officer—Predator or Victim?' *Commonwealth and Comparative Politics* 48 (4).

Schofield, Victoria. 2003. *Kashmir in Conflict: India, Pakistan and the Unending War*. London: I. B. Tauris.

Shah, Ghanshyam. 1987. 'Middle Class Politics Case of Anti-Reservation Agitations in Gujarat'. *Economic and Political Weekly* 22 (19/21), Annual Number.

Sheth, D. L. 1999. 'Secularisation of Caste and Making of New Middle Class'. *Economic and Political Weekly* 34 (34–35).

Shourie, Arun. 1983. *Mrs Gandhi's Second Reign*. New Delhi: Vikas Publishing House.

Singh, Charan. 1959. *Joint Farming X-rayed: The Problem and its Solution*. Bombay: Bharatiya Vidya Bhavan.

Singh, M. P. 1990. 'Patterns of Recruitment, Strategies of Mobilisation and Inter-Party Alignments'. In Richard Sisson and Ramashray Roy (eds), *Diversity and Dominance in Indian Politics. Volume 1: Changing Bases of Congress Support*. New Delhi: Sage.

Singh, M. P. and Douglas V. Verney. 2003. 'Challenges to India's Centralized Parliamentary Federalism'. *Publius* 33 (4).

Singh, Nihal. 1982. *My India*. New Delhi: Vikas Publishing House.

Singh, Tavleen. 1995. *Kashmir: A Tragedy of Errors*. New Delhi: Viking.

———. 2012. *Durbar*. New Delhi: Hachette India.

Sridharan, E. 2002: The Fragmentation of the Indian Party System 1952–1999. In Zoya Hasan (ed.), *Parties and Party Politics in India*. New Delhi: Oxford University Press.

Sridharan, E. 2003. 'Coalitions and Party Strategies in India's Parliamentary Federation'. *Publius* 33 (4).

———. 2004. 'The Growth and Sectorial Composition of India's Middle Class: Its Impact on the Politics of Economic Liberalization'. *India Review* 3 (4).

Subbarao, K. 1985. 'Regional Variations in Impact of Anti-Poverty Programmes—A Review of Evidence'. *Economic and Political Weekly* 20 (43).

Suri, K. C. 2003. 'Andhra Pradesh: From Populism to Pragmatism'. *Journal of Indian School of Political Economy* 15 (1&2).

Swaminathan, Madhura. 1990. 'Village Level Implementation of IRDP: Comparison of West Bengal and Tamil Nadu'. *Economic and Political Weekly* 25 (13).

Telford, Hamish. 1992. 'The Political Economy of Punjab: Creating Space for Sikh Militancy'. *Asian Survey* 32 (11).

Torri, Michelguglielmo. 1974. 'Economic Policy and Political Gains: The First Phase of India's Green Revolution (1966–1971)'. *Asian Studies* 2 (3)

———. 1975. 'Factional Politics and Economic Policy: The Case of India's Bank Nationalization'. *Asian Survey* 15 (12).

———. 2007. *Storia dell'India*. Bari: Laterza.

Tully, Mark and Satish Jacob. 1985. *Amritsar, Mrs Gandhi's Last Battle*. London: Jonathan Cape

Tummala, Krishna K. 1986. 'Democracy Triumphant in India: The Case of Andhra Pradesh'. *Asian Survey* 26 (3).

Vanaik, Achin. 1990. *The Painful Transition: Bourgeois Democracy in India*. London and New York: Verso.

Van Der Veer, Peter. 1994. *Religious Nationalism: Hindus and Muslims in India*. Berkley: University of California Press.

Varma, Pavan K. 2007 [1998]. *The Great Indian Middle Class*. New Delhi: Penguin Books.

Varshney, Ashutosh. 2002. *Ethnic Conflict and Civic Life: Hindus and Muslims in India*. New Haven: Yale University Press.

Vasudev, Uma. 1974. *Indira Gandhi: Revolution in Restraint*. New Delhi: Vikas Publishing House.

Verney, D. Douglas. 1995. 'Federalism, Federative Systems, and Federations: The United States, Canada, and India'. *Publius* 25 (2).

———. 2003. 'From Quasi-Federation to Quasi-Confederacy? The Transformation of India's Party System'. *Publius* 33 (4).

Wallace, Paul. 1980. 'Plebiscitary Politics in India's 1980 Parliamentary Elections: Punjab and Haryana'. *Asian Survey* 20 (6).

———. 1990. 'Religious and Ethnic Politics: Political Mobilization in Punjab'. In Francine Frankel and M.S.A. Rao (eds), *Dominance and State Power in Modern India—Vol. 2*. New Delhi: Oxford University Press.

Wallack, Jessica S. 2008. 'India's Parliament as a Representative Institution'. *India Review* 7 (2).

Wadley, Susan. 2002. 'The Domination of Indira'. In Vandana Madan (ed.), *The Village in India*. New Delhi: Oxford University Press.

Weiner, Myron. 1967. *Party Building in a New Nation: the Indian National Congress*. Chicago: University of Chicago Press.

———. 1978a. *India at the Polls: The Parliamentary Elections of 1977*. Washington: American Enterprise Institute for Public Policy Research.

———. 1978b. *Sons of the Soils: Migration and Ethnic Conflict in India*. Princeton: Princeton University Press.

———. 1982. 'Congress Restored: Continuities and Discontinuities in Indian Politics'. *Asian Survey* 22 (4).

———. 1983a. *India at the Polls: The Parliamentary Elections of 1980*. Washington: American Enterprise Institute for Public Policy Research.

———. 1983b. 'The Political Demography of Assam's Anti-Immigrant Movement'. *Population and Development Review* 9 (2).

Widmalm, Sten. 1997. 'The Rise and Fall of Democracy in Jammu and Kashmir'. *Asian Survey* 37 (11).

Wood, John R. 1975. 'Extra-Parliamentary Opposition in India: An Analysis of Populist Agitations in Gujarat and Bihar'. *Pacific Affairs* 48 (3).

———. 1984a. 'Congress Restored? The 'KHAM' Strategy and Congress (I) Recruitment in Gujarat'. In John Wood (ed.), *State Politics in Contemporary India: Crisis or Continuity?*. Boulder and London: Westview.

———. (ed.) 1984b. *State Politics in Contemporary India: Crisis or Continuity?*. Boulder and London: Westview.

Yadav, Yogendra. 1999. 'Electoral Politics in the Time of Change: India's Third Electoral System 1989–99'. *Economic and Political Weekly* 34 (34–35).

Yadav, Yogendra and Suhas Palshikar. 2003. 'From Hegemony to Convergence: Party System and Electoral Politics in the Indian States 1952–2002'. *Journal of Indian School of Political Economy* 1 (2).

INDEX